W9-AHE-080

Rogues and Heroes from
IOWA'S AMAZING PAST

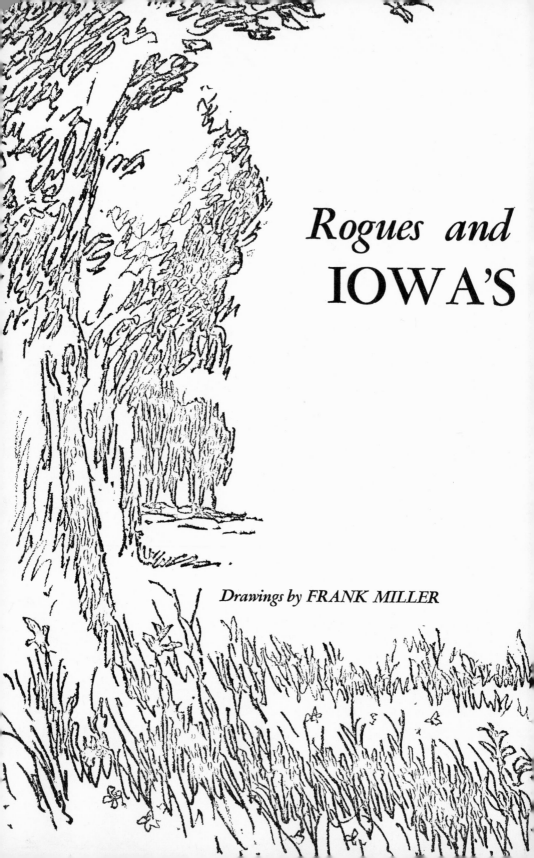

Rogues and
IOWA'S

Drawings by FRANK MILLER

Heroes from
AMAZING PAST

by GEORGE MILLS

THE IOWA STATE
UNIVERSITY PRESS

GEORGE S. MILLS has been an Iowa newspaperman since joining the staff of the *Marshalltown Times-Republican* in 1928 after graduation from Northwestern University with a degree of Bachelor of Science in Journalism. In addition to the *Times-Republican,* he has worked as a reporter and editor for the Iowa Daily Press Association, the Associated Press, the *Cedar Rapids Gazette* and the *Des Moines Register.* He served as legislative reporter and political writer for the *Register* from 1943 to 1971. His professional experience includes eleven years as Iowa correspondent for *Time* and *Life* magazines and he has written for *Look* and *Quick* magazines. In 1950 he won the *Reader's Digest* human interest award for his story "How Four Teen-agers Met Death." He also has won the Iowa Associated Press annual news writing sweepstakes award three times. He has written numerous historical series and articles over the years, including "In Old Des Moines" and "Iowa's Amazing Past" and a series on the United Nations. He is author of *The Little Man with the Long Shadow,* a biography of Frederick M. Hubbell, notable Des Moines pioneer.

Library of Congress Cataloging in Publication Data

Mills, George S.
  Rogues and heroes from Iowa's amazing past.

  Includes bibliographical references.
  1. Iowa—Biography. 2. Iowa—History, Local.
I. Title. II. Title: Iowa's amazing past.
F620.M5   920.0777   77–153160
ISBN 0–8138–0865–0

Composed and printed by
The Iowa State University Press

First edition, 1972

CONTENTS

Foreword, ix

Preface, xi

Acknowledgments, xi

1. **DUBUQUE, 2:** Creek on Fire, 3; Settlers' Homes Saved, 3; One-legged Speaker, 5; Daring General Bypassed, 6; Called a Traitor, 7; Patent on Paper Clip, 10; Thankful He Was Bald, 11

2. **WATERLOO, 13:** "They Sure Were Real Boys . . . ," 14; Prairie Rapids Crossing, 16; Escape from *Main Street*, 17; Rotten Egg Barrage, 17; Gets Notice to Leave, 18; Maytag Two-Cylinder, 18; Teachers Wear Lipstick?, 19; First AT&T President, 20; Letter to a Railroad, 21

3. **BURLINGTON, 22:** Slave Hunters Foiled, 23; Lincoln's Boiled Shirt, 24; Iowa's First Plane Flight, 25; Black Hawk's Bones Burned, 25; Finds Key to Arsenal, 26; *One Foot in Heaven*, 27; A Honey of a War, 28; Speculators Squelched, 30; He Inspired "Hold the Fort," 31; Domination by Railroads, 32; Tried to Buy Cuba, 33

4. **MASON CITY, 35:** Beginning of Bank Robbery, 36; Dillinger Came to Town, 36; She Used a Strap, 40; Whistling Wizard, 42; MacNider Hated War, 44; A Professional Spy, 45; The Genial "Music Man," 47; Fought for Safety, 49

5. **CLINTON, 50:** Schools Spread Disease, 51; Contaminated Water, 51; ". . . Wisdom of Creator . . . ," 54; Whole Streets Gone, 55; Balked Age with Onions, 56; Star Peeled Potatoes, 57; Reckless Driving in 1904, 58; "We Will Meet You at Border," 58; He Upset Prohibition, 59; Two Black "Volumes," 59; A Ghostly Steamboat, 60

6. **CEDAR RAPIDS, 62:** "Cherries Ripe, Cherries Red . . . ," 63; "I Would Be Less Than a Man . . . ," 66; Inspired While Milking, 67; Free Rides on Trains, 69; Jake (The Barber) Sobbed, 71; *The Tattooed Countess*, 73; Argument over Pancakes, 74

7. **KEOKUK, 76:** Unafraid of Mob, 77; Nineteenth-Century Hippie, 77; "Watchful Fox," 81; Disliked in Towns, 81; Found $50 Bill, 83; Born during Opera, 83; Harnessed Big River, 84; $125,000 Year from Movies, 85; Teddy Planted a Tree, 86; "No Soldier on Firing Line . . . ," 86; Nameless Graves, 88; Paid Under Five Cents an Acre, 89; Buried at Night, 90; A Warm Writer, 91

8. **AMES, 93:** Carver Talks with God, 94; A Costly Windmill Prank, 96; Free Tuition at Iowa State, 96; "My Last Wonderful Days," 97; The Margarine War, 97; Cut Cost from $1,000 to under $1, 99; ". . . Liquor Can Not Be Tolerated . . . ," 100; Tama Jim Goes to Washington, 100; Great Highway Builders, 101; Russians Sing Corn Song, 102; ". . . To See Beyond . . . ," 103

9. **MUSCATINE, 104:** Cancer Quack, 105; Great Lumber Baron, 108; Graybeard Soldiers, 109; Daily Prayer Vetoed, 110; Twain Loved Sunsets, 111; Black Susan Won, 111; Clamshell Boom, 112; When Bridge Caved In, 113; Three Explosions, 114; A Homely and Gentle Man, 115; Heaviest Rainfall, 117

10. **MARSHALLTOWN, 119:** Preached to 100 Million, 120; Fist Fight in Cow War, 123; The County Seat Conflict, 124; "You're Dang Right I Ran," 126; Fire Inspired Invention, 127; Mayor Ticketed Self, 128; Laid Rails at Night, 129; $700,000 in Gifts, 130; Carpetbag Governor, 131; "Not out for Dollars," 132; Taught King Tricks, 133; Slums Appalled Her, 134; "America Will Pass Away . . . ," 136

11. **COUNCIL BLUFFS, 137:** $3.5 Million Train Robbery, 138; Abe's Stories Not for Ladies, 140; "Saddest Day of My Life," 141; Warden-Novelist-Pastor, 142; General Gave Up His Pants, 143; Polygamy in Iowa, 145; "We Are Deserting These People . . . ," 146; The Original Bloomer Girl, 147; Long Life Inherited?, 148

12. **IOWA CITY, 149:** Body in a Haystack, 150; Trapped in Belfry, 152; Might Have Been Governor, 153; Suddenly Went Tongue-Tied, 154; Barred from Campus, 154; "A Modest and Majestic Man," 155; Perfectionist Builder, 157; A Souvenir Pie, 158; "We Must Have a School," 158; Key Man in Work Relief, 159; Delightful Stutterer, 160; Collector of Magazines, 161; Salary Cut of 44 Percent, 161; Mr. History of Iowa, 162

13. **DES MOINES, 163:** WAC Did Striptease, 164; Capitol Bribery, 165; President Visited Cemetery, 168; Cigarettes Illegal, 169; Governor Injured, 170; "China Belongs to Chinese," 171; Farmers Jammed Capitol, 172; Questions Progress, 173; Retreat from Railroads, 174; The Barbed-Wire Trust, 175

14. **SIOUX CITY, 177:** Took Hens off Nest, 178; "The King Is with Us," 178; Rickenbacker Won $10,000, 180; "Tax . . . Tax . . . Elect . . . Elect," 181; Foreign Language Row, 182; "Sing It As We Used to Sing It . . . ," 184; Disappointed in Love, 184; The Peacock Girl, 185; Dawn, Blazing Cloud, 186; Won with "Wobbly" Help, 187

15. **OTTUMWA, 189:** Ate Green Corn Eighteen Days, 190; A Pipe of Peace, 190; A Bitter Little Girlhood, 191; He Reduced Sales Tax, 193; Pat Worked in Bank, 194; Criticized Heroes, 195; ". . . Let Me Sow Love . . . ," 195; Industrial Development, 196; She Wrote about Lincoln, 197

16. **FORT MADISON, 198:** They Tried to Forget, 199; Fined for Contempt, 200; The Notable Hamiltons, 201; "I Never Miss Chicago," 202; Black Hawk's Last Speech, 203; Writer in Prison, 204; Greeted by Boos, 206; He Lost School Money, 207; Fountain of Ink, 208

17. **FORT DODGE, 209:** "Human Life Is Too Sacred . . . ," 210; Sent Capone to Prison, 212; Stone Giant Found, 212; Grasshopper Scourge, 216; Wrote Circus Music, 219; Terror in Winter, 220; Fought for Common Man, 221

18. **DAVENPORT, 225:** Medicine from a Horse, 226; "If That Boy Had Lived . . . ," 228; Exceeded His Authority?, 229; Colonel Davenport Slain, 230; Indians Got Fourteen Cents an Acre, 231; Election Skullduggery, 232; *Effie Afton* Hit the Bridge, 233; He Never Shaved, 234; "I Hear the Mountain Stream . . . ," 235; Sold Washers for $10, 237; Exposed Corruption, 238; Iowa Fed Hungry Russians, 238; Tragedy in Hotel Room, 239; Restless Pioneer, 240

Bibliography, 243

Index, 247

FOREWORD
by Clark R. Mollenhoff

ALTHOUGH George Mills is not a native of Iowa, he has embraced Iowa, its politics, and its people with the kind of warm and interested inquisitiveness that cannot be satisfied until all the secrets are known.

The painstaking research that went into the series that appeared in the *Des Moines Sunday Register* under the title "Iowa's Amazing Past" has brought Iowa's history alive in the lives of the men and women Mills writes about. It is as if you were there whether it was the exploits of Julien Dubuque in developing the lead mines along the Mississippi nearly 200 years ago or as Mills dealt with the spectacular events of the Iowans he has covered in the last 43 years as a reporter.

It is as if "Lefty" Mills is always asking himself the question: How did Iowa and the people of Iowa influence these men and women? It is as if Lefty Mills is seeking to explain with a good deal of compassion and understanding the little warnings and inspirations that all of us can get from the lives of others who have walked the same streets and experienced the same experiences.

Mills has covered stories of Iowa politics for more than 40 years, and he has dominated the political scene for nearly 30 years. He covered politics with an energetic enthusiasm that gained the respect of everyone he dealt with except for a few scoundrels on the political scene. Even the competition he so soundly trounced week after week usually had a grudging admiration for his work.

For years the best laid secret plans of Iowa's political strategists—Democrats and Republicans—usually emerged in the *Des Moines Register* under the by-line of George Mills. For 30 years he was the top political reporter in Iowa, and he was one of two or three political writers the reporters from outside Iowa would be certain to contact to learn the significance of the movements of Iowa farm prices and what it meant on a national and regional basis. Mills seldom relied upon second-hand information, and the chances are that he had known the key figures in an important story from the time they entered Iowa politics.

Mills always brought to political reporting the kind of perspective that comes from knowing and understanding the political figures and their aspirations, and the reality of what politics would drive men to do to move ahead. He was realistic about the meanness of men and yet perpetually understanding and looking for the better motivations.

The political atmosphere in Iowa is today a little cleaner because of the influence of George Mills and the often-whispered caution: "What if Lefty Mills finds out?"

The legend of Lefty Mills as the final word on Iowa politics was recognized by the late President John F. Kennedy and his top political aids and by President Richard M. Nixon. "What does Lefty Mills think?" was the first question that either Kennedy or Nixon would ask in trying to make an assessment of political fortunes in Iowa. For years *Time* magazine and the *New York Times* relied upon Mills as a political sounding board in Iowa.

But more important than the technical competence and the objectivity of Lefty Mills is the attention to the kind of detail that makes his subject come alive and move. We have all benefited from his example that combined brilliance, hard work, enthusiasm, and a steady disposition.

It will be a long time before anyone comes along who combines all of his qualities, and I think that it is fortunate that Iowa will have a book capturing the best of this aspect of the George Mills product.

PREFACE

Even some Iowans are wont to say the history of their state is unexciting. That's bosh. Iowa has had at least its share of lively individuals who have sparked the distant and recent past.

There was nothing ordinary or commonplace about these personalities: George Washington Carver, Herbert Hoover, Henry Wallace, Grant Wood, the Sullivan brothers, Billy Sunday, the Cardiff Giant, John Dillinger, Julien Dubuque, Bix Beiderbecke, Mark Twain, Meredith Willson, Chief Black Hawk, Norman Baker, the Cherry Sisters, Carrie Chapman Catt.

The purpose of this book is to picture in the experiences of individuals, some important and some obscure, the great cyclical flow of events in Iowa's bygone days, such as the enormous migration of peoples westward in nineteenth-century America; the displacement of the Indians; the great wars and their effects on communities and families; the advantages and the tragedies of the scientific and mechanical age; the rise of women's rights and the struggles over the rights of blacks and Indians; the humbugs, crimes, and swindles; the profound religious movements; the growing pains of railroads and highways; advances of science in conquest of diseases; the growth and perils of early education; and notable works of compassion to assuage suffering among fellow human beings.

In addition, the book groups interesting Iowans according to the cities with which they were identified. Thus, residents of eighteen Iowa cities are provided with a summary of exciting persons who highlighted the local past in each instance, and the history of the state as well.

ACKNOWLEDGMENTS

The author acknowledges with appreciation permission granted to quote from the following works:

Meredith Willson, "Iowa, It's a Beautiful Name," copyright 1944, the Big Three Music Corporation; Hazel Andre, "My Last Wonderful Days," copyright 1956, *Farm Journal;* Cornelia Meigs, *Invincible Louisa,* copyright 1968, Little, Brown and Company; Edward V. Rickenbacker, *Rickenbacker, an Autobiography,* copyright 1967, Prentice-Hall; unpublished research on the Cherry Sisters in the possession of Orville Rennie of Denver, Colorado.

Special thanks to the *Des Moines Register* and *Tribune* in whose pages much of this material originally appeared and through whose kindness the photographs have been reproduced.

xii

I want also to extend my thanks to the following persons and groups for the help given me in research: Mrs. Lida Greene and her staff in the state historical library in Des Moines; Jon Robison and his assistants in the newspaper division of the state historical department; staff members of the state traveling library, state law library, and Fort Madison and Des Moines public libraries; and last, but certainly not least, the assistance of my wife Marie for her suggestions and for her help in indexing the subject matter of this book.

Rogues and Heroes from
IOWA'S AMAZING PAST

DUBUQUE

Creek on Fire

J ULIEN DUBUQUE outfoxed the Indians.

They refused to do a favor that he asked. Tradition says he threatened to set Catfish Creek on fire "and leave their village high and dry."

Still the Indians did not move. Dubuque's aides thereupon poured a barrel of oil, or turpentine, into the creek one night. When the flammable liquid floated down to the Indian village, Dubuque tossed a firebrand into the creek.

"In a few minutes the entire creek was apparently in a blaze. The terrified Indians made haste to concede all that Dubuque had asked—and supposedly, by the exercise of his will, the fire went out!"

George Washington had not yet become president when Julien Dubuque began mining lead in the Dubuque area in 1788.

> *Dubuque was one of many exciting Iowans who have lived in the Dubuque area over a span of nearly two centuries. These interesting individuals have included a heroic soldier who was the only Iowan ever elected Speaker in Washington; a United States senator who came close to getting the Republican presidential nomination in 1888; a young banker who was awarded the Medal of Honor for courage in the Civil War; an outspoken Dubuquer who was jailed for expressing his opposition to that war; an early Catholic bishop who wrote a dramatic eyewitness account of the aftermath of an Indian massacre.*
>
> *Then there was the O'Connor who was hanged at Dubuque in 1834 in Iowa's first legal execution. More than 100 years later came another O'Connor (no relation) who was chosen to deliver the most significant nominating speech at the 1940 Democratic National Convention.*

Settlers' Homes Saved

J ULIEN DUBUQUE was twenty-six years old when he got permission from the Indians to start mining lead near Catfish Creek. The actual digging was done by "Indian squaws and old men" because the braves were "above work" and could not be hired. By 1805 Dubuque was getting ten to twenty tons of lead a year, which he sold in St. Louis.

He lived with the Indians who liked and respected him despite such incidents as the "creek burning" episode. He reportedly could handle poisonous snakes without fear because he possessed a cure for snakebite.

Dubuque, who was a French-Canadian, was described as "courteous and polite to women." But whether he ever married is one of the big love mysteries of early Iowa. He died in 1810 and is buried on a bluff above Catfish Creek.

For generations there were persistent reports that Dubuque did take an Indian woman as his wife. She was named Potosa and was a member of the Fox tribe. The Dubuque grave site was exhumed on the bluff in 1897 to see if a burial really had taken place there. A skeleton identified as that of Dubuque was found. Also buried nearby were the remains of an Indian woman. Was she Potosa and Dubuque's mate? Romanticists like to think so.

Dubuque claimed as his own a vast tract of land stretching twenty miles along the Mississippi and nine miles inland, and including the present city of Dubuque. He called his extensive diggings "the Mines of Spain." That was to curry favor with the Spanish governor at New Orleans. (Present Iowa was part of Louisiana Territory then and under Spanish control.) The obliging governor gave Dubuque the Spanish title to the property that he asked.

Dubuque proved to be a poor businessman and he was bankrupt at the time of death. He earlier had had to surrender nearly half his claim to Auguste Chouteau, a St. Louis merchant to whom he had become indebted. Chouteau then got the rest of the property when Dubuque died. Or so Chouteau thought.

This was a time when settlers flowed westward by the tens of thousands seeking new homes. Settlers poured into the Dubuque area as well as other parts of Iowa. They obtained titles to their land from the United States government. (The Louisiana Territory had been transferred from Spain to France and then was bought by the United States in Dubuque's time. Also, the Indians had given the Dubuque area and other sections of Iowa to the United States after being defeated in the Black Hawk War.)

The rights of the settlers to their lands soon came under attack in the courts. The Chouteaus claimed ownership of all of Julien Dubuque's claim. The case went to the United States Supreme Court. Thomas S. Wilson, famed Dubuque judge and attorney, argued the case in Washington. He said a decision for the Chouteaus "would place hundreds of families at the mercy of foreign, heartless speculators, turning them from house and home. These men, women, and children would be turned into the wilderness."

In 1853 the high court ruled in favor of the settlers and against the Chouteaus. The unanimous decision was based on the ground that there never had been a legal survey of the Dubuque grant. Thus, the Spanish title was not full and complete.

The ruling touched off great rejoicing in Dubuque where the people rang bells and lighted bonfires in celebration. "Now, for the first time, the settlers felt their homes were their own," says one account.

DAVID HENDERSON

One-legged Speaker

T HE CITY was aglow with pride. Word had come from Washington, D.C., that David Henderson, Dubuque's one-legged Republican congressman, had been elected Speaker of the National House of Representatives.

Henderson, who lost a leg in the Civil War, was the first congressman ever from west of the Mississippi River to be elected Speaker. The year was 1899. Dubuque was a city of 36,000, slightly more than half its present size.

Henderson was a tremendous fighter, in politics as well as on the battlefield. Says one historian: "He fought in the open and not by intrigue. His enthusiasm was as the march of an army. In the clash of angry debate, his voice sounded above the din like a bugle." But his story is one of tragedy as well as triumph.

He was born in Scotland and grew up on a Fayette County farm. When the Civil War broke out in 1861, he joined the Union Army. He first was shot in the neck during a charge on enemy lines. Later he was wounded so badly in battle that his left leg had to be amputated above the ankle. More amputations on the leg followed in later years. But such problems did not keep him from winning election to Congress in 1882 after he had practiced law in Dubuque a number of years.

Henderson finished his first two years as Speaker and then was reelected in 1901.

One year later, however, in 1902, the bluff old soldier stunned the political world by a sudden and complete retirement from politics. He withdrew as a candidate from his Iowa district for reelection to the House. President Theodore Roosevelt asked him to reconsider. But it was too late. Henderson was a strong "standpat" conservative and he sensed the rising Progressive tide in the Republican party at the time. No other Iowan ever has held the Speakership in Washington.

When Henderson died in retirement in 1906, Roosevelt sent a telegram of condolence describing the old warrior as "a gallant soldier and upright public servant."

Henderson's career as Speaker spans the time of Iowa's greatest influence in Washington. Not before or since has this state wielded so much power in the national capital. In addition to the House Speakership, Iowans occupied two posts in the president's cabinet. Leslie Shaw of Denison was secretary of the treasury and "Tama Jim" Wilson of Traer was secretary of agriculture.

Four Iowa congressmen also held chairmanships of House committees. They were J. A. T. Hull of Des Moines, military affairs committee; William P. Hepburn of Clarinda, interstate and foreign commerce; John F. Lacey of Oskaloosa, public lands; and Robert Cousins of Tipton, expenditures in the treasury department.

Most important Iowan of all in Washington, however, was Dubuque's longtime United States Senator William Allison. He served forty-three years in Washington until his death in 1908. He was a congressman eight years and a senator thirty-five years. He was longtime chairman of the Senate Appropriations Committee.

Allison was so highly regarded in national Republican circles that the party chiefs decided at the 1888 national convention in Chicago to nominate him for president. Everyone thought the night before that the stage was set for Allison. But Chauncey Depew, powerful New York leader, upset the deal. He refused to support any candidate of western farmers who were hostile to railroads. The convention nominated Benjamin Harrison of Indiana who then was barely elected.

Allison was reputed to have turned down opportunities to serve both as secretary of the treasury and secretary of state during his career.

WILLIAM ALLISON

Incidentally, Dubuque residents have served a combined total of forty-nine years as United States senators from Iowa. No other city in the state can approach that record. Des Moines is closest with thirty-seven years of such service. In addition to Allison's thirty-five years, Democratic Senator George W. Jones of Dubuque served from 1848 to 1859 and Louis Murphy of Dubuque was a Democratic senator from 1933 until he was killed in an auto accident in 1936.

FRANCIS HERRON

D Daring General Bypassed

UBUQUERS were indignant in the early 1890s over the plans for the proposed soldiers' and sailors' monument on the Statehouse grounds in Des Moines. The plans provided for placing statues of four Iowa generals of the Civil War on the memorial, all mounted on horses.

The monument was built but, despite Dubuque objections, Major General Francis Herron of that city was not one of the honored four. The large statues may be seen today, up on each corner of the monument. They are figures of Major Generals Samuel Curtis of Keokuk, Grenville Dodge of Council Bluffs, and John Corse of Burlington and Brigadier General Marcellus Crocker of Des Moines.

Dubuquers had a strong case in urging a Herron statue be included even though the chosen four all were topflight soldiers. Herron had come to Dubuque in 1855 at the age of eighteen. Despite his youth, he and his brother started a bank.

Herron joined the Union Army in 1861 and was awarded the Medal of Honor in 1862 for bravery at the battle of Pea Ridge in Arkansas. He was reported to have been "foremost in leading his men, rallying them to repeated acts of daring until himself disabled and taken prisoner." He was promoted from lieutenant colonel to brigadier general after returning from captivity.

Herron's brilliant leadership at the battle of Prairie Grove in Arkansas that same year won him promotion to major general while still only twenty-five years of age.

The service and sacrifices of hundreds of Dubuque soldiers constituted a vital contribution to the nation's military effort in the 1861–1865 Civil War. At the same time, Dubuque was a hotbed of opposition to that war and two Dubuque notables were imprisoned for their comments.

GEORGE W. JONES

Called a Traitor

A DUBUQUE DIPLOMAT came home from his South American post and was entertained at dinner in Washington by the secretary of state.

The next day the diplomat, George W. Jones, was clapped into jail.

Asked for an explanation, Secretary of State William Seward said he had "dined the diplomat and arrested the traitor."

Actually, the fifty-seven-year-old Jones was not a traitor although he had been most unwise in things that he said in his letters to Jefferson Davis.

The year was 1861 and firing had started in the Civil War.

Jones had been American minister to what is now Colombia for two years. He had been corresponding with his warm friend Jefferson

Davis. The two had served together in the United States Senate and in the Black Hawk War.

The Jones letters to Davis had been intercepted by federal officials. Davis meanwhile had become president of the rebelling Confederate States of America.

The arrest and imprisonment of Jones jarred the whole nation. He was one of the most controversial of all notable Iowans. He had spent most of the preceding twenty-seven years in public service, including eleven years in United States Senate. He and A. C. Dodge of Burlington were Iowa's first senators. They were Democrats and they took office together in 1848 after Iowa had become a state.

Jones was beaten for reelection in 1859 after the Republicans came to power in Iowa. Democratic President James Buchanan appointed Jones minister to Colombia.

When Republican President Abraham Lincoln took office, Jones resigned and came home. Seward decided that the intercepted letters to Jefferson Davis proved the "disloyalty" of Jones. The letters sympathized with the cause of the South and with slavery. (Jones had been compelled by public opinion at one time to emancipate nine of his own slaves and he did not like it.)

One Jones letter to Davis said, "I love Wisconsin and Iowa for the honors they have conferred on me and because I have always served them faithfully; but I will not make war with them against the South whose rights they have shamefully neglected."

Another Jones letter to a different Southerner said that if he fought at all in the war he intended to fight on the side of the South.

The white-bearded Jones was imprisoned in Fort LaFayette in New York for sixty-five days. He wrote to Lincoln asking for permission to return to Washington to answer any charges against him. He pointed out that he had taken the oath to support the Constitution after he had been relieved of his post in Colombia.

Jones and others finally gained their freedom after pledging they would "render no aid or comfort to the enemies in hostility to the United States."

Dubuque gave Jones an enthusiastic reception on his return. He never attained a high position in government again, however.

Jones carried the honorary title of "General" because he twice had served as "Surveyor General" of Iowa by appointment from the president. The title fitted pretty well anyway because he had extensive military experience. He was a drummer boy in the War of 1812 before he was eleven years old. He saw action again in 1832 when he was on the staff of an army general during the Black Hawk War.

In the realm of politics, he first was elected delegate to Congress in 1835 from Michigan Territory, which extended from the present state of Michigan to lands west of the Mississippi and including the present Iowa. He then got Congress to divide the Michigan Territory and to name the western section Wisconsin Territory. He was elected delegate to Congress from the Wisconsin Territory, which included Iowa.

Then, in 1838, at Jones's urging, Congress created the territory of Iowa out of the western portion of Wisconsin Territory. He also procured from the government parcels of land of 640 acres each to be used as sites for various cities in Iowa.

In a testimonial speech decades later, former Senator Dodge held up Jones's hand at Burlington and told the crowd, "Here, ladies and gentlemen, is the hand that chipped Wisconsin out of Michigan; that chipped Iowa out of Wisconsin; that chipped for us 640 acres of land covering this original town [of Burlington] at a mere nominal price."

Jones wanted in 1838 to be elected delegate to Congress from the new Iowa Territory. But he was defeated because of a duel in which a congressman was killed.

The duel took place in Washington between Congressmen William Graves of Kentucky and Jonathan Cilley of Maine. Jones served with both in Congress. The duel arose from a trivial issue of whether or not Cilley had insulted Graves in a discussion over a news story that charged corruption involving another congressman. Cilley said he had not done so but declined to go as far in retraction as Graves had demanded.

Jones was drawn into the arrangements for the duel because he was a close friend of Cilley. The assailants used rifles against each other. They both shot twice and missed. Each time the spectators, Jones included, tried in vain to reconcile Cilley and Graves. Then they fired a third time. Cilley fell dead.

Jones's opponents accused him of wanting to stir up the duel and of having enjoyed being a participant. These accusations apparently were untrue. But they helped bring about his defeat for delegate from Iowa.

In his extreme old age (he lived to be ninety-two), Jones found himself in financial trouble in Dubuque. His home was heavily mortgaged. The mortgage was about to be foreclosed when J. K. Graves of Dubuque raised enough money to pay off the debt. Jones occupied the home free from worry in his remaining days.

Dennis Mahony was more sharply critical of Lincoln and the Union cause than was George Jones. As editor of the old *Dubuque Herald,* Mahony assailed many acts of the Lincoln administration as unconstitutional and indefensible. He was arrested and held for three months in "Old Capitol" prison in Washington.

He was released without explanation. He returned to Dubuque where "a large part of the people . . . felt that the proceeding was wholly unwarranted and a flagrant violation of his rights as a citizen."

Mahony was given the Democratic nomination for Congress in the northeast Iowa district while in prison. He lost, but carried Dubuque County by 1,457 votes. He later was elected county sheriff.

Patent on Paper Clip

SOME DUBUQUERS became footnotes in history on the basis of one act or idea.

John Plumbe, an early engineer, called a meeting back in 1838 to stimulate interest in building a railroad across the continent to the Pacific. He may have been the first to advance that daring idea. Not until thirty-one years later, in 1869, was the present Union Pacific completed to the west coast.

Patrick O'Connor also received one historical mention, but of a different type. He shot and killed his business partner George O'Keaf in 1834 at Dubuque. A hastily recruited "court" found O'Connor guilty and he was hanged at the corner of what is now White and Seventh streets in the first legal execution ever carried out in Iowa. The hanging was witnessed by a reported 1,000 persons, "many from a steamboat at the landing."

More than a century afterward, Frank O'Connor, Dubuque attorney, was in Chicago to attend the 1940 Democratic National Convention as a delegate. President Franklin Roosevelt stunned the party at that convention by selecting Henry A. Wallace of Iowa as the Democratic nominee for vice-president. O'Connor was chosen by the Roosevelt Administration to deliver the Wallace nominating speech which O'Connor did with competence. Roosevelt and Wallace were elected.

The Reverend Albert Hoffmann of Dubuque was the most decorated American chaplain of World War II. Father Hoffmann lost his left leg in Italy while helping a dying American soldier.

Thomas Kelly attained fame by another route—by burying gold in "Kelly's Bluff" in Dubuque. He was an eccentric bachelor lead miner who struck it rich.

He died in 1867 and searching parties immediately started digging in his bluff for his buried gold. City authorities chased the searchers away for trespassing. Later, however, sums of $10,000, $1,200, $1,800, and $500 were unearthed. His fortune was estimated at $50,000 to $200,000.

Then there were such Dubuquers as John L. Harvey who attracted attention in 1856 by getting a patent on a paper clip and C. A. Mills who got a patent the same year for head rests for chairs.

W. J. McGee, born in Dubuque in 1853, patented several agricultural devices while at nearby Farley in the 1870s. More important, McGee became a nationally known geologist. From 1883 to 1893 he was in charge of all coastal plain operations of the United States Geological Survey. Before that, he made an amateur geological survey covering 17,000 square miles centering in northeast Iowa, an operation which he completed at his own expense.

MATHIAS LORAS

Thankful He Was Bald

FAR LARGER than the territory covered by McGee in his surveys was the diocese of Bishop Mathias Loras who arrived in Dubuque in 1838. He was the first Catholic bishop of Dubuque and his territory included all of present Iowa and Minnesota, and part of the Dakotas as well.

The bishop worked in 1839 to establish a mission in Indian territory where the Sioux and Chippewas were on the verge of war. The rival Indians agreed to sit down and smoke the pipe of peace which was packed with a combination of tobacco and willow bark.

Hopes of continued peace were high until the rival tribes decided to run some foot races. The Sioux won the first race and the Chippewas the second. The third appeared to have been a tie but the Chippewas grabbed the prize, the nature of which is not recorded.

The Indians parted company decidedly unhappy with each other. The next day the Chippewas shot and scalped a Sioux warrior. The Sioux thereupon went after the Chippewas.

Bishop Loras was offering a prayer at the altar one day during a church service when a great noise was heard. He wrote: "I perceived through the windows a band of savages all covered with blood. . . . At the top of long poles they brandished fifty bloody scalps to which a part of the skulls were still attached—horrible trophies of the hard fight of the preceding days. I finished the Holy Sacrifice as well as I could and recommended to the prayers of the audience these unfortunate human beings."

The Sioux had chased the Chippewas sixty miles and had killed 100, only 22 of whom were warriors and the rest women and children. These atrocities shocked but did not discourage the bishop who said he was only inspired all the more to impart to the Indians "the blessings of Christian faith."

Loras was a central figure in a crisis in Dubuque where the old cathedral appeared to be in danger of falling. The priest at the altar ran out of the building carrying the chalice and the other priests also left in a hurry. But the bishop did not stir. Says one account: "The brave old prelate stood calmly at his throne unmoved by the alarm. He had faced danger among the savages in the wilds. He had put his trust in God." The cathedral did not collapse.

Dubuque's famed lawyer and judge Thomas S. Wilson once was appointed by a court to defend a Chippewa charged with murder. Wilson got the Indian acquitted, to the red man's great surprise. The Indian went home. Wilson reported: "He [the Indian] sent word to me that he had for me two handsome Indian girls as presents for wives. My wife very unreasonably objected and the presents were not sent."

George Cubbage was thankful he was baldheaded. Cubbage taught the first school in Dubuque in 1833. He is said to have been captured by the Indians in the Black Hawk War a few years before. He was "sold" by the Indians to a trader for the low price of a plug of tobacco because he could not be scalped.

WATERLOO

THE SULLIVAN BROTHERS: JOSEPH, FRANCIS, ALBERT, MADISON, AND GEORGE

"They Sure Were Real Boys..."

T HE ELDERLY RAILROAD CONDUCTOR moved quietly as he packed a lunch in his weather-beaten home on a wintry morning in 1943.

He did not want to awaken his sleeping wife and their daughter and daughter-in-law. His train left in half an hour.

He heard a car stop outside in the January darkness, then footsteps on the porch. He opened the door and saw the gold braid and uniforms. He knew what the message would be. There had been no letters for weeks, only one ominous report. He called his womenfolk.

. . . Mr. and Mrs. Thomas Sullivan, the United States Navy regrets to inform you that your five sons are missing in action. . . .

. . . George, twenty-nine . . . Francis, twenty-six . . . Joseph, twenty-three . . . Madison, twenty-two . . . Albert, twenty. . . .

They were all aboard the cruiser *Juneau,* lost in the Battle of Guadalcanal against the Japanese in World War II.

. . . Expressions of sincere sympathy . . . tears . . . stunned silence . . . what can a father and mother stand? Had such a heavy wartime blow ever been inflicted on a family before? . . . Probably never in American history. . . .

But life goes on. Mr. Sullivan, fifty-nine, went to work. He was on his Illinois Central freight train when it left at 7:45 A.M. *Sometimes a man can keep from thinking about it when he works. . . .*

14

Missing in action . . . that does not necessarily mean death. . . . But then came a letter. . . .

. . . *George was a special friend of mine. . . . George got off the ship. . . . But he died on a life raft I was on. . . . The other four boys went down with the ship so they did not suffer. . . .*

. . . It was a sad and pathetic sight to see George looking for his brothers but all to no avail. . . .

. . . I don't know whether this sort of letter helps or hurts you, but it is the truth. . . .

. . . I know you will carry on in the fine navy spirit and I truly hope your boys' lives did not go to no avail. . . .

A total of 676 men died in the sinking of the *Juneau*. Only eleven crew members survived.

Another survivor: . . . *George stayed with me on the raft for five days. Then he disappeared. He either died of his wounds, was drowned, or was pulled away by sharks. . . . I remember he kept talking about his brothers all the time. . . . He might have tried to hunt for them in his delirium. He was pretty badly hurt, though. He was injured in the legs and couldn't swim. . . .*

Other letters, many of them. One to Mrs. Sullivan from Mrs. Franklin D. Roosevelt, wife of the president: . . . *You and your husband have given a lesson of great courage to the whole country. . . . I shall keep the memory of your fortitude always in mind, as I hope other mothers with sons in the service will do. . . .*

. . . It is heartening that parents who have suffered the loss you have can always find solace in your faith and your abiding love for our country. . . .

The Japanese staged their devastating attack on Pearl Harbor, Hawaii, on December 7, 1941. Among those killed was Bill Ball of Fredericksburg, Iowa, a friend of the Sullivan boys.

The five Sullivans went to the naval recruiting office together shortly afterwards. Two had had hitches in the navy before. They all said they wanted to enlist to avenge the death of Bill Ball. But they also declared they would join only if they could serve together.

. . . We've fought together a lot. That way we can fight like hell. We don't know how we would do separately. . . .

The Sullivans were accepted by the navy on their terms. They were assigned to the brand new light cruiser *Juneau*.

The *Juneau's* executive officer repeatedly recommended that the Sullivans be separated. But the navy honored the original commitment to keep the brothers together.

. . . They went together . . . as they wanted to . . . and gave their lives for their country and victory. . . .

In the Sullivan family were only the five sons and one daughter Genevieve. She joined the WAVES after the deaths of her brothers.

Time never heals completely. When the war came to a victorious end August 14, 1945, a reporter called Mother Sullivan. *". . . I can't*

*talk . . . I'll let my daughter talk to you." . . . "I think you know
what Mom's reaction is. . . . She feels quite bad. . . . She told me she's
glad for other boys coming home but hers won't be back."*

The Sullivan Brothers Memorial Park was dedicated in Waterloo
in 1964, nearly twenty-two years after the great family tragedy. Mrs.
Sullivan covered her face with her gloved hand when the bugler sounded
taps at the dedication. . . . *Mother is living it all again today. . . .*

There are other Sullivan memorials. A movie was made of the lives
of the Sullivan sons. Dad and mother saw the movie sitting hand in
hand in a New York projection room.

*. . . They sure were real boys, weren't they Mom? . . . It doesn't
seem quite real they're gone. . . .*

> **The lives of many persons in the bygone days of
> Waterloo sparkled with action.**
>
> **A Waterloo contingent invaded Cedar Falls in an
> effort to seize the county government. Waterloo citizens
> got novelist Sinclair Lewis slightly drunk in a successful
> effort to get him to change his mind. F. L. Maytag,
> the washing machine magnate, lost part of his shirt
> making automobiles in Waterloo.**

T *Prairie Rapids Crossing*

HE WATERLOO SITE first was called "Prairie Rapids" and "Prairie
Rapids Crossing" in 1845.

In 1851 settlers authorized Charles Mullan to select a name for the
community when he filed a petition requesting a post office. "He hit
upon the name Waterloo, and, being well pleased with it, and finding
no other place of the same name in the state, he filled the blank with
that name."

Another account says the place first was called "Waterlow" because
of "the original flat appearance of the village."

The Cedar River was anything but low in 1858. Floods washed
away 200 feet of railroad embankment. The river got so high that
a 100-ton stern wheeler steamboat, the *Black Hawk,* easily reached
Waterloo loaded with cargo.

The boat's arrival created wild excitement. Citizens ran up a flag
and fired salutes. Waterloo thought it had become a river port. The
cheaper water transportation costs caused the price of salt to drop immediately from $8 to $4 a barrel. The port dream ended the next year
when low water prevented the boat from getting beyond Gilbertville,
several miles downstream.

Samuel L. May was licensed in 1853 to operate a ferry across the
Cedar. He was unhappy because he was required to carry free all
church-goers crossing the river on Sundays and all voters on election
days.

Escape from Main Street

T RADITION has it that Sinclair Lewis was diverted by liquor half a century ago from using Waterloo as the location of *Main Street,* his famous satirical novel.

Main Street, which came out in 1920, is a biting picture of the narrow quality of life in a small midwestern town. Some critics class the book among the great writings of modern times.

Lewis had been a reporter on the *Waterloo Courier* briefly, following his graduation from Yale University in 1908. He was no newspaper success. He was told by an editor: "Sinclair, I am convinced you will never be a writer. Why don't you try something else, some other business?"

Lewis was transferred to another department, but soon left for California. He worked hard at writing. But when he offered a novel to a publisher in 1912, he was advised to forget the whole thing. He persisted, however, and caught on. He had published five books by the time he came back to Waterloo in 1919 on a visit.

He had Waterloo in mind for the plot of *Main Street* and he mentioned that fact in a letter he wrote to Ben Lichty, a Waterloo friend. Waterloo people did not want that kind of literary limelight.

Lichty and others met the train and gave Lewis a royal and alcoholic welcome. The author became slightly intoxicated that night. The next day his hosts plied Lewis with liquor again. Said one Waterloo resident, "Mr. Lewis was, shall we say, pleasantly plastered and hardly thinking of his book about the city and its people."

Lewis did not get a chance to investigate the possibilities of Waterloo nor to gather any color. He was still sailing high when he left by train to Minneapolis. By the time he had staged a partial recovery, he evidently had forgotten Waterloo. He decided to visit his home town, Sauk Center, about 100 miles northwest of Minneapolis. There he gathered details for *Main Street.* Waterloo escaped.

Rotten Egg Barrage

A BUNCH of the boys were whooping it up one night in Waterloo. When all had reached the point of feeling no pain, they decided to go to nearby Cedar Falls, then the Black Hawk county seat, and seize the county records.

The year was 1854. There had been considerable sentiment for moving the courthouse to Waterloo which is nearer the center of the county.

One O. E. Hardy assumed command of the Waterloo expedition. But Cedar Falls defenders heard what was cooking. They were prepared. They greeted the invaders with a shower of rotten eggs. The Waterloo contingent ignominiously retreated.

Cedar Falls won that battle but lost the war. The issue of locating the county courthouse came before the Black Hawk voters in an 1855 election. Waterloo won. The vote: Waterloo 388, Cedar Falls 260. Cedar Falls charged that many Benton County residents illegally voted in the election. Waterloo similarly charged that Cedar Falls got "all the strangers in town" to vote. Probably both were right.

Gets Notice to Leave

ADVENTUROUS WHITE MEN seeking to make a fast dollar came into the Waterloo area in the 1840s and cut down many red cedar trees along the Cedar River. The logs were rafted down the rivers to St. Louis and sold.

Charles Dyer, a hump-backed individual, was a leading logger. The first settlers did not like at all what Dyer was doing. They went to his shanty to tell him to leave pronto. He was not home.

The settlers stripped the bark off a nearby tree. With a charred brand for a "pencil," they drew a likeness of Dyer on the tree, then riddled it with bullets. He evidently took the hint. He was never seen in those parts again.

F. L. MAYTAG

Maytag Two-Cylinder

F. L. MAYTAG lost $300,000 in the business of manufacturing automobiles in Waterloo.

The original Newton washing machine magnate tried his hand at automobiles in 1909 and 1910. He wished he hadn't.

Maytag got involved when Edward B. Mason, a Des Moines auto builder, said he needed some working capital. Before long Maytag had invested a substantial amount in what became the Maytag-Mason Motor Company and had taken over the management.

Waterloo residents, alert to industrial possibilities, got Maytag to locate the auto factory there. The first cars, featuring a two-cylinder engine designed by Fred and August Duesenberg, proved successful. Prices ranged from $1,250 to $1,750, a lot of money in 1909 America.

The Duesenbergs, among the top car designers in American history, lived in Des Moines then.

The two-cylinder Maytag demonstrated its excellence by climbing all the west steps leading up to the Statehouse in Des Moines. That would be no mean feat for a modern automobile.

Maytag then came out with a four-cylinder car which was an engineering failure. The company collapsed. The mortality among automobile manufacturers was high in those days. The industry was described as "an exciting gamble in which a few won and many met disaster." Maytag said he decided to confine himself in the future to business that he "knew something about"—which was washing machines.

A number of Newton men bought stock in the Maytag-Mason company because they had confidence in Maytag. The stock became worthless. Maytag was bothered by the losses suffered by Newton residents even though he was not personally liable.

On Christmas morning, 1923, says Maytag's biographer, each of the losers found in the mail a Maytag check covering his loss on the automobile stock. The checks totaled more than $20,000. Maytag had gone far out of his way to square accounts.

The automobile loss did not damage Maytag's bank accounts irretrievably. When he died in 1937, the value of his estate in Iowa alone was placed at close to $7 million.

Teachers Wear Lipstick?

SHOULD Iowa high school girls use lipstick and face powder and even have their hair bobbed? Should teachers be so bold as to do the same?

That was a burning issue in 1922 when May E. Francis was elected state superintendent of public instruction. She was the first woman to win election to an Iowa state office after women got the right to vote in 1920.

Miss Francis served notice that she would not try to dictate "cosmetics and dress" to school girls and teachers. She said those were "personal" questions.

Such decisions seem of little consequence now. But there was much headshaking in Iowa over Miss Francis's attitude then, even though she was elected in the decade known as the "roaring 20's."

Miss Francis rubbed some Iowans the wrong way also on weightier issues of the day. She spent four years as the state superintendent and there was hardly a dull moment.

She was accused in 1924, for example, of insisting that high school teachers be high school graduates who had completed at least two years of college! That was a startling position to take in a time when comparatively few people ever were exposed to college. (High school and elementary teachers now must be four-year college graduates and most of them have engaged in graduate work.)

Miss Francis defeated two men for the Republican nomination for state superintendent in 1922. She came under heavy attack in the election but won hands down anyway.

The Iowa House of Representatives conducted an inconclusive investigation of her policies in 1924. At one point the debate became heated. Representative George Potts of Fort Madison accused Representative J. P. Gallagher of Williamsburg of using "unbecoming and profane" language. Potts apologized in part when Gallagher offered to punch him in the nose.

Miss Francis took special pride in the fact that 10,000 one-room rural public schools were operating then in Iowa. (Such schools are obsolete now and there is none operating in the state.) She reported "with pleasure" in 1926 that more than 1,300 such schools had been built in the previous three years, "adding charm to the landscape."

Opposed by teachers and others for various reasons, Miss Francis was defeated in the 1926 Republican primary by Agnes Samuelson, who then began a notable career as state superintendent.

In 1942 Miss Francis ran for state superintendent as a Democrat and went down to defeat with the rest of the ticket. She lived in Waverly when first elected state superintendent but was a resident of Waterloo most of her subsequent life. She died in Waterloo in 1968 at eighty-seven years of age.

First A T&T President

T HEODORE VAIL always called himself "a Black Hawk County boy," even after he became one of the world's top industrialists.

He twice served as president of the American Telephone & Telegraph Company and held other major business posts.

The Vail family settled on a farm near Waterloo in 1866. Theodore, then twenty-one, rode a farm horse into Waterloo where he was a winning pitcher for a semipro team.

He soon got a job as a railroad station agent. He revamped the railway mail service in his area and did such a good job that he was called to Washington to take charge of the nation's entire railway mail system.

Alexander Graham Bell invented the telephone in 1876. Bell's father-in-law selected Vail in 1878 to become general manager of the developing telephone industry. Vail's genius for organization was such that he was named first president of the AT&T in 1880 and held that post until he retired to a Vermont farm in 1887.

Vail thereupon took to traveling. In 1893 he built an electric power station near Cordoba, Argentina. He bought a horsecar line in Buenos Aires, electrified the line with the best cars available in the United States. The streetcar company was financed by British money and the "Black Hawk County boy" maintained his headquarters in London until he returned to his Vermont farm in 1904.

In 1907 Vail yielded to the pleas of telephone officials and again became AT&T president, a position he held for at least ten more years. Along the line, he also became president of Western Union and greatly improved that company's revenues and service. He was given credit for installing the popular "night letter" telegram and deferred cables at reduced rates. He left the Western Union job in 1914 when the AT&T disposed of its interests in that company.

ARCH W. McFARLANE

A *Letter to a Railroad*

A RCH W. McFARLANE demonstrated that a politician can "live down" a major mistake and continue in some capacity in elective office.

McFarlane, a Waterloo coal merchant, served in the legislature over a record forty-four-year period. He first was elected to the Iowa House of Representatives in 1914 and was finally beaten for reelection to the Iowa Senate in 1958.

Twice he was elected Speaker of the Iowa House and twice lieutenant governor. It was while he was lieutenant governor late in 1930 that a letter came to light that he had written to the Illinois Central Railroad. He wanted the railroad to buy coal from his company. He unwisely said in the letter that as lieutenant governor he had been "looking after the legislative matters" of the various railroads in Des Moines.

Such a disclosure might have been expected to end his career altogether. He did cease being a possibility for governor, or for reelection as lieutenant governor. But he went home and succeeded in winning election as state representative in 1932. His achievement in winning on the Republican ticket that year was all the more remarkable in light of the fact that that was a Democratic landslide election.

McFarlane served in one house or the other of the legislature most of the time for the next twenty-six years. He was a highly skilled lawmaker. He occasionally presided over the House in that period. When he served as Speaker, the House really got things done.

He was again a candidate for election as state representative in 1960 when he died suddenly in Chicago while attending the Republican National Convention. The seventy-five-year-old McFarlane was in the headquarters of the Iowa delegation in the Palmer House when death came. The old warhorse died where he would have wanted to die, where the political action was.

BURLINGTON

EDWIN JAMES

Slave Hunters Foiled

A FARM WAGON carrying an elderly doctor and a Negro man stopped in Jefferson Street in downtown Burlington. A crowd gathered. The doctor and his companion sat quietly on the wagon seat.

Two Missouri slave hunters armed with pistols and Bowie knives stood guard. They had forced the physician and Negro to return across the Mississippi River to Burlington from the Illinois side.

The Missourians said the Negro, whom they called "Dick," had escaped from a slave owner named Rutherford in Missouri.

> *Burlington was the setting for many exciting events in the history of Iowa.*
>
> *An escaped slave won his freedom in Burlington when the moment came to identify him.*
>
> *Abraham Lincoln was traveling light when he came to Burlington for a speech.*
>
> *Art Hartman built a plane that surged briefly into the air at Burlington in the first flight ever in Iowa. Senator James Grimes of Burlington saved a president with his vote.*
>
> *Iowa's "Hawkeye" nickname originated with a Burlington man.*
>
> *A Burlington resident failed in Spain to close an international real estate deal.*

The year was 1855. Missouri was a "slave state," Iowa a "free state."

Dr. Edwin James, a physician who lived near Burlington, hated slavery. His home was a station to which fleeing slaves came.

Dr. James had taken Dick across the river to board a train for Chicago. The manhunters caught them before Dick could leave.

An attorney for the slavehunters got a warrant in Burlington for the Negro's arrest. He was taken into custody. A hearing was scheduled for three days later. The outcome seemed certain. Congress had said escaped slaves must be returned to their masters.

Burlington was aroused. Would the fugitive be taken back to slavery or would he be freed? If the ruling went against the Negro, would the people permit him to be taken by the manhunters?

23

Marion Hall in Burlington was "filled to suffocation with excited people" on hearing day.

It developed that the slavehunters could not personally identify the Negro as being Dick. At their suggestion, a son of the slave owner came to the hearing to prove that the prisoner was the runaway slave.

Then came the shocker. Looking straight at the Negro, young Rutherford stunned everyone by saying the defendant was "not Dick!" The young man said he had "never seen" the Negro before!

That ended the hearing right then and there. The judge dismissed the case. A joyous roar went up from inside the hall. Those outside responded even "more vigorously."

The Negro was started by rail to Chicago. His real name never was learned. He undoubtedly was an escaped slave but not from the Missouri Rutherfords.

Dr. James would have been a mighty popular physician today. He reportedly would take no pay for his services. He was "tall and erect, with a benevolent expression and piercing black eyes."

Pike's Peak in Colorado really should have been named "James Peak" after the Burlington doctor. He scaled the supposedly inaccessible peak in 1820 when he went to Colorado as a botanist with an expedition.

The peak is named for Zebulon Pike, a noted explorer, but Pike never climbed the mountain.

Dr. James would have been in the forefront in fighting racial discrimination in the 1960s and 1970s. He declared before the Civil War that "one race is as good as another." He once expressed the belief that slavery "has so deeply polluted the blood and destroyed the stamina of the white race that our restoration is impossible."

Dr. James did not live to see the slaves emancipated. He died at sixty-four years of age in 1861, the year the Civil War started. He fell off a wagonload of wood and the wheels passed over his chest.

Lincoln's Boiled Shirt

ABRAHAM LINCOLN gave a package wrapped in newspaper to a desk clerk in a Burlington hotel.

"Please take good care of that," Lincoln said. "It is my boiled shirt."

Lincoln had little luggage when he got off a Mississippi River boat at Burlington in October 1858. He came to make a speech before 1,200 enthusiastic Republicans in Grimes Hall. He spoke for two hours. Stephen A. Douglas had talked to Democrats five days earlier but only for half an hour. He was too hoarse for more.

Lincoln needed a clean white (boiled) shirt every day because he was out on the speaking circuit. He was engaged in appearing with Douglas in their famed Illinois debates at the time. Their Burlington speeches were extra appearances.

What they said at Burlington was not reported. Lincoln, however, opposed allowing slavery in territories such as Kansas and Nebraska. Douglas favored letting the territories vote on whether to have slavery.

Douglas beat Lincoln for the United States Senate in Illinois that year. But Lincoln defeated Douglas for president two years later, in 1860.

ARTHUR J. HARTMAN

Iowa's First Plane Flight

BACK AND FORTH on the fairways of the old Burlington golf club chugged the little airplane. But it would not leave the ground.

Arthur J. Hartman was not discouraged, however. He had built the plane with a wing span of twenty-eight feet after talking with the Wright brothers, inventors of the heavier-than-air machines.

Hartman tinkered some more with his craft. Finally, on May 10, 1910, the little plane took off, rose perhaps ten feet into the air, and then came down so hard that the undercarriage was damaged. The landing after a flight of "a minute or so" was just in time to miss some trees.

That short ascent was the first recorded airplane flight to take place within Iowa. Hartman was one of the original "Early Bird" flyers. He was different from most in that he lived into his eighties. Many such flyers were killed in accidents in the early 1900s. Hartman's first journey into the sky was a balloon ascension in 1903 when he was a lad of fifteen. Burlington honored its grand old man of flying by naming a road near the airport Art Hartman Drive.

Black Hawk's Bones Burned

THERE IS a Burlington conclusion to the story of Black Hawk, the superb Sac and Fox Indian chief.

He died in 1838 and was buried near Iowaville in Van Buren County. The body was stolen from the grave. Burlington's calm was shattered one day when a son of Black Hawk and fifty other Indians stalked into the city to inform Governor Robert Lucas of the theft. Burlington was the capital of Iowa Territory at the time.

A Quincy, Illinois, dentist later surrendered Black Hawk's bones which he said he had gotten in St. Louis. Black Hawk's widow turned the bones over to Governor Lucas whom she called "that good old man." The bones were placed in a Burlington museum and were destroyed when that building burned in 1855.

JAMES GRIMES

T *Finds Key to Arsenal*

HERE IS REASON to believe that the governor of Iowa arranged for the "theft" of 1,500 muskets from the state arsenal.

The governor was James Grimes of Burlington. The year was 1856. The governor's office was in the present Old Capitol in Iowa City.

Grimes was a bitter foe of slavery. He was much interested in the struggle that was going on in Kansas, which had not yet been admitted to the Union as a state. Open warfare had broken out in Kansas between Southerners favoring legalized slavery there and Northerners determined to keep the state free. Both sides brought in forces from other states.

A band of free-state Northerners bound for Kansas stopped at Iowa City. One of them, Richard Hinton, went to the governor's office. Grimes was not present. There in plain sight on his desk was a key to the state arsenal. A fast visit to the arsenal—and the volunteers took 1,500 muskets along when they marched out of town.

Nobody pursued the marchers. Grimes must have made the key available to Hinton.

Grimes also was reportedly ready in 1855 to take direct action if necessary in the case of the slave identified as "Dick" at Burlington. It has been said that the governor arranged for freeing Dick if the law had called for sending the Negro to slave-owner Rutherford in Missouri. Such action was not necessary, because of the honesty of Rutherford's son in not identifying the defendant as the escaped slave.

Grimes, father of the Iowa Republican party, is best known in American history for his refusal as a senator to vote for removal of President Andrew Johnson from office in 1868 under impeachment proceedings. The courageous Grimes had himself brought to the Senate to vote even though he had been stricken with paralysis a few days before.

Grimes and six other Republicans voted in favor of keeping Johnson in office although the GOP generally wanted the president ousted. Johnson was saved from removal by a single vote. Thirty-five senators voted "guilty." Had thirty-six so voted, Johnson would have been doomed. The president would have been ejected from office had Grimes or any of the other Republicans voted for removal.

Republicans everywhere were enraged. Horace Greeley, New York editor, in effect called Grimes a traitor. He was hissed on the streets of Burlington where he long had been an idol.

Grimes was no fan of Andrew Johnson. But the Iowa senator said he would not be a party to destroying the Constitution "for the sake of getting rid of an unacceptable President." Grimes opposed the idea of Congress using the power of impeachment to gain control of the presidency.

One historian wrote: "The denunciation of Grimes by Iowa Republicans was unmeasured, almost unanimous and brutal in the extreme. For a time reason was ignored, justice smothered and rage ruled supreme. His motives were impugned and his superb and patriotic service to his state and country during the darkest days of the Civil War . . . was ignored."

The storm of abuse proved too much. Grimes resigned his Senate seat in 1869. He died at fifty-five years of age in 1872 following a heart attack.

One of the finest tributes to Grimes came from Chief Justice Salmon P. Chase of the United States Supreme Court. Justice Chase had presided over the long Johnson trial in the Senate. Sitting by the Iowa senator's sickbed following the trial, Justice Chase said, "I would rather be in your place, Mr. Grimes, than to receive any honor in the gift of our people."

HARTZELL SPENCE

One Foot in Heaven

Hartzell Spence, a Methodist minister's son, wrote twelve books that were rejected by publishers. He sent the thirteenth to John T. Frederick, his onetime English professor at the University of Iowa.

"Shall I keep on or quit?" Spence asked. "Why don't you write about what you know best?" responded Frederick. Spence thereupon wrote

One Foot in Heaven, a lively best seller about the life of a minister's family and the family's periodic moves from one place to another.

The Spences lived in Burlington four years during the 1920s when Hartzell was a teen-ager. *One Foot* provides a Sinclair Lewis-like look at staid old conservative Burlington in the years after World War I.

Spence, a onetime Iowa newspaperman, called Burlington "Riverton" but otherwise made no real effort to disguise the identity of the city. He says "Riverton" then "was notable chiefly for its insincerity and entrenched smugness." The real rulers were "a few pioneer descendants of great wealth; with nothing to do, they made a profession of defeatism."

Spence added, however, "Built on five hills overlooking the Mississippi River, Riverton was opulent with handsome homes set in expensive lawns, with clean stores, wide streets and many churches."

Spence enjoyed his father's triumphs in conflicts within the "Riverton" church. Some unfriendly church members planted a rumor that a certain family left town because of a daughter's pregnancy and that Hartzell was responsible. The elder Spence disproved the story and embarrassed the gossips.

A Honey of a War

Robert Lucas was territorial governor at Burlington in 1839 when the "Honey War" broke out between Iowa and Missouri.

The "Honey" conflict was the best possible kind of war. Not a shot was fired by either side.

Some Iowa soldiers felt lousy afterwards, not from fighting but from drinking too much.

Missouri started the trouble by claiming ownership of a substantial southern Iowa area. In the area were bee trees containing wild honey. That's where the war got its "honey" name.

Missouri maintained that Congress intended to fix the boundary between the two states nine miles to thirteen miles north of the present border. Lucas would not buy that. A Missouri sheriff was arrested when he tried to collect taxes in Van Buren County, Iowa.

Missouri's governor called out troops. Lucas immediately summoned the Iowa militia to repel any invaders. Approximately 1,200 Iowans responded. A few had guns. One came armed with a sword made out of sheet iron. Another carried an Indian spear bedecked with red ribbons.

Missouri decided not to fight and there was no confrontation. The issue instead went to the United States Supreme Court which decided in Iowa's favor.

Missouri scalawags did slip over the border and cut down three bee trees during the "hostilities." That caused hard feelings but nothing more.

The war gave Iowans an excuse to stage riproaring parties in Burlington. Said one "pre-war" report: "Drums rattled, fifes whistled and bugles blew in Burlington when the First Iowa militia assembled there to settle the boundary dispute. . . . Roistering groups of soldiers surged through the streets. . . .

"They jostled shoulders in taverns and hunted excitement along the riverfront. Boisterous hilarity and drunken brawls marked their brief sojourn."

When the possibility of actual fighting faded away, one writer said, "I have never seen a wilder set of men and greater carousal than there was that night in Burlington."

One individual who did not take a drink was Governor Lucas. He was an uncompromising dry. He once declared that intemperance and gambling caused "more murders, robberies and individual distress" than all other misdeeds combined.

Lucas, a Democrat, previously had served two terms as governor of Ohio before being appointed governor of Iowa Territory in 1838. He presided over the first Democratic National Convention ever held, in Baltimore in 1832. That convention nominated Andrew Jackson for president.

When the Whigs defeated the Democrats in the 1840 presidential election, Lucas lost his Iowa job. (The president appointed territorial governors on a political basis.) Lucas moved to Iowa City where he built a home called "Plum Grove," which is an Iowa historical landmark today. Lucas died in Iowa City in 1853 at the age of seventy-two.

The old governor objected strongly to the custom of carrying pistols and other weapons in early Iowa. He said such a practice "should not only be considered disreputable but criminal and punished accordingly."

What stirred up the governor was a killing on the streets of Burlington. Cyrus Jacobs of Burlington, a member of the territorial legislature, feuded with David Rorer, widely known Burlington attorney. Sharp-tongued Jacobs had been editor of the *Burlington Gazette*. He demanded an explanation of certain charges made by the pugnacious Rorer. The argument heated up and Jacobs beat Rorer with a cane. Rorer shot Jacobs who died three days later.

Rorer was "appalled by the violence of his deed" but apparently never was prosecuted.

Rorer is credited with nicknaming Iowa the "Hawkeye State." He wanted the Hawkeye label established quickly so that Iowa would not get a worse nickname. Illinois, for example, was originally called the "Sucker State," now is known as the "Prairie State."

Rorer got editor James Edwards of the *Fort Madison Patriot* to promote the Hawkeye name in commemoration of Chief Black Hawk. Edwards afterwards moved his newspaper to Burlington and changed the publication's name to the *Hawk-Eye*.

Speculators Squelched

A GOOD WAY to get lynched in early Iowa was to try to grab the farm of a pioneer.

Thousands of families moved into Iowa and established homes before there were real estate deeds. These families broke the prairie, planted crops, built homes and barns. They increased the value of the properties far beyond the government price of $1.25 an acre.

These pioneers, however, fully expected to get their land in due time from the government for the $1.25 figure. But public sales of land had to be held. Speculators saw a chance to pick up bargains by bidding more than the $1.25 amount.

The first sales were held in 1838 at Burlington and Dubuque. Outsiders quickly got notice that it was not safe to try to buy a pioneer's farm out from under him. "Claims clubs" had been formed to bid in the land of whole townships at $1.25. Heaven help the person who tried to horn in. He was in for some rough handling.

One individual who tried to "jump a claim" in Johnson County was "soundly whipped." A Virginian tried to do the same thing at Burlington. A mob started for his hotel. The frightened man grabbed his bag, rushed out the back door to the river, and disappeared.

Chief Justice Charles Mason of the Territorial Supreme Court ruled in favor of the settlers in a key case. His ruling gave the force of law to the activities of the claims clubs. Defending the clubs, he said it was a good thing for the nation to have families occupying the western lands even if the settlements were unauthorized. He declared the pioneers had been encouraged to move into Iowa at the "almost express invitation of Congress." His decision was called "flimsy law . . . but first class history."

CHARLES MASON

JOHN M. CORSE

He Inspired "Hold the Fort"

THE GALLANT STAND of a Burlington general and his men in a Civil War battle inspired the phrase "Hold the Fort."

Brigadier General John M. Corse, twenty-nine, a Burlington attorney in civilian life, commanded a Union force of 1,800 men guarding a vast store of army supplies at Alatoona, Georgia, in 1864.

A Confederate Army of 7,000 surrounded Corse. The Confederate general gave the Yankees five minutes to surrender to avoid a "needless effusion [flow] of blood." Corse replied, "We are prepared for that needless effusion of blood whenever it is agreeable to you."

General William T. Sherman sent this message by signal flags to Corse: "Hold the Fort. We are coming." Corse signaled back: "I will hold it till hell freezes over."

The Confederates launched an all-out attack but the outnumbered Yanks held. Corse lost 700 men out of his small force, the Confederates more. The 39th Iowa alone reported 165 slain in that battle. One bullet grazed Corse's cheek and another took off the top of his left ear.

Sherman said to Corse afterward, "Your presence alone saved us at Alatoona." The Corse victory inspired a composer to write a gospel song entitled "Hold the Fort." The song was sung in American churches and Sunday schools for generations. Here are the first verse and chorus:

> Ho, my comrades, see the signal
> Waving in the sky;
> Reinforcements now appearing,
> Victory is nigh.
> Hold the fort, for I am coming,
> Jesus signals still;
> Wave the answer back to Heaven
> By Thy grace we will.

Corse had been seriously wounded in 1863 at Missionary Ridge where a cannonball fractured his right ankle. He recovered and returned to action the next year.

He was named internal revenue collector in Chicago after the war and also became involved in railroad building. All his household goods were destroyed in the great Chicago fire of October 1871. Later he was appointed postmaster at Boston, Massachusetts. He died at fifty-eight in 1893 and is buried in Aspen Grove Cemetery in Burlington.

JOHN H. GEAR

T Domination by Railroads

HE BURLINGTON RAILROAD was a major power in Iowa politics in the nineteenth and early twentieth centuries. Much of that power stemmed from the skill and manipulative ability of Joseph Blythe, a resourceful lawyer at Burlington. The railroads in those days bought support by distributing free passes for train travel to politicians.

The railroad's influence was such in southern Iowa that the counties through which the line passed were known as the "Burlington reservation." That was because the Burlington usually controlled the votes of all the delegates of those counties in state political party conventions.

Blythe of the Burlington and Nathaniel Hubbard of the North Western Railroad were long a potent pair in state affairs. Hubbard, also an attorney, lived in Cedar Rapids. Although the railroads did lose considerable control before 1900, what really slowed them down most politically was the election of A. B. Cummins of Des Moines as governor in 1901. He put an end to the free-pass system.

Blythe's wife was a daughter of John Gear of Burlington, governor of Iowa from 1878 to 1882 and United States senator from 1894 until his death at seventy-five in 1900. Having a father-in-law occupying such positions of power was a great asset to Blythe.

It was during the Gear administration as governor that the railroads succeeded temporarily in overturning the Iowa "Granger law" which regulated rates and other rail activities, and which the railroads hated.

Gear was an effective campaigner and personally popular. He once was asked by a Quaker at West Branch if he were addicted to drink.

Gear replied, "I take a glass of whisky when I feel like it." The Quaker commented, "I admire thy candor but I wish thee did not do so."

Another historian said of Gear: "I have seen him lift a glass of whisky to his lips and gulp it down in one swallow without batting an eye. What happened after that I cannot relate for he bade us good night, saying he was old enough to go to bed while still in possession of his senses." Gear was sixty-nine at the time.

Snows were heavy in Des Moines one winter while he was governor. The hill on which the Statehouse is located in Des Moines became a popular coasting ground. Boys watched for the governor in late afternoon. They invited him to ride down the hill.

"He invariably accepted the invitation and there was sharp rivalry between the boys for the honor of carrying the governor down the hill."

Tried to Buy Cuba

AUGUSTUS DODGE of Burlington tried hard to buy Cuba for the United States but the Spanish were not selling.

From 1855 to 1859, Dodge was United States minister to Spain, which owned Cuba.

How different would have been the history of the last 100 years if Dodge's efforts had succeeded! There might not have been a Spanish-American War. Cuba might have become at least one and probably two states in the Union. And there might never have been a "Castro."

Augustus Caesar Dodge is one of the great historical figures of Iowa. A Democrat, he became one of Iowa's first two United States senators in 1848. His father, Henry Dodge, was senator from Wisconsin at the same time. Thus, father and son simultaneously represented different states in the Senate. That has not happened before or since.

The Dodges did not always agree on issues in the Senate. For example, Augustus Dodge wanted to let new states decide by a vote of the people whether to allow slavery within their borders. Henry Dodge voted no on that bill.

Augustus Dodge was appointed register in the federal land office at Burlington in 1836 and was thereafter always identified with that city.

He pushed early for giving, instead of selling, homestead lands to settlers. Dodge said, "If every quarter section of public land was the bona fide property of an actual settler, it would do more to perpetuate our liberties than all the Constitutions, state and national, that have ever been devised." Years later, in 1862, Congress enacted such a free-homestead law.

Upon his return from Spain, Dodge was given the 1859 Democratic nomination for governor of Iowa. He ran a good race but lost to Republican Samuel Kirkwood, 56,500 to 53,300.

The courtly Dodge arrived at a political meeting at Washington,

Iowa, in a carriage drawn by "four splendid horses." In contrast, Kirk-wood came into town on a hayrack drawn by two oxen. Kirkwood be-came known as the "plowhandle candidate" and undoubtedly gained lots of votes from the common people as a result.

Dodge served as mayor of Burlington in his later years. It is said that his pity for offenders appearing in his mayor's court caused him to pay their fines himself.

One Republican editor said Dodge, a Democrat, was "as honest a man as ever lived." Another writer said he was incorruptible and he left public office "without the smell of smoke on his garments."

Henry Dodge, the father, died at the son's home in Burlington in 1867 at the age of eighty-five. Augustus Dodge died in 1883 at the age of seventy-one in the home which was at 829 North Fifth Street.

Augustus Caesar Dodge lies in Aspen Grove Cemetery beside his father "with whom he remains in death as he always was in life—a com-panion."

The epitaph for Augustus Caesar Dodge says, "Life is not a pleas-ure nor a pain but a serious business which it is our duty to carry through and to terminate with honor."

MASON CITY

Beginning of Bank Robbery

A MAN who said he was looking for a certain house number stopped at the Harry Fisher residence in Mason City one cold March evening.

Fisher directed the stranger to a home up the street.

The individual stared hard at Fisher for a moment and then walked away, in the opposite direction. He had no interest in going to the other street number. But he did want to be able to identify Fisher in the grim business of the morrow. Fisher was an assistant cashier of the First National Bank of Mason City. It was his job to open the bank vault daily.

Fisher wondered what the guy was up to but dismissed the matter from his mind. He would have been scared to death, however, had he known. The episode on Fisher's front porch was one step in a sensational bank robbery staged by the notorious John Dillinger gang on March 13, 1934.

Many famous persons, and some highly infamous such as Dillinger, highlight the past of Mason City. They include Carrie Chapman Catt, the renowned feminist who once spanked unruly Mason City pupils; Bil Baird, famed puppet-show artist; Hanford MacNider, a great soldier and statesman who was once Dwight Eisenhower's boss; and Meredith Willson, the composer, whose nostalgic musical about Mason City has entertained millions.

JOHN DILLINGER

WILLIS G. C. BAGLEY

Dillinger Came to Town

JOHN DILLINGER, thirty-one, was Public Enemy No. 1 in the early 1930s. He and his cohorts robbed nearly a dozen banks. He intimidated a guard with a "gun" whittled from wood and escaped from jail at Crown Point, Indiana. His goal in 1934 was to get a lot of money quickly. He wanted to leave the country and live it up. He never made it.

The Dillinger gang of six (perhaps seven) bandits robbed the First

National Bank at Mason City of more than $52,000 on March 13, 1934. The bank happened to have $300,000 in cash on hand that day.

Eddie Green and Homer Van Meter were "advance men" for the Dillinger mob. They came to Mason City early to lay the groundwork for the robbery. They roomed at the YMCA.

Green was the man who went the night before to get a good look at Fisher, who was an assistant cashier.

In their scouting, Green and Van Meter missed getting one important bit of information. They did not learn that guard Tom Walters, seated in a bulletproof glass cage above the lobby in the First National, was armed with tear gas. Such gas would have thwarted the robbery— if Walters's gun had not jammed after firing one shell. One weeping bandit complained, "If we had known we were going to run into this damned tear gas, we wouldn't have tried it."

A few hours before the robbery, Van Meter and Green drove a blue Buick to a sandpit four miles southeast of Mason City. There they met Dillinger, "Baby Face" Nelson, Tommy Carroll, and John Hamilton, all cold-blooded criminals. They got into the Buick and drove to Mason City. (Some sources said there was a seventh bandit. If so, he was never identified.)

There are three dramatic chapters in the bank holdup story: the Robbery itself inside the bank, Terror in the streets outside, and the Escape.

At 2:20 that afternoon, the First National's serenity was shattered by an outburst that "sounded like a pack of wild Indians yelling." Three bandits invaded the bank, shouting and waving machine guns.

"Get down on the floor, all of you!" shouted an outlaw at the thirty employees and twenty customers in the bank. He fired a burst of bullets over their heads.

The three desperadoes were Green, Van Meter, and Hamilton.

Hamilton made a beeline for Willis G. C. Bagley, the president. Bagley ran into his office and tried to shut the door. Hamilton put his gun muzzle in the way. Hamilton pulled out the gun and Bagley slammed the door. Hamilton fired through the door. A bullet went under Bagley's arm and splinters from the door lodged in his coat sleeve. But he was unharmed.

Walters fired a tear-gas shell from his upper cage into the bank lobby. The missile struck Green in the back but caused no wound. Tear gas started spewing around the bank.

The bandits fired a fusillade at Walters's cage, which was struck by thirteen bullets. A couple of bullets entered the gun slit and wounded Walters slightly on the chin and ear. He tried to fire more tear gas at the robbers but could not get an empty shell out of the gun. He also was prevented from firing real bullets because the bandits used employees and customers as shields.

Another employee tossed a tear-gas candle onto the floor. Breathing became difficult but not impossible. The robbery proceeded.

Green plucked Fisher out of a cage and shouted, "Now open that vault or I'll fill you full of holes." Fisher recognized Green as the man who had come to his door the night before. At gunpoint, courageous Fisher handed out bundles of $1 and $5 bills to the desperado, but very slowly. The impatient robber warned, "If you don't hurry up, I'll shoot you."

The robbers would have been most unhappy had they known they were departing without having gotten a quarter million dollars still stored in the vault.

Outside the bank, Dillinger and the other two gangsters, all armed with machine guns, held downtown Mason City at bay for ten minutes or more.

Dillinger stood in front of the bank on Federal Avenue, a machine gun cradled in his right arm and a pistol in his left hand.

Around the corner on State Street, "Baby Face" Nelson, who delighted in killing people, held the sidewalk. Stationed in the doorway of a prescription shop on the other side of State Street was Tommy Carroll, also ready to kill without notice. The getaway car was parked close by.

Dillinger, wearing a dark hat and overcoat, coolly maintained control of the avenue with occasional bursts of gunfire.

City detective James Buchanan took cover behind the Civil War Memorial boulder in the city park across the street. Buchanan was armed with a shotgun but dared not shoot for fear of hitting Douglas Swale of Mason City whom Dillinger used as a shield.

"I yelled to Doug to get out of the way," Buchanan said. "Doug tried to move but Dillinger wouldn't let him."

Dillinger blasted at the boulder which was chipped by the bullets but could not hit Buchanan.

Meanwhile, Mason City Police Judge John C. Shipley went into action in his office up in the bank building. He got out an old pistol, fired, and struck Dillinger in the shoulder. Dillinger fired back but only pierced a window in the office of Dr. B. Raymond Weston.

Blood also had been shed by this time around the corner. R. L. James, secretary of the Mason City school board, started into the rear door of the bank. When he stepped back out to see what the noise was all about, a desperado shot him twice in the right leg.

One of the State Street bandits, perhaps "Baby Face" Nelson, acted "crazy" and interspersed his firing with outbursts of laughter. A new Hudson automobile came down the street. A bandit punctured the radiator with several shots. The driver frantically backed up the car as fast as he could.

The "inside" bandits with six bank employees as hostages, came hurrying out of the bank front entrance and went around the corner with Dillinger to the getaway car. Rounding the corner last was John Hamilton. Judge Shipley again fired from up in the bank building and hit Hamilton in the shoulder. Shipley was two for two that day—two shots fired and two bandits wounded.

Twelve Mason City hostages, six men and six women, went on the most frightening ride of their lives.

They were forced to get on the outside of the Dillinger escape car. Some were ordered to stand on the running boards on both sides (cars don't have running boards now), two had to ride on the front fenders and others on the back bumper. They all thus formed a "human shield" which kept the police from shooting at the car.

The car rounded the corner and started slowly northward on Federal Avenue, at a speed of maybe twenty-five miles an hour, with Van Meter at the wheel.

As they moved through the city, the gangsters continued to terrorize the hostages. At the sight of a following police car, one bandit growled, "If the cars don't stop following us, we will kill all of you."

Curious Clarence McGowan was out riding with his wife and five-year-old daughter. McGowan did not know about the robbery. He drove up close to the bandit car. A bullet fired out of the back window hit the McGowan auto. The bullet shattered into three pieces. One fragment wounded McGowan in the abdomen slightly and the other two pieces hit his knees. His wife and daughter were uninjured.

The getaway car, with its cargo of scared human beings clinging to the outside, rolled out into the country west toward Clear Lake. The driver speeded up to forty miles an hour.

The desperadoes sprinkled sacksful of roofing nails on the roads to puncture tires of any pursuing cars.

The robbers turned south beyond the Mason City country club and then east. The hostages were freed unharmed at various places.

The getaway car proceeded back to the sandpit. There the gang purposely ran the auto into the ditch and left for St. Paul, Minnesota, in two other cars. They made a clean escape. The wrecked car had been stolen in Indiana a few months before.

Dillinger and Hamilton both had their comparatively slight shoulder wounds dressed that night by a frightened doctor in St. Paul.

Today such a bank robbery and escape would be difficult indeed. Bank security is much better. Highway patrolmen and other officers also would be swiftly mobilized in several states to apprehend such a gang. There was no Iowa highway patrol at all in 1934. The crimes of such gangs as the Dillingers may have been a factor in the decision to set up an Iowa patrol in 1935.

The Mason City bank robbery was one of the final outrages of the Dillinger gang. Within nine months all six who staged the First National robbery had been shot to death. Dillinger died under FBI guns July 22, 1934, as he emerged from a movie in Chicago. Eddie Green was slain by FBI agents April 11 in St. Paul and John Hamilton was fatally wounded there April 23. Tommy Carroll was shot to death by police in Waterloo, Iowa, June 5. Homer Van Meter was killed by police in St. Paul August 23.

George "Baby Face" Nelson, the last to go, was found dead November 27 at Barrington, Illinois, with seventeen bullets in his body. He had killed two FBI agents in his final battle with the law.

CARRIE CHAPMAN CATT

M
She Used a Strap

OST of Mason City's 3,500 inhabitants were shocked.

A twenty-four-year-old single woman had been appointed superintendent of schools!

That was no job for a young woman! Discipline in the grade schools was bad. What was needed was a big, tough man.

Nevertheless, Carrie Lane got the job. She was promoted from high school principal to superintendent. She was the daughter of a Floyd County farmer and was an 1880 graduate of Iowa State in Ames.

Carrie knew she had to prove immediately that she was forceful enough to handle the superintendent job.

The first day she went to the worst school, armed with a leather strap two feet long. She called the most unruly children from their rooms, one by one. She whaled each vigorously on the seat of his pants. The cries of each victim deeply impressed the other pupils.

She used the strap with energy on nine troublemakers in two schools. After that she kept the strap in plain sight on her desk. Apparently there was little more disciplinary trouble during the rest of her career as superintendent.

Despite all this, she was not one to emphasize physical punishment in running the schools. She was known as a person of "natural dignity and kindly authority." Her schools career gave no indication that she would become a famous national and world leader in the long battles of the nineteenth and twentieth centuries for the rights of women and for universal peace.

As Carrie Chapman Catt (she was widowed twice), she became president of the National American Woman Suffrage Association. She founded the League of Women Voters in 1920. (That was the year that women got the right to vote in national elections.)

She served as president of the International Woman Suffrage Alliance from 1904 to 1923. Without question she was one of the great feminine figures in human history.

Carrie was only six years old when she first became angry over what she thought was discrimination against women. All the girls in her schoolroom wore hoopskirts. A little girl's skirt fell off one day.

"The boys tittered," Carrie said. "One of them, a red-haired lad a bit larger than the others, chuckled audibly behind his book. Every little girl blushed and we felt very much ashamed. We all had the feeling our sex had been insulted."

The red-haired boy laughed again at recess and Carrie slapped his face.

In 1872, when she was thirteen, she watched her father and the hired men drive away in a buggy to the polling place on election day. She asked her mother why she didn't go too. Carrie was astonished when her mother said she "had no legal right" to vote.

That night Carrie defiantly told her father that when she grew up she was going to tell everybody that women should have the same voting rights as men.

"Where do you think our daughter ever got that notion about woman suffrage?" her father asked. "I don't believe she'll ever get a husband."

Carrie observed years later, "That was the first of the suffrage arguments which I eventually won, and my father was wrong too because I did get a husband."

She first married Leo Chapman, a fine Mason City newspaper editor.

In 1884 Carrie had her English classes write news stories about events in their schools. She got Chapman, editor of the *Mason City Republican,* to agree to print the stories. He also fell for her. She quit her school job. They were married in 1885. She became assistant editor of the paper, a job she enjoyed very much.

She did an expert job of mobilizing Mason City women behind a bill in the Iowa legislature to give women the right to vote in municipal elections. The bill did not carry but the Iowa Suffrage Association was impressed by her organizing ability.

Chapman decided he wanted a larger newspaper. He sold the *Republican* in 1886. He went to California looking for a paper to buy. Carrie was to follow him. She got a telegram saying he was critically ill of typhoid fever in San Francisco. He died before she could get there. She was a widow at twenty-seven.

After pulling herself together, she got a newspaper job in San Francisco. She became incensed, however, at the spectacle of other women doing more work than men but getting less pay for it. She determined that fighting discrimination against women was to be her life's work. She returned to Iowa and settled in Charles City where she launched a career that brought her to a position of world preeminence in fighting for the rights of women.

One of her speeches in Stockholm, Sweden, was translated into twenty-four languages and distributed all over the globe.

She was an organizing genius. When her program for organizing women into a regular political force took hold, a Chicago political boss complained, "I wish to God I c'd make this district organizing as fascinating to the party workers as it is to these danged women!"

Carrie did find, however, that the attitude of some women was a major obstacle. She said, "The lethargy we met with in some women was just as hard to combat as the opposition of men."

In 1890 she married George W. Catt, a well-to-do engineer who had been a classmate at Iowa State. He died in 1905.

Turkey issued a commemorative postage stamp in her honor that same year.

One forgotten part of her early history was her militant insistence in the 1870s that the girl students at Iowa State be given the same opportunity to take military training as the boys. The obliging college drillmaster provided broomsticks for "weapons" and the girls furnished their own blue uniforms. Their organization was known as "Company G," the "G" standing for girls. The popular girl unit at Iowa State lasted more than a generation and was disbanded only at the outbreak of World War I.

More to the point were her later strenuous efforts in behalf of world peace. In 1922 she delivered a peace speech in Cleveland that still rings with fire and intelligent concern. Addressing a convention session of the League of Women Voters, she condemned America's refusal to join the League of Nations. Her voice filled with conviction, she went on: "The people in this room tonight could put an end to war if they would set themselves to it! Let us put an end to this aloofness, this deadly silence! We can do it! This is an infinitely greater call than any of us will ever hear again.

". . . God is calling to the women of the world to come forward and stay the hands of men and say to them: 'No! You shall no longer kill your fellow man!' "

One commentator said: "I can still hear the tremendous applause that followed that appeal. I can still see women wiping away their tears . . . in solemn promise to heed the warning uttered by this great woman."

But peace was not to come, then or now. Mrs. Catt lived to see the beginning and ending of World II in 1939 to 1945. She died in 1947 at eighty-eight years of age.

I *Whistling Wizard*

IN A WAY, the Whistling Wizard and Flannel Mouse are products of Mason City.

They are famed puppets created by Bil and Cora Baird, the most notable marionette artists since the old Punch and Judy shows.

As a boy and teen-ager, Baird lived in Mason City. His chemical-engineer father managed the sugarbeet plant there. When the youngster was seven, his dad gave him a homemade puppet. That was the first step in the brilliant Baird career. Years later a reporter wrote: "The Baird house in Mason City had a wonderfully big attic. Up there the puppets and marionettes came into being. . . . That Iowa attic was the scene of scores of free shows."

Another report in Baird's own book gives credit to the inspiration he got in 1921 when he saw Tony Sarg's superb puppets present *Rip Van Winkle*. Baird, then sixteen, decided, "This is the life for me." But he first finished high school and the University of Iowa, worked as a steeple-jack, even spent three years building big balloons for the annual Macy's Thanksgiving Day parade in New York.

Somewhere along the line he shortened his first name from "Bill" to "Bil." It is said he did so to qualify for membership in a club limited to persons with names of no more than three letters.

He launched Bil Baird's own marionettes at the Chicago World's Fair in 1934 after a five-year apprenticeship with Tony Sarg. Bil met and married his wife Cora in 1937. She was an actress. Together they created thousands of puppets which delighted children and adults alike through three decades of stage shows and television. They took part in the Ziegfield Follies in the 1940s and were on television almost continu-ously throughout the 1950s.

The Columbia Broadcasting System was deluged with letters from indignant children when the Baird Whistling Wizard program was dropped in 1952. Flannel Mouse also was a beloved character as was Charlemane the Lion, and similarly delightful but in a different way were Bubbles La Rue, the stripteasing doll, and Slug O'Brien, a honky-tonk piano player with a cigarette dangling from his lips.

The United States government was happy to have the Bairds go abroad to perform in India, the Soviet Union, and Afghanistan in 1962. Before that their puppet shows were used effectively in a nutrition drive to get children in Latin America to drink milk and eat vegetables.

The Bairds built their own playhouse in their Greenwich Village residence in New York and presented adult-level puppet shows that won wide acclaim.

Cora once pointed out the necessity of making the dolls seem hu-man. She said: "You have to feel as though you are the character the puppet is to imitate. Even though Bil and I are back of the puppet stage and no one can see us, we go through wild facial contortions."

Baird's brother George gained fame in a totally different field. He was a great quarter miler in track and was a member of the United States Olympic team in 1928. He previously had been captain of the University of Iowa track team and before that was a Mason City high school track star.

HANFORD MacNIDER

I *MacNider Hated War*

HATE WAR!" declared Mason City's great General Hanford MacNider. He meant what he said.

No one fought harder than he in 1940–1941 to keep the United States out of World War II. He joined Charles A. Lindberg in the "America First" campaign against this nation becoming involved in that bloody conflict.

Yet, when the Japanese attacked Pearl Harbor and the war was on, MacNider hurried to Washington to offer his extensive military skill in the service of his country.

"They had me branded as a political undesirable," he said, "but I raised so much hell they finally called me just to keep me quiet."

As a campaigner for peace, he had said, "I am interested in one country, the United States of America."

That was his philosophy when the United States came under attack. He wanted to do all he could for his country once the firing had started. What he did for the United States in the two world wars was monumental.

He was wounded in action in World War I in France where his remarkable bravery and accomplishments led to his being awarded more military decorations than any American other than General of the Armies John Pershing.

As a fifty-two-year-old brigadier general in World War II, he was wounded in combat in New Guinea. He suffered eight wounds, one of which ultimately cost him the sight of his left eye, from fragments of a Japanese grenade. He was awarded an oak-leaf cluster, in lieu of a third Distinguished Service Cross, for "extraordinary heroism" in action.

He was commended for his "courageous personal example of coolness under fire" and his fortitude after he was wounded was termed "an inspiration to the men" under his command.

Consistent with his longtime opposition to war, General MacNider did not at all like our involvement in Vietnam. He said: "Look at history. Europe has always settled its affairs in one way or another without outside intervention.

"It would have in World War I and World War II without us being there. I feel the same way today. We have no business meddling in the affairs of other nations.

"Once we are in—such as Vietnam—then we should either stomp hell out of them and get it over with, or get out."

MacNider was a strong personality who left his imprint on his times, during peace as well as war. He was elected national commander of the American Legion in 1921 when he was only thirty-one years old. He was assistant secretary of war and acting secretary of war in Washington from 1925 to 1928. Dwight Eisenhower, the great World War II commanding general and later two-term president, was MacNider's assistant executive officer in the war department.

As minister to Canada in 1931 and 1932, MacNider negotiated a St. Lawrence River treaty with Canada. He received 178½ votes for the Republican nomination for vice-president on the one ballot taken for that nomination in the 1932 GOP National Convention. Vice-President Charles Curtis was renominated with upwards of 600 votes.

MacNider was president and general manager of the Northwestern States Portland Cement Company until his retirement in 1960. As president of the First National Bank in Mason City (as was his father before him), he helped set up Northwest Bancorporation, one of the nation's largest bank holding corporations.

He did not always obey orders and sometimes at least he was correct in his disobedience. As an officer in France, he was told on November 11, 1918, to send 2,000 men across the Meuse River to establish a beachhead. That was the day the Armistice to end the war was signed.

"We knew the cease fire was set," he explained. "The whole thing was simply first class murder so I didn't do it."

When he heard about MacNider's decision, his commanding officer exclaimed: "Thank God somebody around here has some sense. Take my car and give yourself a few days' celebration in Paris."

When MacNider died in 1968 at the age of seventy-eight, one of his old-time military associates said, "I consider General MacNider to have been the greatest citizen-soldier in the history of the United States."

HANS V. TOFTE

International Spy

A FORMER Mason City businessman was disclosed to have been a longtime professional spy with the CIA (Central Intelligence Agency).

He is Hans V. Tofte, who once operated Klipto Loose Leaf Company in Mason City.

Tofte, a native of Denmark with an exciting past, was fired in 1966 from his $25,000-a-year job as a CIA undercover agent. The firing perhaps had international repercussions in the spy world.

Tofte was accused of taking secret CIA material to his Washington home in violation of regulations. Other CIA agents got into his home and seized the material. Tofte contended that his constitutional rights had been violated by the search and seizure. He also said $20,000 of his wife's jewelry turned up missing at the same time.

Tofte declared that what he did was nothing new, that many agents took home documents to work on them. He said the documents were hidden in a blanket in his third-floor library.

He said the seized papers included an analysis of the disastrous "Bay of Pigs" invasion of Cuba which was thwarted by Castro's forces in the early 1960s. Also in the papers, he said, was a critical analysis of the Vietnam situation. He said he long had been working on a plan to "revolutionize the entire CIA and make it do the work it is supposed to do."

Tofte and his wife Marlys bought controlling interest in Klipto in Mason City in 1948 from Mrs. Tofte's uncle, John Corsaut. Tofte said he planned to spend the rest of his life as a businessman. He joined various Mason City clubs and became chairman of the airport commission.

The Toftes considered Mason City their home from 1949 to 1957. But he was gone a lot, beginning almost immediately. When the Korean War broke out in 1950, he was given the secret assignment of setting up CIA operations in Korea. As a young man he had spent many years in the Orient where he learned to talk Chinese, Japanese, and Russian. In a letter to General Douglas MacArthur at Tokyo, General Hanford MacNider wrote: "Colonel Tofte has spent a good part of his adult life in the Far East, particularly in Manchuria and China, and would seem to have all the necessary background to be of definite service to you in the present emergency. I have faith in his ability, his loyalty and his resourcefulness."

Tofte had lived a life of intrigue and danger since he was a young man. He was part of the resistance movement in Denmark when that country was occupied by the Germans in World War II. He made one round trip in a kayak through the Nazi water patrols to Sweden in that period.

After slipping out of Denmark again, he reached Burma where he organized guerrilla fighters and engaged in combat intelligence behind the Japanese lines. As an American undercover agent, he managed to run a fleet of forty ships through the German blockade with guns, ammunition, and other supplies for Tito's resistance forces in Yugoslavia. He also became a paratrooper in Palestine so that he could drop behind enemy lines for reconnaisance.

For such deeds Tofte was awarded the Legion of Merit for Valor by the United States and the Yugoslavian Medal of Merit.

He had had his espionage troubles before. He was suspected in

1956 of being a Soviet agent but cleared himself, partly by means of a lie-detector test. In 1944 he said he was "up for court martial" during the Yugoslav operation but instead ultimately was decorated by the Yugoslav government.

MEREDITH WILLSON

The Genial "Music Man"

MEREDITH WILLSON has contributed considerable glow and cheerfulness to the largely grim world in which we live. He is the onetime Mason City flutist who wrote the gaily nostalgic smash hit *The Music Man.*

One reviewer called the work "a warm and genial cartoon of American life." Another said, "The brass band rhythm is so infectious, the comedy so simple and honest, the romantic scenes so droll, and the smalltown scenes so hospitable that *The Music Man* emerges as Americana in an authentic tradition."

The Music Man takes place in the Mason City of 1912. Willson was a ten-year-old Mason City boy then. The Music Man was a traveling salesman of musical instruments who blew into town to sell his wares. He promised to give instruction in how to play the instruments. (But he couldn't read a note.) His plan was to organize a band, sell uniforms as well as instruments, then clear out. Only this time there were hilarious complications.

Willson was born in Mason City. He has always called himself an Iowan although he has lived away from this state since he was in his teens.

After the prize-winning *Music Man* became established as one of the great musicals of the century, Meredith recalled how things had been with him as a little boy.

"I took piano lessons," he said. "Everybody took. But one day the piano teacher, who also was the band director, talked my mother into letting me take the flute. We found out later that it was because it was the only instrument in the band for which he had no one to play."

Meredith also became highly proficient on the piccolo. He played piccolo in the band which came with the Mason City high school football team to Des Moines to play North High.

The score was 0–0 until the last few seconds of the game when a Mason City player drop-kicked a field goal for three points. There was some question as to whether blasts from the piccolo and other noise may have diverted the referee's attention while the ball was in the air. There was a heated dispute over whether the ball really went over the bar. Willson later recalled with a chuckle that the morning paper the next day carried a story saying, "An educated toe and a jazz piccolo player beat North High School out of the championship."

In addition to *The Music Man,* Willson put together such other notable productions as *The Unsinkable Molly Brown, Here's Love,* and *1491* and such books as *And There I Stood with my Piccolo* and *Eggs I Have Laid.* Among many other songs, he also composed "May the Good Lord Bless and Keep You" (written especially as a good-night radio song for Tallulah Bankhead).

Nothing in the wide Willson repertoire, however, ever will top his rousing "76 Trombones." The buoyant, rhythmic cadence of that *Music Man* number is a John Philip Sousa-type of march flavored by Meredith Willson's own brand of lilt. Willson in fact was a flutist with the great Sousa for three years, from the time Meredith was nineteen until he was twenty-two.

Willson, who highly treasures his Iowa ties, wrote the song "For I for S Forever" for Iowa State University in 1953 and the Iowa Fight Song for the University of Iowa in 1951. In 1959, following the Iowa football victory in the Rose Bowl at Pasadena, California, Willson wrote another marching song called "The Band." He explained: "What would the Tournament of Roses parade be without bands? What would a football game be without a band? I realized how important bands are. That's why I wrote the song."

A big, bespectacled fellow with a shock of hair, Willson's droll outlook on life is pointed up by what he has termed "Willson's Law," which is, "Always be on time, but barely." He apparently has driven people crazy on important occasions by being nearly, but not quite, late.

Iowans will be forever grateful to Meredith Willson for the haunting nostalgia in the "Iowa" song he wrote in the 1940s and which became the centennial song for the state's 100th birthday celebration in 1946. Here is the chorus:

> IOWA, it's a beautiful name
>   When you say it like we say it back home,
> It's the robin in the willows,
>   It's the postmaster's friendly hello.
> IOWA, it's a beautiful name,
>   You'll remember it wherever you roam;
> It's the sumac in September,
>   It's the squeak of your shoes in the snow.
> It's Sunday school and the old river bend,
>   Songs on the porch after dark;
> It's the corner store and a penny to spend,
>   You and your girl in the park.

IOWA, it's a beautiful name
    When you say it like we say it back home,
It's a promise of tomorrow
And a memory of long ago.
IOWA, what a beautiful name
    When you say it like we say it back home.

W. EARL HALL

Fought for Safety

MOTOR VEHICLES kill a lot more Iowans each year than do bullets fired by wartime enemies. Yet traffic deaths are almost taken for granted while angry demonstrations against war have been frequent.

This apparent inconsistency bothered W. Earl Hall, editor of the *Mason City Globe-Gazette*. As a longtime fighter for highway safety, he fervently believed people had to be awakened to the tragedy of highway killings.

Hall's never-ending drive to promote safety began in 1926 and earned for him in 1954 a $10,000 tax-free national prize awarded by Mutual of Omaha insurance company.

He was a key man in the organization of the old Iowa State Safety Council in 1934 and served as its president until 1939. As a member of the state board of regents from 1937 to 1949, he helped promote the first driver training courses in Iowa high schools.

In 1946 Hall became chairman of the national committee for traffic safety and he was appointed by President Truman in 1948 to head the committee for the president's Highway Safety Action Program.

Hall never was happy with the increasing danger to everyday living stemming from accidents. He said in 1946, "Between Pearl Harbor and VJ day [the day the Japanese surrendered], some 260,000 American soldiers were killed [in World War II] . . . but 355,000 other [Americans] were killed in all kinds of accidents in the U.S."

Hall died in 1969 at the age of seventy-two.

CLINTON

Schools Spread Disease

POOR HEALTH CONDITIONS in thousands of Iowa schools brought sickness and suffering to children in every part of the state before 1900.

More than a fifth of the schools did not even have suitable privies for their youngsters.

Henry Sabin pointedly called attention to such shocking situations in his reports to the people. He was a Clinton educator who served eight vigorous years in the 1880s and 1890s as Iowa superintendent of public instruction.

His comments undoubtedly paved the way to better health practices in the schools, and to improved teaching as well. He is one of the forgotten heroes of nineteenth-century Iowa.

Strong individuals such as Sabin marched through every decade of Clinton's stirring past.

A big-time Clinton lumber baron was not satisfied with the speed of the water flowing in the Mississippi River, and did something about it. . . . One of America's greatest stage beauties was born in Clinton. . . . A Clinton black man, a giant athlete of his time, achieved distinction as a judge. . . . A debt-ridden riverboat owner moved fast to avoid bill collectors.

HENRY SABIN

Contaminated Water

THE AMOUNT of sickness and the number of deaths among children were distressingly high in Iowa's "good old days."

Diphtheria, scarlet fever, smallpox, tuberculosis, and other diseases took a toll that would be intolerable today.

Henry Sabin held the schools at least partly to blame. His 1889 report said 2,745 schools lacked suitable outhouses. That was more than 21 percent of the 12,877 schoolhouses then operating in the state.

The privies were found to be in "wretched condition" in some school yards while other schools had no outbuildings at all. Sabin termed the state of affairs "almost beyond belief." He demanded a law to compel school boards to provide separate and decent outhouses for each sex on all school grounds. (Flush toilets were still far in the future for schools.)

Sabin also charged school conditions with being responsible for children's "weak eyes . . . distorted spines . . . unstrung nerves . . . aching heads . . . unnatural languor . . . weakness and debility." These ailments, he said, originated "in the impure water children drink; in the vitiated [polluted] air they breathe; in the forced and constrained positions necessitated by ill-fitting seats; in the light, deficient in quantity . . . ; in the method of warming, which heats the head while the feet are freezing."

The state superintendent declared that drinking water in a school well sometimes was contaminated by seepage from a nearby privy. He added: ". . . the floors of many schoolrooms are not washed oftener than once a year. . . . The desks, which may have been occupied by children coming from families in which some member is sick with a contagious disease, are seldom if ever cleansed. . . . The walls are never treated to a thorough coat of whitewash."

He was critical of the "heaps of rubbish and litter" accumulated in "dark corners" and under school stairs. He said that if doctors "would place themselves in position to catch some of the vile odors which come from cellars and basements, and in the country schools from under the buildings, but which find their way through crack and crevice to mingle with the air the scholars and teacher breathe—they would no longer wonder at the mysterious outbreaks of diphtheria and scarlet fever among the children of the neighborhood."

Sabin, a native of Connecticut, came to Clinton as superintendent of schools in 1870. He was chosen head of the state teachers association in 1878. He was elected state superintendent in 1887 and 1889 and again in 1893 and 1895. He was widely known nationally. He died in California in 1918 at the age of eighty-eight.

Sabin was deeply concerned over two other major Iowa school problems of his time: Many children did not go to school at all and many teachers were woefully young and incompetent.

He said in his 1888–1889 report that 13,000 of 96,000 children of ages eight through sixteen were not enrolled in any school. He expressed belief that the number of nongoers was even higher than shown in the survey.

"In all our cities there is a large number of children who are not in attendance upon any school," he said. "Here is an evil for which there ought to be some remedy. We have thousands of children growing up in ignorance which is a prolific source of crime. They will become a perpetual menace to the safety and peace of the community in which they live. The education of the street, the companionship of the idle and vicious, is every whit as potent as that of the school, of books and the influence of a cultured home."

Sabin observed that "an ignorant populace, armed with the ballot, is the most dangerous enemy republican institutions can have."

He asked for a strong compulsory school attendance law. (There was no law saying that children had to go to school.) He recommended, "Every person having under his care a child between the ages of seven and eleven years, inclusive, shall keep such child in school during the whole time that the schools are in session." Every person having a child twelve to sixteen inclusive "shall keep such child in school at least sixteen consecutive weeks each year." No child under twelve "shall be employed in any store, mine or factory, or in other labor, when the schools are in session."

School laws and child labor laws were scanty indeed in those days.

The reports showed the average child attended school for less than four years in the 1880s. Many dropped out after the fifth grade.

Assailing country school boards for hiring incompetent teachers, Sabin asked: "What can be expected of an untrained, immature girl of sixteen or seventeen years of age, whose education scarcely entitles her to a third-grade certificate?

"She can keep school, it is true, so far as filling out the six hours each day is concerned, but she has neither the amount of knowledge, the discipline of mind, nor the maturity of judgment necessary to make a teacher in any sense of the word."

He declared that "economy is a sin" if achieved at the expense of the children by hiring poorly qualified teachers. He commented, "Here as elsewhere money should not be weighed against the welfare of the child."

Sabin once said: "A teacher who can give thorough instruction in reading, writing and spelling, in the daily, practical use of the English language, and in the fundamental rules of arithmetic, ought to be honored with a certificate empowering him to teach these branches in any county in the state. To do this is no mean requirement, and a teacher who possesses it has a right to be proud of it."

Some of Sabin's ideals might be treated with disdain in certain areas of modern American society. He believed that schools should instill in pupils' minds "love of country, reverence for the flag and obedience to law." He added: "The world does not need men of genius so much as it needs men of sense. Not so much great men, whom it is fashionable to admire, as God-fearing men, with clean hands and clear hearts, whom it is safe to follow."

He said the schools had failed "to make our teachings reach out into the homes of the pupils.

"The mental growth of the child at school can not be separated from his mental growth at home," Sabin said. If the lines of direction at both school and home are close to identical, "the greatest progress is made." But if those lines go in opposing directions, either the school or the home will predominate "and become the character of the man."

Sabin did not have his head in the clouds over the education process. He once observed, "There are men who are forever learning, yet never really know anything." He added, "Our American education, if it is to retain the confidence of the people, must be wholly on the side of that morality which has truth for its basis; it must stand for law and order and decency; its instructors must first *know,* and then *practice,* those eternal, immutable principles of right and wrong which are the foundations of a permanent republican liberty."

Sabin maintained that the American flag "should be displayed in every school room and children should be taught what it signifies. . . .

". . . the growth and resources of this country, the history of the past and the possibilities of the future should be so impressed upon the child that he may be proud to say 'I am to be an American citizen.' "

T *". . . Wisdom of Creator . . ."*

HE MISSISSIPPI flowed southward at the rate of 2½ miles an hour. That was how fast huge rafts of logs were carried down the river from the northern forests to such lumber cities as Clinton, when all went well.

But things did not go well frequently. Winds blowing upstream sometimes brought the rafts to a virtual halt. Crosswinds pushed the logs against one shore or the other. One unlucky rafter averaged less than four miles a day with his logs over a period of a month and a half.

William J. Young of Clinton was the first major sawmill operator to quit depending entirely on the natural flow of the river. In 1864 a steamboat pushed a raft down the river at increased speeds to Young's big mill. This not only saved weeks of time but also permitted reductions in the size of raft crews, hardy men who made their living riding logs down the Mississippi. Before long all rafts on the river were being pushed or pulled by boats.

Hundreds of rafts were brought down the Mississippi each year in the robust logging days of the late 1800s. Largest rafts were as much as 275 feet wide and 1,400 to 1,500 feet long. They must have been an imposing sight.

Rafting continued for perhaps sixty-five years and faded out when great forests in Wisconsin and Minnesota became depleted. The last raft reached Fort Madison, Iowa, in 1915.

Young's milling operation at Clinton cut 100 million feet of lumber and 40 million shingles in its top year. Others in Clinton and other river cities also produced nearly as much. One foot of lumber is defined as a piece one foot long, one foot wide, and one inch thick.

These tremendous supplies of new wood products were a vital factor in the great building booms that developed in the midwestern states which were rapidly filling with people.

Iowa showed spectacular population gains in the 1800s. The state's population increased 519,000 in the 1860s, from 675,000 to 1,194,000. The gain was 430,000 in the 1870s, from 1,194,000 to 1,624,000. In the 1880s the Iowa gain was 288,000, from 1,624,000 to 1,912,000, and in the 1890s the increase totaled another 320,000, from 1,912,000 to 2,232,000. Iowa more than tripled its population in the forty years between 1860 and 1900. Other states also showed extraordinary gains in the great westward migrations from the eastern seaboard and from European countries.

One riverboat captain expressed belief that the logs and the river to carry them were part of a divine plan. He wrote, "One can not contemplate this vast amount of building material so admirably suited for houses, barns and fences without recognizing the wisdom of the Creator in providing extensive forests at the headwaters of the Mississippi and its northern tributaries on whose waters the logs could be floated down at so little expense."

The cost of rafting logs from well up in Minnesota down to the eastern central Iowa area was about $1.10 per thousand feet, or $1 a ton for the resultant lumber.

Clinton was reputed to have developed seventeen millionaires from the lumber industry. The hard-working Young probably was the richest of them all when he died in 1896. Thirty years later, Courtland Young, scion of the family, was reputed to be worth $30 million. He was said then to control the Clinton waterworks, the street railway system, and the gas and electric systems. A 1952 report listed the Young interests as owning the *Clinton Herald,* a large bank, a toll bridge, and the street railway.

During the late nineteenth century, Clinton had the reputation at times of being the leading lumber-producing center between Minneapolis and St. Louis and was reported in some years to have cut more lumber than any other city in America.

Clinton lumber shipments once averaged 20 to 40 railroad carloads a day. In 1880, a peak year, the Clinton shipments totaled 13,000 carloads. Sawdust long was a problem for the city. Stretches of the Clinton shore on the river have been underlaid with sawdust as much as twenty feet deep.

Fire was always a major threat. Chancy Lamb of Clinton, whose mills had a capacity of 80 million to 100 million feet of lumber a year, went through four major fires in twenty years but nevertheless survived and prospered.

Lamb came to Clinton in 1857 and scarcely had gotten his first mill in good running order when it burned in 1859. He rebuilt and expanded. Other mills caught fire in 1876 and 1877 and in 1879 he lost a brick building and lumberyards. His combined fire losses totaled $300,000.

Lamb made a major contribution to raft logging when he invented a large metal-and-rope device to control the movement of a vast field of floating logs.

Whole Streets Gone

T HE JUNE THUNDERSTORM ended and the warm evening air grew quiet in Clinton. Lightning flashes continued in the east. The moon and stars peered occasionally through the retreating clouds.

Abruptly Clinton's calm was broken by the sound of a horse madly galloping through the streets. The rider shouted: "Camanche is destroyed by a tornado! Half the inhabitants are buried in the ruins! Send all your doctors!"

Clintonites sprang into action. Volunteers jumped into carriages and wagons and rushed to Camanche, a neighboring town downstream on the Mississippi. Railroad handcars were pressed into service. A relief train and a steamboat were hurriedly gotten ready.

There were no signs of storm damage on the way to Camanche. The moon shone bright and strong. Some thought the alarm might have been a hoax. That notion was abandoned at the first house where three children with broken arms and legs were found. Far worse scenes were ahead.

Confronting the rescuers in town was indescribable devastation. All but 50 of the 350 homes had been damaged and many were flattened. Forty-one persons died and eighty others were injured. Bodies were being pulled from under collapsed buildings. Frantic parents searched for their children and frightened children for their parents.

Whole streets had disappeared. Thirty-nine business buildings were destroyed, including two hotels and two churches, all this within a few miles of untouched Clinton. Said one account: "God save us from ever seeing again such a sight as the village presented. To describe it would be impossible. . . . You had to see it to believe it. Once seeing it would haunt the memory forever."

The 1860 tornado that hit Camanche was one of the worst in Iowa history.

LILLIAN RUSSELL

S *Balked Age with Onions*

SHE WORE a $3,900 jeweled corset and embroidered stockings that cost $400 a pair. Her Japanese spaniel sported a collar containing $1,800 in gems. She lived in a thirty-room mansion, rode a $1,900 bicycle that sparkled with diamonds, and earned the spectacular sum of $5,000 a week.

Her stage name was Lillian Russell. She was the No. 1 glamour girl of her time. She was born on the second floor of the old Hotel Clinton in Clinton in 1861. Her real name was Nellie Leonard. Her father, Charles Leonard, was founder and editor of the *Clinton Herald.*

She did not wear fabulous jewelry and fancy clothes in her early days in Clinton, however. In fact, she did not get to see much of Clinton as a child. The family moved to Chicago in 1863 when she was two years old. She never lived in Clinton again.

As an actress and singer in light operas and other stage productions, Lillian never failed to pack 'em in. She once was called "perhaps the most beautiful woman in facial features in the history of the American theater." She was too hefty to have been much of a threat in modern beauty contests, however. She weighed from 145 to 165 pounds, a lot for a lady. But the customers seventy-five and more years ago really loved her in such productions as *H.M.S. Pinafore* and when she sang such songs as "After the Ball is Over," "Come Down My Evening Star," "The Last Rose of Summer," and "Brighten the Corner Where You Are." President Grover Cleveland listened to her sing a song over the first long-distance telephone hookup. Even though she was forty-six years old, Clinton fans found her still terrific when she came back to her hometown for an appearance in 1908.

She delayed old age by taking cold showers, eating big bunches of green onions, punching a bag, and rolling on the floor to keep her hips under control.

Lillian drew wide acclaim during World War I when she appeared in a marine uniform and personally urged young men to join the marine corps. (Some 10,000 did.) She died in 1922 after returning from a European tour.

DUKE SLATER

Star Peeled Potatoes

F RED (DUKE) SLATER of Clinton earned his three meals a day by peeling a bushel and a half of potatoes at Iowa City.

That fact is important now only to recall that a great athlete, whatever his color, had to work to pay his bills in college fifty years ago.

Slater, a black, was an all-American tackle on the University of Iowa football team in 1921. He was large for his time, six feet two inches, 210 pounds. He previously had been a Clinton High star.

He was awarded his law degree at Iowa in 1928 and was elected a municipal judge in Chicago in 1948. He was one of two Negroes on the

---

Chicago municipal bench at the time. The other thirty-five judges were white.

Slater was a Chicago circuit judge when he died in 1966 at sixty-seven years of age. The chief Illinois circuit judge said: "Judge Slater was a good lawyer and a perfect gentleman. He was highly regarded by his associates; a religious man who set a fine example for youth."

Reckless Driving in 1904

SPEED! DANGER! THRILLS! A Clinton resident experienced all those sensations when he rode 161 miles in nine hours from Clinton to Chicago in an automobile in 1904. That was at a blinding average speed of nearly eighteen miles an hour!

A few of the new-fangled automobiles were just coming into use in Iowa. F. L. Butzloff of Charlotte, Iowa, got one (termed a "devil wagon") and took an unnamed Clinton citizen with him on the trip to Chicago. Here is how the citizen described the bouncing ride: "You soon learn that you partake of the motion of the machine. You feel sure when you leave it that it will be in the right place when you come down. . . .

"After a while you get confidence in your destiny. A succession of hair-breadth escapes forces on you the conviction that you were not born to die so soon. Then you begin to appreciate the sensation. You would not go slow if you could, and if you ride with Fred Butzloff you could not go slow."

The passenger said he and Butzloff were "wonderfully lucky . . . the car went over rutty roads as boys skip stones over smooth water, slid through droves of cattle like a walleyed pike through a rocky torrent, dodged fractious horses like a fox the baying hounds." It is scary even to read about it now, sixty-eight years later.

"We Will Meet You at Border"

THE HAWKEYE RANGERS were not a football team but a Civil War company of cavalry recruited by William E. Leffingwell, Clinton attorney.

The 100-man company was equipped, horses and all, without expense either to the federal or state governments.

The unit went to war under a homemade blue silk banner bordered with gold stars on one side. On the other was an emblem consisting of a hawk and an eye.

In the hawk's talons was a motto, "We will meet you at the border." The motto did not say which border.

The rangers became Company B of the First Iowa Cavalry and saw plenty of fighting. Leffingwell was captain but is listed as having been "dismissed" in 1862 after a year of war. He must not have been disgraced, to any lasting degree at least, because he twice was a Democratic nominee for Congress after the war. (He was not elected.)

Leffingwell liked to drink. He campaigned in 1856 for Democratic President James Buchanan. Henry O'Connor of Muscatine campaigned in the same area at the same time for General John Fremont, the Republican nominee.

Leffingwell got liquored up. His team of horses ran away and threw him out of the buggy. A farmer, strongly opposed to liquor, pulled Leffingwell from the ditch. Tipsy Leffingwell was quick-witted enough to tell the farmer that he was O'Connor and was out "stumping the state for Fremont." As a result, Buchanan got "nearly all the votes" in that dry precinct.

He Upset Prohibition

I N 1882 the people of Iowa approved a state constitutional amendment forbidding the manufacture and sale of liquor, wine, and beer in the state.

District Judge Walter I. Hayes of Clinton stirred consternation among the drys by holding the amendment unconstitutional.

The constitution says an amendment must be approved in identical form by two consecutive legislatures before going to a vote of the people. Judge Hayes held that the wording was changed a little between sessions. The Iowa Supreme Court agreed with the judge and the state's stringent Prohibition amendment never went into effect. The drys were furious but helpless. They never again were able to get such an amendment approved by the people.

It may be said that the Clinton judge alerted all future legislatures to be painstakingly careful when considering constitutional amendments.

Hayes later was elected to Congress four times on the Democratic ticket, a major political achievement in his time. Twice, in 1888 and 1892, he was the only Iowa Democrat elected to Congress.

Hayes was a leading sponsor in Congress of the bill which provided for construction of the Hennepin Canal which connects the Illinois River near LaSalle, Illinois, with the Mississippi River below Rock Island, Illinois. The seventy-five-mile canal was finished in 1907 at a cost of $7.5 million and was long used for transportation of coal and grain.

Two Black "Volumes"

C . S. CAMPBELL of Clinton got a mysterious letter in 1859 from George Weston of Low Moor, Iowa.

The letter said "two volumes of 'The Irrepressible Conflict,' bound in black," would reach Campbell's home the next night.

Campbell understood the message. He prepared for the arrival of two runaway Negro slaves fleeing from their masters in southern states.

Campbell and Weston were members of a secret organization which helped fugitive slaves on their way to safety, perhaps in Chicago or Canada. The Campbell and Weston homes both were "stations" on the famed "underground railroad." The Civil War was still two years in the future. Clinton was a notable underground railroad center.

There was no underground railroad as such, of course. That was the name given to the routes over which helpful people transported the runaways hidden in wagons from one station to another. The stations were ten miles to fifteen miles apart, about as long a round trip as a person would want to drive a horse in one night.

One of the larger groups to escape through Clinton consisted of nine persons, a father and mother and four children and three other men.

A Ghostly Steamboat

G AY PASSENGERS filled the steamboat *Envoy*.

They were going on a Mississippi River excursion from the Clinton area to Dubuque.

Up stepped an officer of the law who said, "You are not going anywhere." He slapped a lien on the *Envoy* for unpaid debts. He tied the boat to a stout post with a strong rope to make certain the vessel did not leave until the debts were paid.

N. C. Roe, owner of the *Envoy*, was in deep financial trouble, which was nothing new for him. He was some $50,000 in the red at the time, a huge sum in those pre–Civil War days of 1855 and 1856. He was always scurrying up and down the river to avoid bill collectors.

This time Roe appeared to have been immobilized at last.

Or was he? Without warning, the tied-up *Envoy* started to move away from the wharf. Evidently there was considerable slack in the rope. The boat picked up speed.

Everybody held his breath as the rope tightened. There was a sudden jerk. The *Envoy* careened and almost capsized. The rigid rope yanked the post out of the ground on shore and into the water.

The crew happily pulled the post on board as a trophy while the discomfited officer watched helplessly. The freed *Envoy* churned to Dubuque where further legal troubles waited.

Dubuque officers also seized the boat. They sought to make certain that the *Envoy* would not leave. They removed the pistonheads from the engine. The officers went ashore, confident they had Roe hog-tied this time.

During the layover, the resourceful Roe had his carpenters construct and install temporary wood pistonheads made of oak.

When the time came for the boat to leave, the engineers quietly got up steam. Without warning, "the lines were quickly cast off, the bells jingled and before the eyes of these astonished officials, the crippled craft, as if by magic, floated out into the broad stream."

The *Envoy* vanished down the river "with bands playing and whistles screaming in derisive triumph."

The *Envoy* was a legendary will-o'-the-wisp in its comings and goings on the Mississippi. Steamboats burned wood in those days. Scattered along the shore were supply yards where skippers bought wood and other needed items.

The *Envoy* specialized in getting free wood. The boat cruised slowly on the river until a woodyard was spotted where there was nobody around. The crew hurriedly landed and filched so much fuel that the *Envoy* looked like a floating woodpile. Left behind for the frustrated supplier was a worthless receipt for the wood taken "on credit."

Nobody could be certain where the *Envoy* was going when she left a wharf. The boat might depart upstream in an evening, blazing with lights which would soon be doused. Then, with exhausts muffled, the darkened *Envoy* might creep downstream on the other side of the channel, fade into the darkness, and perhaps next be heard from on the far-off Ohio River.

Histories do not say what finally happened to the *Envoy*. Probably the boat was seized and sold for debts. Or maybe it is still slipping around ghostlike on the Mississippi, in the darkness of the night.

CEDAR RAPIDS

T "*Cherries Ripe, Cherries Red...*"

HE CHERRY SISTERS disliked dodging eggs.

They usually did not complain too much when the missiles were cabbages, onions, turnips, cigar butts, and the like. They did not object strenuously when a wash boiler was tossed at them on the stage. But eggs . . . !

The sisters served notice during one New York appearance that if anybody threw an egg they were going home. The threat got results. The audience fired no eggs. The show, such as it was, went on.

The Cherry Sisters of Cedar Rapids and Marion were among the most celebrated, and the most awful, stage performers of their time. They acted, sang, danced. They appeared intermittently from 1893 until 1938. There were five sisters in the spinster group at first, three in the later years. The three were Effie, Jessie, and Addie. They were so terrible they were exciting.

Crowds packed the old Olympia Theater in New York for four weeks in 1896 to jeer and to heave things at the Iowa girls.

Vegetables and debris rained on the stage the second night. The audience departed in an "advanced state of hysteria." The sisters were not bothered at all. Said one reviewer, "They never missed a note, or found one either."

Oscar Hammerstein the elder took in a lot of money at the Olympia box office that he badly needed to stave off creditors. (The prosperity was only temporary, however. Hammerstein went broke and lost the Olympia in 1898.)

Another New York drama critic commented: "Never before did New Yorkers see anything like the Cherry Sisters. It is to be hoped that nothing like them ever will be seen again." Back in Iowa one writer said their presentation in Des Moines was the "cleanest show ever seen, also the worst."

Most famous of all observations about the Cherry Sisters was made by Editor Billy Hamilton of the *Odebolt Chronicle* at the turn of the century. After the sisters appeared in Odebolt, he wrote:

Effie is an old jade of 50 summers. Jessie a frisky filly of 40, and Addie, the flower of the family, a capering monstrosity of 35. Their long skinny arms, equipped with talons at the extremities, swing mechanically, and anon frantically at the suffering audience.

The mouths of their rancid features opened like caverns and sounds like the wailing of damned souls issued therefrom. They pranced around the stage . . . strange creatures with painted faces and a hideous mien. Effie is spavined. Addie is stringhalt and Jessie, the only one who showed her stockings, has legs with calves as classic in their outlines as the curves of a broomhandle.

The *Leader*, a morning newspaper published in Des Moines, re-printed the Odebolt comment.

The angry Cherry Sisters thereupon sued the *Leader* for libel in

Polk County District Court in Des Moines. District Judge C. A. Bishop in 1901 ruled that the comment was justified and dismissed the case against the newspaper. The Iowa Supreme Court upheld the verdict.

Effie made a bad mistake in the trial in Des Moines. She presented part of the Cherry Sisters' act in the courtroom. The judge decided that Hamilton's scathing criticism was fair!

Their singing of the song "Oh Don't You Remember Sweet Alice, Ben Bolt?" was described as "a riot the way the Sisters murdered it." Actually, how they sang did not make much difference because the noise from the audience usually was terrific. One critic wrote: "The pianist left after the thing was half over. He could not stand the racket."

Sometimes the sisters stopped the performance to admonish a noisy audience. One sister would say to rowdy spectators: "You don't know anything. You have not been raised well or you would not interrupt a nice, respectable show."

Sometimes they took direct action. Jessie once went down into an audience at La Porte City and "tapped a hoodlum on the head with a board."

Another time a theater patron aimed a piece of calf liver at the girls. The meat struck the sisters' manager in the face. He pursued a small boy in the audience. Another patron hit the manager on the head with a chair.

There were no reports of the Cherrys ever being injured by flying objects. Maybe that was because they knew how to dodge or said objects were squishy. The sisters insisted that reports of rowdyism were exaggerated anyway, and maybe they were. But every young sport who was anybody boasted of having hurled a cabbage at the girls. Effie herself reported this incident at Dubuque: "We had hardly started the act when one of the ruffians in the front row turned a fire extinguisher on the stage. Instead of hitting us as intended, it struck one of the boxes." Occupants of the box were drenched and had to leave.

The Cherrys indignantly denied that they ever performed behind a screen put up to protect them against thrown objects. There is reason to believe they are telling the truth. But the screen story was widely reprinted, and helped build their crowds.

Their theme song was "Cherries ripe, cherries red, Cherry Sisters still ahead; Ta-ra-ra boom-de-ay Cherry Sisters here to stay."

Their main act was "The Gypsy's Warning"; Effie played the part of the Gypsy woman. Addie was an evil Spanish man and Jessie was the Lady. The Spaniard had designs on the Lady and she was willing. But the Gypsy once had a daughter in the same fix. The daughter came to a sad end. The Gypsy did not want the Lady to suffer the same fate. The Gypsy pointed offstage and said dolefully, "Lady, in that green grave yonder lies the Gypsy's only child."

But the Lady did not heed the warning. She left with the Spaniard anyway, while the audience guffawed. Author of the skit is not known. Probably the Cherry Sisters wrote it themselves.

Despite their box-office success for a time, the sisters wound up with

THE CHERRY SISTERS: EFFIE, JESSIE, AND ADDIE

little money. Effie mentioned receiving sums varying from $200 to $1,000 a week for their first New York appearances. From their complaints, however, they often were not fairly compensated.

The sisters originally came from a twenty-acre "farm" near Marion. Their first appearance was in an opera house at Marion. The three main Cherrys lived in Cedar Rapids a major part of their lives. When their stage fame faded away, they opened a bakery in Cedar Rapids. They also sold milk.

Effie twice ran for mayor of Cedar Rapids but got nowhere. Once she polled but 347 votes. In 1926 she ran on a platform of opposition to "high taxes, high skirts, high life, high utility rates." She declared that public officials "waste too much time playing golf." She said, "Ankle-length skirts will be the style if I have my way." The voters were unimpressed. One source said the Cherry Sisters each wore seven underskirts.

In 1935 the Cherry Sisters appeared in New York. Reports said their performance was so pathetic that "Gracie Allen sobbed and Tallulah Bankhead wiped her eyes." Effie, the last Cherry, died in 1944.

The Cherry Sisters really are only a chuckle in the history of Cedar Rapids. Much more important are numerous other exciting persons who are part of Cedar Rapids' past. The list includes a heroic couple involved

in a great ocean tragedy; famed painter Grant Wood;
Carl Van Vechten, leading American man of letters; and
Nathaniel Hubbard, a potent railroad boss of politics.

"*I Would Be Less Than a Man . . .*"

W HEN THE *Titanic* struck an iceberg and sank in the Atlantic in 1912, Walter D. Douglas of a noted Cedar Rapids family refused an early opportunity to leave the doomed ship.

"I would be less than a man," he is reputed to have said, "if I left before every woman was saved."

The fifty-one-year-old Douglas was one of 1,513 persons who died.

Among those saved was his wife Mahala. Her lifeboat was picked up by the ocean liner *Carpathia*.

The Douglases had gone to Europe to procure furnishings for the palatial home they had built on Lake Minnetonka near Minneapolis, Minnesota. He was reputed to have been worth at least $4 million.

He was a member of the Douglas family which, with the Cedar Rapids Stuarts, had started the American Cereal Company, predecessor of the present Quaker Oats Company.

The Walter Douglases had moved from Cedar Rapids to Minneapolis in about 1905. But close Cedar Rapids connections, family and otherwise, remained. Walter Douglas was a director of Quaker Oats, secretary of the Douglas starch works in Cedar Rapids, and director of Security Savings Bank of Cedar Rapids. His body was recovered from the Atlantic and brought to Cedar Rapids for interment in the family vault in Oak Hill Cemetery.

The shaken Mrs. Douglas said the shock of the *Titanic* hitting the iceberg "seemed slight" and everyone on board believed there were sufficient lifeboats available to accommodate all. Many passengers thought the alarm was only temporary anyhow. The huge *Titanic* was brand new and provided the latest luxuries in ocean travel. One unworried husband said to his wife boarding a lifeboat: "You are going out there and play around a while. You will be back in a few minutes."

In describing her husband's refusal to leave the *Titanic,* Mrs. Douglas said he expressed hope that he "soon would be with me again." When she last saw him, she said, "he was turning to assist several women and children waiting to get into lifeboats." One report said he assisted another man in launching the last lifeboat filled with women.

The Douglases' French maid was among those saved.

The rescued Mrs. Douglas said the *Titanic* gave one great heave and sank and the scene was wild for a few minutes and the air was pierced with terrible cries of women and children thrown into the water. The ship went down at 2:20 in the morning.

She added: "Two or three times I moved about to see if I would not awaken from a dream. It seemed impossible that such an awful thing could be taking place. When we saw the lights of the big steamer sink beneath the waves, it seemed as though the world was coming to an end. Everyone shrieked and wept."

Mrs. Douglas recalled that a *Titanic* officer thoughtfully put candles and lights into her lifeboat. Without such lights, she said, "the loss of life would have been much greater." The signal lights of her boat brought all the other bobbing boats together. The officer on the lifeboat put a lantern on a pole and "told me to hold it," she said. She held the pole against the back of another woman.

Sailors on board the approaching *Carpathia* said they saw that light from a distance of ten miles. The *Carpathia* captain expected all the *Titanic* passengers would be saved. He had 3,000 breakfasts prepared. But only 711 were taken aboard his ship.

Mrs. Douglas was sharply critical of the lack of safety measures on the *Titanic*. The ship had no searchlight to check the sea for icebergs, she said, and floating remnants of cork indicated that some life preservers were faulty and incapable of keeping human beings afloat.

There were seventy women who had suddenly become widows taken aboard the *Carpathia* and "all were wonderfully brave."

The men passengers also apparently were brave for the most part, "but there were some cowards." Mrs. Douglas said one man forced his way on to a lifeboat at pistolpoint. That man "took blankets from women and children to protect himself." During the rest of the *Carpathia* voyage to New York, the other men "spat at him when they noticed him at all."

GRANT WOOD

Inspired While Milking

A NEW YORK NEWSMAN once asked Iowa artist Grant Wood where he got the inspiration for his paintings.

"All the really good ideas I've had," Wood replied, "came to me while I was milking a cow."

That reply was thoroughly in keeping with Wood's reputation as a major rural midwestern painter.

"Wood planted art as the men and women he painted planted corn and oats," said one critic. Another called his work "vision rooted in the soil itself." A third writer said, "Wood is 'Ioway' today and rural America always."

Few artists of his era (he died at fifty years of age in 1942) attracted so much attention and aroused so much controversy as Wood.

He did perhaps his greatest painting during the eleven years he occupied a studio in the loft of an old carriage house provided by a Cedar Rapids undertaker family. In that period he completed such paintings as *American Gothic* and *Stone City* (1930); *John B. Turner— Pioneer* and *Woman with Plants* (1929); *Midnight Ride of Paul Revere, Birthplace of Herbert Hoover,* and *Fall Plowing* (1931); *Daughters of Revolution* (1932); and *Dinner for Threshers* (1934).

The portrait of John Turner is considered a turning point in Wood's career. Turner was a Cedar Rapids funeral director and father of David Turner, Wood's patron. Wood painted the elder Turner in 1929 upon returning to Cedar Rapids from Europe. The artist had gotten out of his system the belief that a painter, to be somebody, had to belong to a European school of art. One critic said Wood "came into his creative maturity" at that time.

Wood himself said a painter "should try to express what he knows best." In his case, that meant "midwestern farm life" rather than "French modernism." He was born on an Iowa farm and he loved the settings of rural existence. Even in his studio he wore farm overalls while painting. He was particularly happy with his existence upstairs in the carriage house. He said later, "Things worked out best for me in the studio in Cedar Rapids where I lived, ate, slept and worked, all under one roof."

All his painting, however, was not done with brush and easel. As a young man, he painted the exteriors of barns and houses. His farmer-father died when he was ten. He became a house painter to earn money for food for his mother, sister, and himself. He also did carpenter work and truck gardening.

Wood even built a house of sorts for the family on the outskirts of Cedar Rapids. The family subsisted at times largely on rabbits he trapped and roasted outdoors, and on gathered berries and mushrooms. There was no ADC (aid to dependent children) to help such families in those days.

The common people usually liked Wood's paintings, and some artists and critics did also. A display of his paintings outdrew all rival exhibits at the 1934 Chicago World Fair. Also, sales of photographic reproductions of his paintings led those of all artists at the Fair.

But not everybody liked what he did. A farm woman once told him over the phone he ought to have his "head bashed in."

One farmer examined the painting *Stone City* carefully at the Iowa State Fair and commented, "I would not give 35 cents an acre for that land."

Wood's landscape trees are bulbous in shape. He picked up that design from the patterns on his mother's china.

The satirical *Daughters of Revolution* brought down on Wood the wrath of the Sons of the American Revolution. Wood pictured three dour and stern-jawed women, with a hand holding a teacup. A San Francisco chapter of Sons of the American Revolution called the picture "disgraceful and scandalous and destructive of American traditions." But such comments merely served to generate extra publicity for his works.

His search for old-fashioned red flannel underwear drew attention all over the country in 1935. He wanted such underwear to get the genuine red coloring for a planned picture called *Bath 1880*. The picture was to show an old man wearing red flannels about to take a bath in a washtub.

Wood got the underwear he wanted from a Minneapolis man for $10. But the artist abandoned the planned picture when he was criticized for seeking publicity in his underwear search. The accusation hurt Wood.

As a youngster, he was a topflight art student in the Cedar Rapids schools. Later he was an art instructor. (He taught five years at McKinley High.) The final years of his life were spent on the University of Iowa faculty where he became a professor of fine arts. He was born at Anamosa in 1892 and died in University Hospitals in Iowa City in 1942.

Just where Wood will rank among the painters of the centuries probably remains to be seen. Some believe he was good enough to rank with some of the early Italian masters. But a show critic once said that Wood "contributes nothing. It [his work] is a culmination of a trend of escapism."

Nevertheless, his paintings are prized museum pieces and also are found in important private collections. But he never received a lot of money for his work. He reportedly was paid $300 for *American Gothic,* now in the Chicago Art Institute, and $3,500 for *Dinner for Threshers,* plus nearly $2,000 for the *Thresher* drawings.

Forgotten now is the fact that a Grant Wood lithograph was too risqué for the mails. Wood recalled how farmers in the last century went to the horse tank after a hot day's work, stripped, and drenched themselves with pails of water. Wood drew a picture of such a naked farmer taking a bath, front view. Said one writer, "It is about as pornographic as a statue of Apollo."

Free Rides on Trains

A GOOD WAY to get a public official under obligation was to give him free rides on trains.

Railroads found that out in Iowa a century ago. Using free passes and other inducements, the railroads became the most powerful pressure group in the Iowa legislature and in Iowa politics generally.

Nathaniel M. Hubbard of Cedar Rapids, attorney for the North Western Railroad, was a particularly potent leader of railroad forces.

It is difficult to realize today how vital rail transportation was to the people of Iowa 75 and 100 years ago. There were no hard-surfaced highways (except an occasional plank road), no autos, no trucks, no airplanes.

If a person had any distance to go, or anything to ship, he had to use trains or horse power. River transportation was helpful in some areas but only at certain times of the year.

Hubbard and other railroad lobbyists demonstrated their power in the 1878 legislature. They wanted the hated "Granger law" of 1874 repealed. The lawmakers did as they were told. The law was repealed.

The Granger law was passed in the first place because members of the Grange, a farm organization, were unhappy about high railroad shipping charges. The new law fixed reasonable maximum charges for both passenger and freight service. The cost of passenger tickets was fixed at three cents to four cents a mile.

The law also required each railroad to report its annual earnings to the state in January of each year. Perhaps most important of all, railroads were forbidden to charge one customer any more than any other customer for the same service. The railroads wanted none of these limitations.

The railroads had the battle for the Granger law repeal half won before the 1878 legislature even convened. In every county, the railroads had given strong support in the 1877 election to candidates for state representative who favored repeal. A prorail majority was elected. The railroads had control of the Iowa House in their hip pockets.

This does not mean the winners were necessarily rail puppets. Some legislators sincerely believed that the railroads never would extend tracks into their counties unless the restrictive law first was repealed. Many parts of the state still badly needed rail service.

The big problem of the rail forces was to line up sufficient votes in the Iowa Senate to insure repeal.

Many Iowans rode trains on free passes to Des Moines to urge the legislature to rescind the Granger law.

"Large delegations visited the capitol and appeared before the Senate railroad committee," said one historian. "Shippers who were in full enjoyment of secret rebates expressed their gratitude by . . . appearing before the committee. Others, thankful for 'favors to come,' joined the army of petitions for repeal.

"Construction companies came in with statements to the effect that, with 'ruinous' restrictions removed, railroad building in Iowa would be renewed."

The committee voted approval of the repeal bill, and so did the Senate and the House.

As a substitute for the repealed regulatory law, the legislature created a railroad commission which could only advise and not enforce any laws. Salaries of the commissioners were paid by the railroads. The commission was largely a sham.

It took ten years, or until 1888, to restore some semblance of state regulation over railroads in Iowa.

Hubbard, called "one of the strongest railroad lawyers in the state," represented the North Western from 1867 until his death in 1902. He served as a district judge from 1865 to 1867. He was known for his incisive comments.

An attorney who had been governor once tried a case before Judge Hubbard. The attorney recalled that he had appointed the judge to the bench and indicated that Hubbard ought to do him a favor now in return.

Hubbard retorted, "Yes, I remember that [appointment] very well as being the only decent act of your term of office."

One leading Iowa Republican said he never saw Hubbard drink whisky. Hubbard offered this advice, "If you ever drink such stuff, always drink a little less than the others do so that you will have sense enough left to pick up the secrets that fools babble about in their cups."

A very pompous physician asked permission to leave the courtroom to visit his patients. Hubbard said, "Better stay here and give your patients a chance to get well."

Hubbard appeared as an attorney to argue an appeal before the Iowa Supreme Court in Des Moines. The opposing attorney pounded the table vigorously during his argument. When it came his turn, Hubbard said: "I have been a blacksmith in my time. I will pound this table to splinters if it will help me win this lawsuit."

Hubbard once was an attorney in a trial involving John Weare, pioneer banker. During a recess, Weare mopped his brow with a red bandanna handkerchief. Hubbard called across the room, "John, it makes you sweat to tell the truth, doesn't it?"

Hubbard once was accused of giving 500 free tickets, presumably railroad passes, to delegates to a state political convention. He replied: "That's a lie. I gave 1,100 tickets this year."

In one instance, the railroads paid all the expenses in taking the entire Iowa legislature to Chicago to see an opera. Half the legislators were transported on the first trip and the other half on the second trip.

The opera junket may have been set up, in part at least, by James E. Blythe, Mason City attorney. He represented five north Iowa railroads in the 1890s and later. He was a half-brother of Joseph E. Blythe of Burlington, who was general counsel for the Burlington Railroad.

James E. Blythe was elected Republican state chairman in 1892. Strangely, his hobby was oriental rugs and he became an authority in that field.

Jake (The Barber) Sobbed

SPECTATORS WATCHED a scene from the Chicago underworld unfold in Cedar Rapids federal court in 1943.

The notorious Jake (The Barber) Factor, internationally known confidence man, sobbed as he tried to withdraw a plea of guilty. He said he had pleaded guilty some time before only because of a fear of gangland vengeance. He felt he would be safer in prison than out.

"I was told I would be killed on entering this courtroom," he told the judge.

Factor had come to Cedar Rapids to be sentenced on a charge of embezzling receipts for large supplies of whisky stored in warehouses. He and others were accused of bilking investors in the warehouse receipts out of $1 million.

Factor's fear of being shot down had nothing to do with the whisky case. He said two vicious Chicago gunmen, Roger Touhy and Basil (The Owl) Banghart, wanted to kill him for an entirely different reason.

Factor had been kidnaped ten years before by Touhy and Banghart. They collected $70,000 ransom. They were caught and sentenced to ninety-nine years in prison. Factor testified against them.

Touhy vowed he would kill Factor when he got out of prison. Touhy and Banghart escaped from an Illinois penitentiary at about the same time that Factor and ten others were indicted at Cedar Rapids for the whisky fraud. The frightened Factor lived in a state of constant suspense. He decided the best thing to do was to plead guilty at Cedar Rapids and get inside the protecting walls of a federal prison.

Touhy and Banghart were recaptured, however, and returned to the penitentiary before Factor's time of sentencing at Cedar Rapids.

The judge refused to allow Factor to withdraw his plea of guilty. He was given a ten-year sentence and a $10,000 fine. He paid the fine and was released on parole in 1949 after serving six years. He lived a respectable life afterwards as a prosperous real estate executive in Beverly Hills, California. He donated a $1 million recreation center to the predominantly Negro riot-torn Watts area in Los Angeles in 1967.

Factor got his "barber" name from the fact that he was a barber in Chicago in the days when the cost of a haircut was fifteen cents. He developed into a large-scale gambler and crook. He reportedly once took Edward VIII of England for a lot of money in a gambling game before Edward ascended the throne in the 1930s. Factor also was charged with fleecing British investors out of $7 million by manipulating mining stock prices. He avoided extradition on that charge and settled civil damage suits for $1.3 million. He also once reportedly broke a gambling casino bank at Letouquet, France, by winning $650,000.

The Cedar Rapids indictment was based on the misappropriation of warehouse receipts held by 300 investors. They said they surrendered the receipts on a promise that they would realize $100 a barrel for the whisky instead of the usual $60 or $70. The extra profit was to come from bottling the liquor as soon as it had aged four years. But there wasn't any profit in the end and the whisky had been removed from the warehouses.

Fifteen of the victims were residents of Cedar Rapids, including one leading clergyman.

Factor evidently did not fear Touhy and Banghart would get him after his release in 1949. Both were then still in prison. Touhy was shot down in Chicago in 1959, only twenty-three days after he was freed.

Factor was in Chicago at the time of Touhy's death. Factor said, "This really breaks me up and I'm sorry to hear it."

The sixty-one-year-old Touhy may have been slain by other gangsters who felt he knew too much and might talk.

CARL VAN VECHTEN

The Tattooed Countess

A s a young man in Cedar Rapids about 1897, Carl Van Vechten once blurted out in typical teen-age fashion, "I'm so damn bored with this town I'd like to put on a bath towel and run through the streets naked."

Mahala Douglas went into the house and returned with a towel. "Go ahead, Carl," she said.

This incident took place perhaps fifteen years before Mrs. Douglas's tragic *Titanic* experience. Also, far in the future was Van Vechten's career as one of America's great men of letters.

Mrs. Douglas was an older woman and appears to have been married twice. A Van Vechten biographer said that beyond playing piano and going to Greene's opera house "Carl usually parked himself on the doorstep of Mahala Dutton Benedict Douglas." The biographer added: "Because the town considered the lady too emancipated, Carl was warned by his family to avoid her. He promptly interpreted this as an order to see her more, and did so whenever the opportunity arose."

She may have been the model for *The Tattooed Countess,* Van Vechten's once-famous novel published in 1924. The "countess" was an Iowa girl who went away to marry money. Her husband soon died. She had a number of affairs with young Europeans and then returned to her home in "Maple Valley" (Cedar Rapids). Bored, she became involved with a handsome seventeen-year-old boy and finally took him to Europe.

A Van Vechten brother read the book and wrote Carl, "If you don't get murdered when you go to Cedar Rapids, I miss my guess." But the Cedar Rapids reaction was not hostile. In fact, a number of Cedar Rapids residents claimed to have been the inspiration for many of the book's characters.

One critic said Van Vechten's writings evoke "images of . . . erratic and erotic individuals who trip lightly from novel to novel, living a cream puff existence, engaging themselves in very improper affaires d'amour, and conversing on impossible situations."

Carl Van Vechten was born in Cedar Rapids in 1880 and went away to school, and for good, in 1899. He died at eighty-four in 1964. Few native Iowans have had so marked an impact on the culture of their times. He wrote 7 novels, more than 200 magazine articles and book reviews, and established a number of important library collections.

"Almost singlehandedly, he was responsible for the popular recognition of the Negro as a creative artist during the Harlem renaissance," Van Vechten's biographer said. Among other things, Van Vechten edited the selected works of Gertrude Stein; published works on dancers Nijinsky, Isadora Duncan, and Pavlova; has been described as the first music critic to write about George Gershwin and Igor Stravinsky; produced nine volumes of music and literary criticism.

In his later years he became a superb portrait photographer. He took some 15,000 pictures, many of them of leading personages of his time. He refused money for his photography. To take pay, he said, would give his subjects "control" over his photographic work. He once said of his writing: "I possess only sufficient skill to write about what happened to interest and please myself; and in a manner that pleases myself; with the further limitation that I never entirely succeed in doing that. If then, I succeed in pleasing others, that largely must be in the nature of an accident."

Another writer said of a Van Vechten book, "It has the charm of a pair of patent leather dancing slippers, the sparkle of wine glasses and diamonds, the beauty of a girl with thick dark hair, the seducing delightfulness of a cafe at the dinner hour."

Argument over Pancakes

A CORPULENT former president of the United States provoked an argument at a breakfast table in Cedar Rapids.

The former president was William Howard Taft and he was a guest in the home of Luther Brewer, publisher of the old *Cedar Rapids Republican* newspaper. Other guests included Iowa Governor William Harding and Cyrenus Cole, editor of the *Republican*. The year was 1918 and the United States was involved in World War I.

Taft loved to start a fight and then sit back and enjoy the battle. Over pancakes he soon had Governor Harding and Cole in a wrangle.

There were a lot of native Germans in Iowa at the time and Germany was an enemy in the war. The use of German in conversations was common in many Iowa communities and was the cause of much friction.

Harding had issued a proclamation forbidding the use of any foreign language in Iowa. Cole, who came from Holland Dutch ancestors at Pella, strongly objected to the proclamation.

Cole related later: "I went so far as to tell the Governor that if my mother were still living, I would call her up on the telephone and in his hearing talk with her in a foreign language. If he arrested me for doing that, I would announce myself as a candidate for office and defeat him."

Cole maintained that the proclamation was unconstitutional.

When Harding retorted that Cole would be more likely to find himself "in a cell than the Governor's office," Taft brought the dispute to a close by saying, "What is the Constitution of Iowa among friends seated around a breakfast table, with more buckwheat cakes awaiting immediate consumption?"

Cole reported that Taft's appetite for buckwheat cakes was prodigious. The former president weighed 300 pounds. Cole said Taft ate three plates of buckwheat cakes, floating in melted butter and syrup and with sausages heaped around the cakes. Taft said he would go on a restricted diet after that breakfast. But he never did, for very long at least.

Taft, who was president from 1909 to 1913, often stopped at Cedar Rapids between trains or to fill speaking engagements there. He was a close personal friend of Brewer.

Cole became a congressman after retiring from the newspaper. He was in Congress twelve years, from 1921 to 1933. He acquired the title of "Corn Sugar Cole" for advocating increased use of sugar made from corn. His purpose was to boost the price of corn from the low levels that prevailed in the 1920s.

Cole wrote history as a hobby, particularly after a notable newspaper and political career. He said: "I count myself fortunate to have writing as a hobby. . . . An unoccupied mind is like an unoccupied house into which bats fly through open windows."

Cole went to Cedar Rapids in 1898 after a newspaper career in Des Moines.

"The Cedar Rapids of which I became a part was a city of no mean importance in Iowa," he wrote thirty-eight years later. "What it was then . . . was due to the fact that men of vision came to live there and do business." He added: "It is now the fashion to under-estimate what is called rugged individualism. But it was by that kind of individualism that the City of Cedar Rapids has prospered, and those who have had less of such individualism have prospered with them."

KEOKUK

Unafraid of Mob

T HE SHABBY, bearded individual calmly faced 100 angry soldiers. He seemed unafraid that he might be hanged at any moment to a lamppost in downtown Keokuk.

His name was Henry Clay Dean. He bitterly opposed the war. . . .

> *Newspapers carried reports regularly of Iowans killed and wounded in action. . . .*
>
> *There were strong objections to the draft and insistent demands that the war be ended by negotiation. . . .*
>
> *Patriots blasted peace advocates. . . .*
>
> *Whites feared their jobs would be taken by blacks. . . .*
>
> *Organizations were formed to embarrass the government in its prosecution of the war. . . .*
>
> *Officials jailed some dissenters but worried about making martyrs out of them. . . .*

The above recital could have been a portrayal of war-weary Iowa and the United States in the 1960s and early 1970s. Actually what the report does describe are difficulties of the 1861–1865 Civil War era, which was torn by many of the same griefs, resentments, frictions, and doubts as existed during the Vietnam conflict a century later. There is very little completely new under the sun. . . .

HENRY C. DEAN

Nineteenth-Century Hippie

H ENRY CLAY DEAN, an Iowa preacher and lawyer, was so unkempt that he might have been called a hippie in modern America. But he was a tremendous public speaker and a person of great courage who assailed Lincoln and the Union cause without letup during the Civil War. He in turn was denounced as "an advocate of slavery, a sympathizer with traitors, a friend of the rebels and disloyal to the Union."

Returning from Illinois in the spring of 1863, Dean stopped at a friend's house in Keokuk.

He had scarcely arrived when he was grabbed by 100 soldiers who were in Keokuk recovering from wounds and illnesses in the army hospitals there.

The soldiers marched Dean to the corner of Second and Main streets in downtown Keokuk. They formed a hollow square, with Dean in the middle, standing on a dry-goods box. They demanded that Dean disown his past statements. This he "stoutly refused to do." There is no question but that he was threatened with immediate death.

James B. Howell, editor of the *Keokuk Gate City* newspaper, pleaded with the crowd not to lynch Dean. Howell was strongly loyal to the Union and "popular with the people." His plea may have saved Dean's life. The soldiers voted to turn their prisoner over to a military police officer instead of injuring him.

When the crowd was ugliest, Dean "uttered not a single word, nor did his nerve desert him for a second."

He was locked up in the guardhouse. Federal officials considered "deporting" him into the South. An official at St. Louis expressed belief that Dean was "a very disloyal man and a dangerous influence." But Dean was released after a few weeks. Maybe the authorities decided he would cause less trouble with his uncensored talk than if he were made a martyr as a political prisoner.

Dean might have been associated in Iowa with the Knights of the Golden Circle, a secret organization of southern sympathizers.

Iowa Governor Samuel Kirkwood was deeply concerned over the Knights in 1863 and said their goal was "to embarrass the government in prosecution of the war, mainly by encouraging desertions from the army, protecting deserters from arrest, discouraging enlistments, preparing the public mind for armed resistance to conscription."

Kirkwood said the government was being accused of wanting to end slavery so that freed slaves could come north and "compete with the poor white man" for jobs.

Also, the governor said, the draft was criticized as designed to force "only the poor white man into the ranks of the army."

When the draft did come to Iowa, two officials looking for draft evaders were murdered in Poweshiek County.

All this is not to be taken to mean that most Iowans were disloyal to the Union. On the contrary. Iowa volunteers fought, bled, and died by the thousands in Northern armies. Iowa sent 75,780 men to fight for the Union cause, or more than 10 percent of her population at the time.

While it is true that 1,474 Iowans were listed as deserters, approximately 13,000 men from this state died in the service of their country, nearly as many as in the two World Wars, the Korean War, and the Vietnam War combined.

But there also was a sizable body of Iowans who were strongly antiwar, and quite a few favorable to the cause of the South.

When Henry Clay Dean's blasts against Lincoln are examined, it is understandable why he aroused so much anger.

In a speech at the 1864 Democratic National Convention, Dean said Lincoln had failed "for all the vast armies placed at his command. . . . And still the monster usurper wants more men for his slaughter pens. Blood has flowed in torrents, and yet the thirst of the old monster is not quenched. His cry is for more blood."

Even in 1868, three years after Lincoln had been assassinated, Dean wrote such statements as the following about the war: "Every household yielded its first-born to the battlefield. Lincoln had filled a new graveyard in every neighborhood, whose white monuments were reared to commemorate his bloody reign. . . .

"Lincoln was cunning, treacherous and fickle. . . . [He] grew wealthy from spoils of office."

Quite different from the usual picture of Abraham Lincoln, rated by most historians as a gentle and sincerely kindly man.

Dean's slovenly appearance became a legend. He was called "Dirty Shirt Dean" and once was described as having appeared on a platform "disguised in a clean shirt." Says one account, "In warm weather he would make a speech in his shirt sleeves, his collar unbuttoned, one suspender slipped from his shoulder and perhaps one or both shoes untied."

He often ate with his fingers and with his hat on. He swilled coffee, five or more cups to a meal.

Mark Twain, the great American humorist and writer, saw Dean in Keokuk. Twain wrote that Dean had the habit of sitting down on a Keokuk curb with a book, "careless or unconscious of the clatter of commerce and the tramp of the passing crowds, and bury himself in his studies by the hour, never changing his position except to draw in his knees now and then to let a dray [cart] pass unobstructed."

Twain described Dean's clothes as differing "in no way from a wharf rat, except that they were raggeder, more ill-assorted and inharmonious . . . and several layers dirtier."

Twain also wrote this account of a Dean speech in Keokuk: A lecturer had failed to appear. Dean was plucked off the street to serve as a substitute speaker. He came on to the platform "shoes down at the heels; socks of odd colors . . . damaged trousers, relics of antiquity and a world too short, exposing some inches of naked ankle; an unbuttoned vest, also too short and exposing a zone of soiled and wrinkled linen . . . ; a long black handkerchief wound round and round the neck like a bandage; bobtailed blue coat . . . with sleeves which left four inches of forearm unprotected."

Laughter greeted Dean but he did not mind. He started speaking even though hardly anyone was listening. Then he said something that suddenly gripped the audience's attention. Twain continued: "He [Dean] followed it quick and fast with other telling things; warmed to his work and began to pour his words out . . . ; grew hotter and hotter, and fell to discharging lightnings and thunder—and now the house began to break into applause, to which the speaker gave no heed but went hammering straight on; unwound his black bandage and cast it away, still thundering; discarded the bobtail coat and flung it aside, firing higher and higher all the time; finally flung the vest after the coat; and then for an untimed period stood there, like another Vesuvius, spouting smoke and flame, lava and ashes, raining pumice stone and cinders, shaking the moral earth . . . with a crash, explosion upon explosion, while the mad multitude stood on their feet in a solid body, answering back with a ceaseless hurricane of cheers."

Eugene Field, noted Chicago newspaperman and poet, said of Dean: "He talked so fascinatingly that ladies at first revolted against his unkempt appearance were attracted to him by the brilliance of his wit and the prodigality of his erudition; once under the spell of his remarkable conversation powers, it became easy to grow blind to the man's grotesque personal appearance and repelling raiment."

Dean had been a circuit-riding preacher in Virginia and chaplain of the United States Senate in Washington before coming to Iowa in 1850. He lived in Mount Pleasant for a number of years.

Friends said Dean was opposed to slavery in principle but felt that slaves should be freed by purchase and not by force.

Dean came to Des Moines in later years and delighted Democratic audiences by blistering attacks on James "Ret" Clarkson, then editor of the *Register*.

Clarkson long had been a sharp critic of Dean. Nevertheless, they were fast personal friends and Dean was one man who could come to the *Register* office and "smoke cheap tobacco in an old strong pipe and be welcome." Clarkson intensely disliked tobacco smoke.

Older persons were skeptical of Dean but "nearly all young people who knew him were his fast friends."

Iowa Wesleyan College students at Mount Pleasant horrified their elders by inviting Dean, then a fellow townsman, to speak on the campus. The oldsters feared he would be blasphemous and would appear sloppily dressed.

An immense crowd gathered. Lo and behold, for once Dean showed up faultlessly dressed, "with a shirt bosom of frills as white as snow and with that bearing of dignity he could so easily assume."

Rather than impiety, he lectured on the topic "God is Love" and he "swept everybody before him with his eloquence, enemies and friends alike."

Dean moved his family and library of 4,000 books to Putnam County, Missouri, in 1871. The library and many valuable papers were destroyed by fire in 1876. He died in Missouri in 1887 at the age of sixty-five.

"Watchful Fox"

T HE FIRED-UP INDIANS were impatient to dash off to war against the whites.

Okay, said Chief Keokuk, but first we should kill all our women, children, and old people. They will die anyway if the palefaces win. And Keokuk made it clear that he expected the whites to win.

The ardor of Keokuk's tribesmen cooled quickly. They of course did not want to see their loved ones die.

They decided not to join forces with Chief Black Hawk in the ill-fated Black Hawk War of 1832 in which the Indians were defeated and a great many lost their lives.

Keokuk, a great orator, simply could not see any way for the Indians to win. He warned his fellow red men that white soldiers "are springing up like grass on the prairies." He said in a contest where the numbers were so unequal "we finally must fail."

Keokuk, who was one-quarter white, was realistic and was an appeaser. His name, Ke-o-kuck, meant "watchful fox" and "he-who-has-been-everywhere."

He was born in the Sac tribe near the Rock River in Illinois in about 1790 and died in about 1848 in Kansas.

In 1883 his remains were brought to Keokuk and reburied in the city's Rand Park bordering on the Mississippi. The grave site is marked by a big monument on which is mounted a statue of Chief Keokuk more than ten feet high.

J. C. WRIGHT

Disliked in Towns

J . C. WRIGHT was cordially disliked in a great many small towns in Iowa but he didn't mind.

He insisted on closing small schools which were unable to provide instruction that children need in this age of exploding knowledge.

Redheaded Jim Wright became state superintendent of public instruction in 1955 after twenty-seven eventful years in the school system at Keokuk.

The state superintendent has much to say about how Iowa high schools and grade schools shall be operated.

Wright led the way in getting many small school districts to merge into fewer larger ones. In his six years as state superintendent, the number of school districts in Iowa was cut from 4,417 to 1,901 and the number of high schools from 819 to 510.

"Get out there and close those small schools," he told his department fieldmen. They did but it was a tough battle. Towns were enraged over losing their high schools (and high school basketball teams). One fieldman said he did not even dare buy gasoline in one hostile central Iowa town.

Rural and small-town forces held complete control of the legislature at the time even though they did not constitute a majority of the people of Iowa. Thus, Wright's days in the state superintendent job were numbered, particularly since he had to be confirmed every four years by the Iowa Senate. The 1959 Senate failed to confirm his appointment. He resigned in 1960.

He made it clear throughout his state career that many Iowa children were being shortchanged in the quality of education they were getting. He was quoted as saying in 1956: "Less than half the high schools [in Iowa] offer physics and only one in six offers chemistry as often as once in four years. Foreign languages are almost unknown and art courses are virtually nonexistent in the small schools."

He sought to give full credit to others for the improvements being achieved. He once commented, "It is heartening to observe that the citizens of Iowa . . . are moving in the direction of making it possible for boys and girls to receive a sound modern educational program which will enable them to compete successfully with those of other states in this satellite age."

Wright, a native of Kansas, also was prominent in drives to boost minimum standards in courses of study in all Iowa schools and to increase the requirements in teacher training.

Wright started at Keokuk in 1928 as a high school science teacher and head basketball and track coach. (He majored in physics and chemistry at Drake and got his master's degree in English at the University of Iowa.)

In the next ten years, Wright's Keokuk basketball teams won 75 percent of their conference games, captured several titles, and never finished below a tie for second. He became high school principal in 1938 and Keokuk superintendent in 1940. He held that job when appointed state superintendent, a post, incidentally, that he did not seek.

Keokuk came to national notice during Wright's stay there because of the advanced architecture of a new $1.5 million high school.

Wright left Des Moines in 1961 to become secretary in Washington of the Committee for Advancement of School Administrators. In 1963 he became director of education in American Samoa in the South Pacific. He served in the late 1960s as a professor of education in Northeast Missouri State Teachers College at Kirksville, Missouri.

When Wright resigned his Iowa state job, the state board of public instruction said in a statement: "The people of Iowa have followed his courageous leadership in the field of reorganization of their school districts so that our state has led the nation the last 5 years in elimination of small and inefficient districts.

"Through his leadership, and under the mandate of the Legislature, the standards for approval of school districts have been raised and the whole level of elementary and secondary education has been definitely improved."

Wright had a hard time as a college student. He worked his way through Drake University entirely on his own. Once he lived for a couple of days on a pie brought home by his roommate from a cafe where the roommate worked. Also, the roommates brewed and sold (nonalcoholic) punch to fraternities for parties. Wright said: "We got a lot of citric acid and a few lemons. We made punch at a cost of 50 cents for five gallons. We sold the stuff for $1 a gallon. It was good too. Our buyers were happy. So were we."

Found $50 Bill

MARK TWAIN found a $50 bill on a Keokuk street in 1856.

He was about twenty-one years old and far from well-heeled. His unbelievable find was "the largest assemblage of money" he had ever seen.

He advertised his find in the newspaper "and suffered more than a thousand dollars worth of solicitude and fear and distress in the next few days lest the owner see the advertisement and come and take my fortune away."

After four such days he could stand "this misery no longer."

"I felt I must take that money out of danger," he wrote, "so I bought a ticket to Cincinnati and went to that city."

Twain lived in Keokuk perhaps fifteen months. His brother Orion owned a job-printing office in Keokuk. Orion published the first Keokuk city directory in 1856 and Mark set most of the type. Mark humorously listed himself in that directory as an "antiquarian."

Mark's mother lived in Keokuk at least the last eight years of her life. She died there at eighty-seven years of age in 1890 and was buried in Hannibal, Missouri, the original home city of the family.

Born during Opera

THE ARRIVAL of Elsa Maxwell in Keokuk was spectacular.

Elsa, internationally famous as a thrower of parties, was born in the Keokuk town hall in 1887. Her mother was watching a presentation of an opera *Mignon* at the time.

"I'm afraid I interrupted the aria," Elsa said half a century later. The opera was staged by a touring French company from New Orleans.

Elsa did not tarry in Keokuk. The family moved to California when she was eighteen months old. Her mother was a Keokuk native.

As a chubby, gay adult, Elsa became a legend in top society. In her autobiography, she wrote immodestly, yet with considerable truth: "I am recognized as the arbiter of international society and the most famous hostess in the world. I have entertained more royalty than any other untitled hostess."

Her motto was "Do good and have fun," and have fun she did. She traced her career as a swinging party-giver to a rebuff when she was twelve years old. She was told in San Francisco that she came from a family too poor for her to be invited to a certain party. She said, "I made up my mind I would give great parties all over the world," which she did.

She wanted her epitaph to be "Die happy." But she had no tombstone when death came at seventy-six years of age in 1963. The body was cremated and the ashes scattered over the Adriatic Sea, which she loved.

Elsa never married, which was quite different from the record of Amelia Folsom, who lived in Keokuk as a youngster. Amelia became the twenty-sixth wife of Mormon leader Brigham Young in 1863. Young had twenty-seven wives and fifty-seven children all told. None of the Young offspring was Amelia's. She was childless.

Amelia was twenty-five and Young sixty-two at the time of their marriage. She was thirty-one when she appeared with sixty-eight-year-old Young at the inaugural ball of President Grant in Washington in 1869. She died in 1910 at seventy-two years of age.

H *Harnessed Big River*

UGH COOPER harnessed the mighty Mississippi River at Keokuk.

Cooper, one of the great builders of his time, commanded an army of 2,500 workers who constructed the big power dam at Keokuk between 1910 and 1913.

The project cost $24 million. The dam is 4,649 feet long and has a maximum height of 53 feet. Poured into the structure were 2.3 million tons of materials, including 3 million sacks of cement.

There was good reason to locate the dam in the river at Keokuk. The Mississippi drops less than one foot to the mile on the average between St. Louis and New Orleans. But the fall averaged two feet to the mile from Keokuk to a point eleven miles upstream, a total of twenty-two feet in a relatively short distance. The steeper descent created the "Des Moines Rapids," which was an area with a fast-moving and dangerous current but nevertheless ideal at the time for production of electric power.

The dam's fifteen turbines, each weighing sixty-five tons, now have a production capacity of 150,000 horsepower. Most of the electricity is transmitted to St. Louis, 145 miles away.

Hugh Cooper was forty-eight years old when the dam was finished. Born in Sheldon, Minnesota, it was said that he built over the nation hydroelectric plants costing more than $80 million and with a capacity upwards of 800,000 horsepower. He was vice-president and chief engineer of the Mississippi River Power Company, which built the Keokuk dam. The body of water back of the dam was named Cooper Lake in commemoration of the noted engineer.

RUPERT HUGHES

$125,000 Year from Movies

T HE TROUBLE with me is that practically everything interests me," Rupert Hughes once said. "I should like to live a thousand years and a thousand lives."

Hughes, a leading modern American writer, spent his boyhood in Keokuk. The family moved there from Missouri when he was seven. His father was president of the old Keokuk & Western Railroad.

Hughes wrote sixty books and many short stories and radio and movie scripts. His work includes an excellent three-volume biography of George Washington whom he considered "the greatest man who ever lived."

A man of short stature, Hughes did almost all his writing in longhand at night. He said he never learned to think on a typewriter. His income was as high as $125,000 a year at one time from movie rights alone.

He saw considerable military service and emerged from World War I a major. He once said: "Perpetual peace strikes me as no more attainable than perpetual motion. Such a thing is contrary to human nature. It is inconceivable and undesirable that human beings should have no opinions in which they believe so strongly that they would die for them. . . .

"It would not mark a very high civilization to have all men say: 'There is not one principle and cause that I believe in enough to fight for.' "

Hughes, who was an uncle of Howard Hughes, the mysterious Nevada tycoon, died at eighty-four years of age in 1956 at Los Angeles.

Teddy Planted a Tree

Sᴇᴇɪɴɢ a president in person was a great experience in pretelevision days.

Special trains from Centerville, Moulton, and elsewhere brought thousands of spectators to Keokuk when President Teddy Roosevelt came to town in 1903.

He planted a tree in the park, pressed a button that started the machinery in a new Hubinger starch factory, and made a speech that would have delighted the Iowa Development Commission today.

The president congratulated Iowa on its "great natural advantages, a rich soil . . . a state that lends itself to diversified industries." He said Keokuk had expanded industrially "to a degree that would not have seemed possible" a few years earlier. But the "greatest of all things to have, as Iowa has," were men and women of high quality and ability.

In 1907 Roosevelt was still president and he came to Keokuk a second time and boarded a steamboat for a trip down the Mississippi to Memphis.

"No Soldier on Firing Line..."

Tʜᴇ sɪxᴛᴇᴇɴ-ʏᴇᴀʀ-ᴏʟᴅ soldier, seriously ill of typhoid fever, could not stand even to look at the unappetizing food that was offered.

"If you don't eat this you will have to do without," said the hospital attendant. "There is nothing else."

A visitor, Mrs. Annie Wittenmyer of Keokuk, was furious that a sick young soldier should be offered such terrible food. She gave this description of the offered breakfast: "On a dingy-looking wooden tray was a cup full of black, strong coffee. Beside it was a leaden-looking platter on which were a piece of fried fat bacon, swimming in its own grease, and a slice of bread."

Mrs. Wittenmyer was particularly angry because the sick youth was her own brother David who had joined the Union Army some months before. He was ill in the army hospital at Sedalia, Missouri. The year was 1862 and the Civil War with all its bloodshed and suffering was agonizing the nation.

Mrs. Wittenmyer, one of the great angels of mercy of the war, had come to the Sedalia hospital as a field worker for the Keokuk Aid Society.

She determined to do something about food served in the army hospitals. (David, incidentally, recovered.)

She found that all Union Army soldiers, well and sick, usually got the same food. Too often that meant only bacon, beans, bread, and coffee.

Such meals most certainly would not tide over the perfectly healthy serviceman today and would be most unsatisfactory for a patient running a high fever and/or suffering from an infected wound.

In 1863 she got the military authorities to approve a large number of diet kitchens to prepare special foods in each hospital for the sick and wounded. She was put in charge of the kitchens in the entire vast Union Army hospital system. Says one historian, "There is no doubt that hundreds, perhaps thousands of lives were saved by this . . . change in food."

She sent out urgent calls for donations of foods for hospital use. One such call said: "The articles most needed are potatoes, onions, sour-krout, corn meal, pickles, dried fruit, cranberries, molasses, soda crackers, toasted rusk, butter, eggs, condiments, and stimulants. Cider vinegar would also be acceptable."

Women of Iowa and other states responded in a big way. Women volunteers also performed nobly in operating the diet kitchens. The volunteers were described as from "the highest circles of society, educated, refined and accomplished, and each was required to maintain the life and character of an earnest Christian. They thus commanded the respect of officers and men, and proved a powerful instrument of good."

General Ulysses S. Grant, Union Army commander-in-chief and later president, once said of Annie, "No soldier on the firing line gave more heroic service than she rendered."

Service to humanity was her lifelong philosophy.

When she and her husband came to Keokuk in 1850, she personally hired a teacher and opened a free school for children. (There were no public schools as we know them today.) Nearly 200 youngsters were enrolled. Many were "ragged, dirty and neglected." She had them "washed and clothed," with church women helping in the project.

When the war started, widowed Annie began her arduous and dangerous work with troops in the field—and in the hospitals. She left this painful picture of a military hospital:

The restless tossing of the fever-stricken ones . . . the groans of the wounded, the drip, drip, drip of the leaking vessels hung over the worst-wounded ones to drop water on their bandages and keep them cool and moist, put every nerve on the wrack, and pulsated through heart and brain till it seemed as though I should go wild.

It was an inside view of the hospitals that made me hate war as I had never known how to hate it before.

The pitiful cry of the helpless ones calling "Nurse, nurse! Water, water!" and perhaps the weary nurses making no response—sitting there fast asleep, yet willing to do their duty when I aroused them—still rings in my ears.

Army nurses in those days were men who were not fond of their jobs. The doctors and hospital directors were badly overworked, too often drunks, and sometimes crooked. (Annie uncovered one case in which a hospital director dried out old coffee grounds and used dogwood as coloring for the "coffee" served to patients. The regular coffee supplies then were stolen.)

Mrs. Wittenmyer also spearheaded the successful Iowa drive to set up state homes for children of soldiers who died in the service. The present Annie Wittenmyer children's home in Davenport was established largely as a result of her urging.

A bill was filed in Congress in 1898 to pay Annie a federal pension. A statement submitted to congressmen said of Mrs. Wittenmyer:

> She collected supplies for the sick and wounded amounting to $200,000 in value, she established diet kitchens. . . . [She] also used about $3,000 of her own money in furnishing food delicacies, etc., for the soldiers.
>
> She is now old and in straightened circumstances. A generous government that she did not desert when it needed heroes and heroines will not desert her now. The case is a worthy one.

Congress voted a pension of $25 a month, not as low in 1898 as it seems now.

Annie spent her final years mostly fighting liquor and handling such Methodist Church assignments as the organization of home missionary societies. She served as national president of Women's Christian Temperance Union (WCTU). She also wrote a number of published hymns. Here is a verse of one hymn:

> The burdens of life may be many,
>   The frowns of the world may be cold,
> To me it will matter but little,
>   When I stand on the streets of gold.
> With joy I shall enter the city;
>   The face of my Savior behold,
> And I shall change and be like him,
>   When I stand on the streets of gold.

She was active to the end. She lectured during the day of February 2, 1900, at Pottstown, Pennsylvania, then died that night at seventy-two years of age at her home in Sanatoga, Pennsylvania.

Nameless Graves

KEOKUK has not one but twenty-one Unknown Soldiers.

They served and died for their country in the Civil War.

Their identities got lost somehow in death. They are buried in nameless graves in Iowa's only national cemetery at Keokuk.

The cemetery is mute evidence that Keokuk was a key city in the nation's all-out war effort in 1861–1865. Tens of thousands of soldiers went through Keokuk en route to the battlefronts of the south—and thousands returned maimed and sick, to be cared for (and some to die) in the six military hospitals operated in the city.

An 1869 report said 606 soldiers had been buried in the cemetery up to that time, including 8 Confederates and the 21 Unknowns.

Allie Smith was a little twelve-year-old Keokuk girl who became highly popular with the soldiers.

Using a barrel as a platform, Allie sang war songs for the men, "cheering the homesick ones [and] causing the hearts of all to throb with renewed patriotic resolve."

As Mrs. Allie Smith Cheek later in life in Des Moines, she was summoned to sing whenever old soldiers gathered for their colorful campfire programs. Those who remembered her as a child in Keokuk nostalgically said her voice had "lost none of its sweetness and flexibility" with the passing years.

The national cemetery, more than twenty acres in size, contained the graves of more than 2,200 servicemen of the nation's wars in the early 1970s, including some who died in the Vietnam War.

H Paid under Five Cents an Acre

UGH T. REID of Keokuk bought 119,000 acres of Lee County land for less than a nickel an acre.

Reid, an early Keokuk attorney, paid $5,773 at a sheriff's sale in the 1840s for the entire area which was known as the "half-breed tract." The area included all of Lee County south of a line from Fort Madison west to Farmington.

Reid thus is known as having been the most extensive landowner in Iowa history. His ownership did not last long, however. The United States Supreme Court ruled the deal illegal in 1850 and Reid lost possession.

The "half-breed tract" was a region set aside in 1824 for persons whose fathers were white and mothers Indian. The "half-breed" arrangement caused endless legal problems. It was difficult to know who owned certain lands and had the right to sell. Also, white settlers had moved in and had established farms without even first asking questions as to ownership.

The courts ruled one way and then another in the numerous resultant lawsuits. Francis Scott Key, distinguished in American history as the composer of "The Star Spangled Banner," came to Keokuk. He was attorney for the New York Land Company which was involved in the ownership lawsuits. Key is said to have drawn up the court order which became the permanent basis of land titles in the area.

Hugh Reid was another Keokuk resident who achieved distinction in the Civil War. Colonel Reid was wounded in the neck and knocked off his horse at the Battle of Shiloh. His regiment lost nearly 200 men in that one battle, an appalling toll. The full strength of a Civil War regiment was 1,000 men. Reid was promoted to brigadier general.

Reid was one of the notables who rode from Keokuk on the first railroad train to reach Des Moines August 29, 1866. The arrival touched off a wild celebration in Des Moines. Reid had been an early president of the railroad which was the old Des Moines Valley line. Others from

Keokuk on that train included United States Supreme Court Justice Samuel Freeman Miller, Civil War General William Belknap, and Samuel Younker, a Keokuk merchant and one of the original Younker Brothers of the widely known merchandising chain.

Keokuk was the "Chicago" of the Des Moines River valley area in the prerailroad days. Large Keokuk warehouses stored goods which were sent up country by boat on the Des Moines River and by wagon in dry and cold seasons. Keokuk also was a key point in Mississippi River navigation, with as many as eleven steamboats crowding the wharfs at one time.

Buried at Night

ALARM SPREAD over the three-state area around Keokuk in 1882.

Dreaded smallpox had broken out among students in the medical college at Keokuk. Two students died. Other cities were deadly afraid of an epidemic. Merchants in Warsaw, Illinois, and Alexandria, Missouri, were reported to have posted signs forbidding Keokuk residents entering their stores.

The smallpox fear was one of the prices Keokuk had to pay for having a medical college. Indeed, Keokuk twice had not one but two medical colleges operating at the same time, from 1853 to 1858 and again from 1890 to 1899.

State health officials blamed the smallpox outbreak on a body received in a medical school from Chicago for dissection. Many students hastily left the college. Said a state health department report: "The foolish and unfortunate dispersion of the students carried the disease to many points, which were mostly in the State of Illinois." The epidemic, if any, died out shortly, probably because a vaccinated person is safe from smallpox. Why all the 1882 students were not vaccinated, if indeed they were not, is a mystery.

Forty cases were reported among students in 1881 and 1882. Henry Hubman, twenty-two, of Seneca Falls, New York, died on New Year's Eve. There was a big argument over whether the cause of death was smallpox or measles. Authorities took no chances. They quickly buried the body at midnight. Burial of smallpox victims at night was a common practice in those days. A few days later P. C. Sheppard of Douds, Iowa, died. That body also was immediately buried.

One student went home to Peoria, Illinois, to attend the wedding of a sister. He developed smallpox. The fifty guests who attended the wedding all were hurriedly vaccinated and there were "50 sore arms for the next 14 days."

Keokuk acquired a medical college in 1850 because of some energetic "chamber-of-commerce" work. The town offered to build a hospital and building. The offer was accepted and the Keokuk College of Physicians and Surgeons started operations. The college functioned under one name or another for forty-nine years, from 1850 to 1899. The college was connected with the University of Iowa until that institution opened its own medical school in 1870. Keokuk Medical College, the last such institution in the city, was absorbed by the old Drake University medical school of Des Moines in 1908. Over the years, Keokuk medical colleges graduated some 3,200 physicians, or more than the number of doctors practicing in Iowa now.

The medical schools and the six hospitals used for treatment of wounded and ailing soldiers during the Civil War made Keokuk a major health-care center in the nineteenth century.

CORNELIA MEIGS

A Warm Writer

CORNELIA MEIGS decided that children were not getting enough good books to read.

She started writing stories for youngsters at her home in Keokuk in 1913.

She was widely acclaimed for her books, especially for *Invincible Louisa,* a biography of Louisa May Alcott, noted author of *Little Women.* The biography earned for Miss Meigs the 1933–1934 Newbery Medal for distinguished contribution to American literature for children.

At the Newbery ceremony, Miss Meigs said, "If I could stretch my voice across the years, I should say 'Louisa, this medal is yours.' "

Cornelia wrote more than two dozen books and many other works, some of them prize winners. She was born in Rock Island, Illinois, in 1885 but the family moved to Keokuk when she was a month old. Her father, Montgomery Meigs, was an expert engineer who devoted his life to dams and structures involving the waters of the Mississippi.

Cornelia lived mostly in Keokuk and taught English at St. Katherine's school in Davenport until her dad died in 1931. After that she lived and wrote in a rural setting at Brandon, Vermont, and later at Havre de Grace, Maryland.

She was a tall, slender person, with hair parted in the middle and drawn down tight, "a quiet charming person, very gentle and very shy." She dictated her stories to stenographers. One Keokuk stenographer reported: "She [Cornelia] would lie flat on her back on a couch, look at the ceiling, and dictate fluently and exactly, including punctuation marks, as if she were reading the story from the ceiling."

She advised ambitious writers to "work hard and practice a great deal, not to be discouraged when you can not express exactly what you want to, not to trust the feeling that you are doing no good. It is almost always better than you think if you have really put your all into it."

Cornelia's warmth and sensitivity are demonstrated in *Invincible Louisa*, the Alcott biography.

Cornelia said Miss Alcott wrote *Little Women* to obtain money to help support her father and the whole family.

Louisa's father died in 1888. She died two days later, not knowing he was gone. Miss Meigs concluded the biography with these sentences about Louisa: "What she did know was that she had taken care of her father to the very last of his needing her, that she had been able to guard and protect and watch over the entire family.

"That, indeed, was the happy ending; that was the whole of what she wanted from life—just to take care of them all."

AMES

GEORGE WASHINGTON CARVER

Carver Talks with God

D ID GOD PROVIDE direct aid to George Washington Carver in his great scientific accomplishments?

Some persons who knew Carver well as a student at Iowa State and Simpson College thought so.

Carver was a gentle and devout Negro who developed some 300 useful products from peanuts, 118 from sweet potatoes, and many others from clay. He refused to cash in on his discoveries. He gave them to the world.

Carver attended Simpson at Indianola in 1890 and Iowa State almost all of the five years from 1891 to 1896. He was Iowa State's first Negro student.

Charles D. Reed said Carver's discoveries were a manifestation of the "Holy Spirit." Reed, who long served as weather bureau chief in Des Moines, was a fellow student with Carver at Ames. They studied, ate, prayed, and roomed together.

Reed said Carver never was outstanding in higher mathematics and in the abstract reasoning other scientists "find necessary for a career in research." Reed said Carver "barely got through" some courses. Yet he was responsible for "hundreds of useful discoveries which will bless humanity for all time."

"There is only one way to account for this," Reed commented, "and that is day by day his mind was keenly sensitive to the guiding Holy Spirit of the Creator and that wonderful discoveries were revealed to him through channels not open to the scientist who is a physical scientist only. . . . Divine intelligence spoke through him and he could not explain it."

During an Iowa visit many years later, Carver told how he had asked God about the peanut. He quoted God as saying, "Take some peanuts apart and find out for yourself." Carver continued: "He looks at me and I looks at Him. 'Now,' He says, 'I suppose you know just what a peanut is.' I let it drop right there because I didn't.

"He says: 'Now put those elements of the peanut back together again, observing the law of compatibility.' And I did that and I found there is no end to the number of things that can be made by this synthetic process."

Carver developed pigments, paints, and face powder from Alabama clay; "milk," "cream," "buttermilk," "coffee," paper, insulation, medicine, and plastics from peanuts; tapioca, mock coconut, syrups, and stains from sweet potatoes; paving blocks from cotton.

He believed that "God helps him who helps himself" and he regularly got up at 4 A.M. to work. He never was satisfied with his findings but kept "improving, evolving . . . and creating."

Louis H. Pammel, Iowa State's famed botanist, called Carver one of his most brilliant students. Yet Carver was born in slavery in about 1864 and as an infant was exchanged for a horse worth $300.

Carver graduated from high school in Kansas and was accepted by an Iowa college which then refused him admittance upon learning that he was a Negro. He never told which college it was and he never expressed bitterness. He said, "It is forgotten."

Carver got a job in Winterset. He walked twenty-seven miles from Winterset to Indianola where he was accepted as a student by Simpson. After paying his tuition, he had ten cents left. That bought enough cornmeal and beef suet to keep him alive the first week. He earned money ironing and as a janitor in an Indianola bank. He said later he discovered at Simpson that he was "a human being."

Reed said Carver's life was "almost one continuous prayer." His public prayers made one feel that here is a man "who actually walks with God." Reed said there were "8 or 10 prayer circles" which met two or three times each week on the Iowa State campus.

Carver was a good friend of the family of Henry C. Wallace, father of Vice-President Henry A. Wallace. The elder Wallace was a student and then a dairy instructor at Iowa State and later became secretary of Agriculture in Washington.

Carver took small Henry A. Wallace, then about eight, into nearby meadows in Ames and showed him differences in plant life. Young Henry became a foremost developer of hybrid seed corn and served nationally as secretary of agriculture as well as vice-president. He said later of Carver, "His outstanding characteristic was a strong feeling for the eminence of God."

Carver was awarded a master's degree at Iowa State in 1896, then went to Tuskegee Institute in Alabama where he did the bulk of his tremendous work. He died in 1943.

The history of Ames, which is the home of Iowa State University and the state highway commission, is replete with forceful and deeply human individuals. In addition to George Washington Carver, the list includes a housewife who serenely prepared herself and her family for her approaching death; a topflight economist who resigned rather than yield to a dairy pressure group; a famed atomic scientist; and a sculptor who continued immersed in his work until the final hours of his life.

I A Costly Windmill Prank

T MAY BE that hard feelings over a windmill cost Iowa State University $1 million.

Back in 1903, a flagpole on the campus was blown over. LaVerne W. Noyes, a notable alumnus, graciously donated a windmill to be used as a flagpole. He was a wealthy Chicago windmill manufacturer.

Engineering students did not want a campus windmill which they felt was a symbol only of agriculture. They put the unerected windmill on wagon wheels one dark night. They allowed the wheels and the load to roll down a hill and to crash. Various segments of the windmill were badly bent. It had no future either as a windmill or flagpole.

Noyes was furious. Official apologies did not help matters. He thereupon donated $500,000 to build a dormitory in his wife's name, not at Iowa State but at the University of Chicago. Overall he gave Chicago $1 million. Some Iowa Staters always have believed that that money would have come to Ames had it not been for the windmill incident.

Noyes, an 1872 graduate, did give $10,000 later to help landscape the Iowa State campus. The body of water now ruled by swans on the campus is known as Lake LaVerne.

S Free Tuition at Iowa State

TUDENT LIFE was rugged when Iowa State formally was dedicated in 1869. There were ninety-three freshmen enrolled, seventy-seven men and sixteen women.

Students brought their own bed ticks from home which they filled with straw provided by the college. The boys wore derbies, sometimes stovepipe hats, and boots, stiff collars, scarves ten feet long and two feet wide. Red flannel underwear was an absolute necessity. The single college building was too warm in some places, freezing cold in others.

An 1876 report said: "The pupils receive their tuition and room-rent free of charge and are boarded at actual cost. Each county is entitled to send three scholars." The college board of trustees was authorized to distribute any excess scholarships to the counties according to population.

"The law requires that all students shall engage in manual labor an average of $2\frac{1}{2}$ hours each day (except Sundays)."

On the first day of each month, the president assigned students to department superintendents to perform various tasks. At the end of the month each superintendent reported "the labor performed by each scholar and its value. . . . The students received credit on their board bills at the rate of 3 cents to 9 cents an hour, according to the value of the work performed."

HAZEL B. ANDRE

"My Last Wonderful Days"

IN A FEW WEEKS—or maybe a few days—I shall die. . . . Every relentless tick of the clock measures off what remains of my life. Yet I am a happy woman. . . . For I am one of the lucky ones who is granted the opportunity to prepare for death."

So wrote Hazel Beck Andre, wife of the dean of agriculture at Iowa State, in 1956. She died that year at forty-two of cancer.

Her final story appeared in the *Farm Journal* under the title "My Last Wonderful Days."

She ruled out bitterness and resentment. "None of this 'why should it be I?' Why shouldn't it? Cancer kills indiscriminately. My background of science made this a logical fact to accept."

The hardest part, she wrote, was the awareness that she was "walking out" on her family. "I must confess that tears dampened my pillow when I wrestled with that one."

But she expressed no regret—"my life has been rich and full and I have loved every minute of it."

"But if I were to live it over," she added, "I would take more time for savoring of beauty—sunrises; opening crabapple blossoms; the patina of an old brass coffee pot; the delighted surprised look on a tiny girl's face when she pets a kitty for the first time. . . .

"There would be more time for the family and for close personal friends.

"I would get closer to people faster. When death is imminent we open our hearts quickly and wide. How much more Christian love there would be if we didn't wait for death to release our reserves.

"I would live each day as if it were my last one, as I am doing now."

The Margarine War

DAIRY FARMERS were boiling mad.

An Iowa State pamphlet said oleomargarine "compares favorably with butter both in nutritive value and palatability."

For anybody to have the gall to class oleo with butter was bad enough in dairy eyes. But to have such a statement come from Iowa's own agricultural college was akin to treason!

The pamphlet even went on to say that dairy interests had been "rather effective in suppressing" the value of oleo despite its merit.

A rural spokesman demanded that the pamphlet be repudiated and the author and four others on the faculty be dismissed.

Iowa State yielded to the pressure and revised the pamphlet although not altogether to the liking of all dairy people. Nobody was fired, but Dr. Theodore Schultz resigned as head of the Iowa State department of economics and sociology. Schultz blasted Iowa State President Charles Friley for restricting "academic freedom."

The margarine war in 1943 was one of the great crises in Iowa State history.

The controversy broke out when the nation was straining every nerve to win World War II.

The world was in the throes of a major food shortage. The goal in agriculture was to get as much production of needed food from the smallest possible amount of scarce labor. Title of the Iowa State pamphlet was *Putting Dairying on a War Footing*. O. H. Brownlee, an Iowa State research associate in economics, was the author.

He said in effect that drinking whole milk instead of eating butter would provide human beings with more food value for a smaller outlay of work. He suggested that vegetable or other animal fats be used instead of butter as a conservation measure. He said one-half the cropland and one-eighth the labor needed to turn out the butter being consumed would produce enough margarine to "entirely displace butter."

In a statement criticizing the University, Iowa Farm Bureau President Francis Johnson said: ". . . farmers are alarmed over the apparent tendency to make over Iowa State into a tax-supported blueprint of Harvard. . . . Iowa farmers are not ashamed of the 'cow college' label sometimes used to describe Iowa State. We only hope it will continue to be worthy of that label."

As the dairy storm deepened, President Friley retracted the pamphlet and ordered its revision. He said the right of an individual faculty member to publish something on his own responsibility "has never been in question." But articles appearing under Iowa State sponsorship should be submitted to "approved methods of review." He also emphasized that Iowa State primarily was "an educational arm of the State of Iowa."

But in his resignation letter, Dr. Schultz said Friley had "undermined the morale" of the economics and sociology department. Schultz said Friley's actions "have created widespread uncertainty among faculty members and have jeopardized the institution's reputation for scholarship."

Schultz added: "Resources of the institution as a whole must be mobilized to create safeguards against undesirable pressure groups' actions if the college is to continue the social sciences on a level worthy of the time and energy of scholars." Schultz went to the University of Chicago as head of the department of agricultural economics.

Brownlee rewrote the pamphlet under supervision of a joint committee of faculty members and dairy representatives. The new version was described as "milder and longer" than the first pamphlet. Instead of directly comparing margarine favorably with butter, the new version said "fortified oleomargarine is nutritious and acceptable by many consumers as a spread."

Brownlee ultimately joined the faculty of the University of Minnesota as a professor of economics.

T Cut Cost from $1,000 to under $1

HE COST of extracting uranium from a chemical compound was cut from $1,000 a pound to less than $1 a pound at Iowa State.

Dr. Frank Spedding and his associates in nuclear research were responsible for that tremendous advance in the 1940s.

The contribution of scientists and workers on the Iowa State campus to the nation's atomic successes has been monumental.

Dr. Spedding, who came to Iowa State in 1937, was a member of the team of topflight scientists whose work led to the first nuclear chain reaction on December 2, 1942. That awesome event took place at the University of Chicago. Out of that initial reaction came the atom bombs dropped on Hiroshima and Nagasaki in Japan, the development of atomic-powered ships and submarines, the construction of atomic-powered plants for industrial use, and many other items of modern civilization.

Production of atomic energy required thousands of tons of high-purity uranium in metal form. But by 1941 science had not been able to process more than the equivalent of a "few thin dimes" of such uranium.

Scientists at Iowa State developed the method which resulted in a tremendous reduction in the cost of extracting uranium from uranium fluoride. Iowa State shipped two tons of uranium to Chicago in October 1942 for use in the atomic energy pile which produced the December 2 chain reaction. Iowa State provided about one-third of the metal used in that pile.

Much of the metal used in making the first A-bomb dropped at Hiroshima in 1945 also came from the Iowa State campus where "millions of pounds" of uranium were processed. An unimposing building near the University Press was the highly secret processing plant and laboratory.

Uranium extracted at Ames also was shipped to Hanford, Washington, Oakridge, Tennessee, and wherever needed elsewhere in the atomic energy program. Iowa State got an "E" award for $2\frac{1}{2}$ years of excellence in production of a vital war material. Spedding once estimated that the processes developed at Iowa State saved the federal government $100 million in the intermediate stages of the A-bomb's development. He also maintained that use of the bomb against the

Japanese actually saved some Japanese lives in the overall picture by bringing World War II to a quick end in 1945.

Spedding said in 1946, not long after the use of the two A-bombs on Japan, that a world state is absolutely essential. He commented: "Either we will get a world state by evolution or there will be another war in which one country will come out on top. World order is inevitable."

"... Liquor Can Not Be Tolerated..."

CHARLES FRILEY was president of Iowa State from 1936 to 1953. Educational television got its start during his time. WOI-TV, a pioneer in the educational field, was launched at Iowa State in 1950.

Friley once commented: "It might seem that we are working at opposite extremes at Iowa State. Our atomic energy program, on one side, deals with what could be a horrible destructive possibility.

"Television, on the other hand, has amazing possibilities for giving us a better, wiser, broader view of the world. Education must be in the possession of all of our people."

When he became Iowa State president in 1936, Friley warned, "My experience both as a student and as a teacher has convinced me unalterably that liquor can not be tolerated in a college or university."

Tama Jim Goes to Washington

UNCLE HENRY" WALLACE, Des Moines farm paper publisher, declared Iowa State was not doing a good job of teaching and of serving agriculture.

The publisher, who was a grandfather of Vice-President Henry A. Wallace, first got his dander up about Iowa State in 1880. He went to Ames seeking advice on how to overcome hog cholera in his swine. He angrily asserted that the hogs at Iowa State also had the cholera and the head veterinarian did not know it.

Wallace joined forces with James "Tama Jim" Wilson and others in staging a drive that shook up the Iowa State organization in 1890. Tama Jim was named professor of agriculture although he had been largely self-educated.

Tama Jim farmed 1,200 acres near Traer in Tama County where as a young man he memorized Robert's Rules of Order while husking corn. Wilson was called Tama Jim to differentiate him from "Jefferson Jim" Wilson of Fairfield in Jefferson County. Jefferson Jim was a United States senator and had been a congressman. Tama Jim had been Speaker of the Iowa House and also had been in Congress.

Tama Jim had served in Congress with William McKinley of Ohio. When McKinley was inaugurated as president in 1897, he summoned Tama Jim from Iowa State to serve as secretary of agriculture. Wilson served in that position for sixteen years, from 1897 to 1913, and under three presidents. No other official has ever served so long in that key agricultural post.

It was said that whenever McKinley was in doubt over an issue, he "called in the canny Scot" from Iowa for advice. Wilson was born in Scotland.

Wilson was sixty-two years old when he left Iowa State to go to Washington and seventy-eight when his federal career ended. He died in 1920 at the age of eighty-four. He is credited with having been an excellent secretary of agriculture. He introduced durum wheat, promoted the sugarbeet industry, encouraged development of hog cholera serum, promoted protection of milk supplies against tuberculosis, promoted inspection of packing plants, and helped bring about enactment of the pure food and drug act.

FRED WHITE

Great Highway Builders

W HEN MY JOB is done," Fred White once observed, "I want my children to be able to say that their dad handled a lot of public money and none of it ever stuck to him."

Fred White retired in 1952 as chief engineer of the Iowa Highway Commission. It is safe to say that none of the hundreds of millions of dollars spent under his direction ever "stuck to him."

White acquired a lot of enemies in his constant push for better highways. Twice he came close to losing his job by action of the legislature. Bills to eliminate White from official life failed only on tie votes in the 1917 and 1921 sessions. But no one ever questioned his integrity.

White first went to work on highways in 1908 when the only unit with any semblance of statewide interest in roads was Iowa State College. He was one of only three employees on the payroll when the beginnings of the present state highway setup were established in 1911. There were only 44,500 autos and 100 trucks in all of Iowa then. (Upwards of two million motor vehicles are registered in the state now.) The pay scale for highway work in 1911 was twenty-five cents an hour for a sixty-hour work week.

Iowa had no paved roads at all in White's early years. Indeed, there were only twenty-one miles of concrete paving in use when he became chief engineer in 1919. Many Iowans in that era looked upon such highways as extravagant. White urged, cajoled, and teased voters of various counties into voting bond issues for highway paving. (The state took over the duty of highway financing from the counties in the 1930s.)

When White left office, Iowa had 5,900 miles of concrete paving and 1,500 miles of blacktop paving.

It was while White was president of the American Association of State Highway Officials in 1924 that he suggested the designation and marking by numbers of highways. Thus, highways today bear such designations as No. 30, No. 6, Interstate 80, and so on.

Another notable fighter for good roads in the early years was Engineering Dean Anson Marston of Iowa State. He was a member of a state highway unit at the college beginning in 1904 when he already was urging better highways.

The Iowa Highway Commission as such was created in 1913 with Marston as chairman. He continued on the commission until 1927. It once was said that Marston "buried old man mud under 6,000 miles of paving."

Marston had a notable career at Iowa State where the campanile was built under his direction, as were the engineering hall, engineering annex, the central building, and the Ames YMCA. He also was a member of the federal interoceanic canal board which spent two months in 1931 surveying the possibilities of constructing another canal connecting the Atlantic and Pacific through Nicaragua. (Such a canal never has been built.)

It was Marston's fate to die at eighty-five years of age in 1949 on one of the highways he fought so hard to improve. He was a victim in an auto accident west of Tama on Highway 30.

A Russians Sing Corn Song

RUSSIAN FARM DELEGATION came to Iowa State University in 1955 to acquire American know-how in agriculture. The Soviet visitors also admired such American luxuries as dishwashers. They even learned to sing the "Iowa Corn Song," which they practiced in the hotel at Ames.

The group visited Iowa in response to an invitation from Lauren Soth, editor of the editorial pages of the *Des Moines Register* and the *Des Moines Tribune*. Soth suggested in a Pulitzer prize-winning editorial that the Russians come "to get the lowdown on raising high-quality cattle, hogs, sheep and chickens."

"We ask nothing in return," the editorial said. "We figure that more knowledge about the means to a good life in Russia can only benefit the world and us."

The Russians were in Iowa close to two weeks and engaged in intensive study at Ames as well as elsewhere. Many foreign delegations have come to Ames and to Iowa over the years to study agriculture. The longtime Russian premier, Nikita Khrushchev, was a visitor during his spectacular tour of America in 1959.

At the time of the 1955 visit, one eastern writer said in a dispatch from Ames, "The Soviet expedition to Iowa is proving once again the truth of what many Americans have often said—the best way of selling the American way of life to the people in the lands of Communism is to let them see it."

CHRISTIAN PETERSEN

"... To See Beyond ..."

CHRISTIAN PETERSEN was in a hurry.

He knew that death was waiting only a few weeks hence. He wanted in his remaining time to finish a statue which would show one generation of man helping the next generation "to see beyond."

Petersen was a Danish-born sculptor who taught and worked at Iowa State for twenty-seven years. Many of his statues adorn the campus. He did numerous commissioned figures around Iowa.

Petersen learned from his doctors in December 1960 that his days were limited. The clay for his final project was delivered in January 1961 and he started to work. His condition was such that he could work only two to four hours a day.

In February he had to undergo surgery. He was back in the studio late the same month.

By this time he had to be lifted around so that his hands could mold.

By March the figures were ready to be cast in bronze. On Good Friday he approved the depth of a portion of the casting. He signed his name in strong lines. Four days later, the Tuesday after Easter in 1961, his vibrant hands were still. He died at seventy-six years of age.

His final work is a big figure of a man holding his small son aloft and may be seen at the Fisher Community Center in Marshalltown.

"I have carried out an idea," Petersen wrote. "I have an 8-foot figure there, holding aloft a child. I want to symbolize this generation helping the next generation to see beyond what it has been able to see . . . so the child is looking into the future, having a little more light."

Another writer said: "It was a great source of satisfaction to him that his last sculpture, completed with much pain, prayer and effort, conveyed an inspired message, directed to all men. Thus is an artist's work impressed upon the world after he is gone."

MUSCATINE

NORMAN BAKER

Cancer Quack

F LAMBOYANT Norman Baker (purple shirts, orchid-colored cars) was not a doctor. He didn't even finish high school.

Yet by radio and printed word, he lured thousands of desperate persons to Muscatine in the late 1920s and early 1930s with his slogan, "Cancer is conquered."

> *Muscatine has had more than its share of forceful and interesting people during the city's 137-year history.*
>
> *A lumberman disregarded prophets of gloom and earned millions. . . .*
>
> *An eighty-year-old man joined the army—and saw service. . . .*
>
> *A little black girl won a notable victory in the Iowa Supreme Court. . . .*
>
> *A pioneer's weather records helped Rock Island get the federal arsenal. . . .*

Norman Baker owned and operated Radio Station KTNT and he printed the magazine *TNT (The Naked Truth)*. The magazine once said, "Mr. Baker's investigation and observations have proved that the worst cancer cases can be cured."

It was claimed that 32,000 persons attended an open-air meeting held to demonstrate that "both external and internal cancer were curable by Baker methods."

All this brought in a large flow of money. The Baker "hospital" was reported to have realized profits of $75,000 for the month of June 1930 alone. Baker said another time that his hospital netted him $35,000 a week.

He did not seem to care that he was victimizing families that were hard up. A seventeen-year-old Des Moines youth told of borrowing the money to pay $100 a week for care of his sick mother in Baker's institution. That was a heavy fee in an era when hospitals regularly charged only $5 a day for a bed. The mother died despite the injections given at Muscatine. Said Dr. Morris Fishbein, longtime spokesman for the American Medical Association: "Of all the ghouls who feed on the dead and dying, the cancer quacks are the most vicious and heartless. Most vicious of all is Norman Baker."

A quack is defined as a medical imposter. Baker did not mind the title. Over a door at the Baker building in Muscatine were these words, "A quack is one who thinks and does things others can't do."

Baker said he used a secret "cure" originated by a physician. Baker never divulged the contents of the liquid which was injected into a patient's muscles. Chemists found the liquid consisted of one-third carbolic acid, one-third glycerine, one-third alcohol, and a trace of oil of peppermint.

Baker used a powder of some sort for treatment of external cancer. He also sold for $30 a pint an "after treatment" medicine. An expert testified that the "after treatment" was syrup of red clover blossoms which could be bought at that time (1936) for $2 a gallon.

Baker sucked in some prominent personages. Charles Curtis, vice-president of the United States from 1929 to 1933, supported Baker. And when Baker launched in 1930 his daily newspaper, the *Midwest Free Press,* President Herbert Hoover in Washington pressed a gold key to start the publication's machinery in Muscatine.

Baker, who was a native of Muscatine, had been a hypnotist on the stage. He also worked as a tool-and-die maker at one time. In 1914 he started making calliopes in Muscatine. A calliope is a large musical device which plays tunes in whistles.

After radio came in, Baker got a broadcasting license and sold all sorts of products over the air—tires, typewriters, flour, coffee, canned fruit, alarm clocks, brooms.

Then he woke up to the fact that there was a lot of easy money to be picked up from gullible people desperately fighting the dread foe cancer.

Baker did not get by with his cancer quackery very many years, although he raked in a lot of cash while it lasted. He embarked on his cancer activities in 1929. He had left Iowa by 1938 after a number of hectic battles. He went to federal prison on a four-year sentence in 1941.

He was repeatedly blasted by Dr. Fishbein in the *Journal of the American Medical Association* (AMA) and by other medical societies, doctors, and newspapers. Baker sued the AMA for $500,000, did not get a dime.

The state of Iowa charged Baker and his associates with practicing medicine without a license. After a brisk battle, the courts upheld the charges and Baker was forced out of business in Muscatine.

All this time Baker used scathing language in attacking his foes over the radio. He called a state health department investigator "a dirty cur . . . lower than a rattlesnake in a ditch." He termed certain newspapermen "immoral drunkards, contemptible curs, scoundrels, and cowards." He similarly scorched the AMA and physicians in general.

The torrent of abuse was too much for the then-Federal Radio Commission which canceled the license of his KTNT station in 1931. A federal hearing officer said, ". . . nothing which tends to vulgarity, immorality or indecency has any place in radio communications."

Baker used the radio to broadcast talks by patients who said they had been helped by his treatments. On one occasion, Baker said a patient in the studio was "now a well man" after four weeks of treatment. The patient, however, broke in and said, "I am not a well man but I hope to be some time again." But he died. His widow said they had come to Muscatine from their home in Washington, Iowa, and had paid $250 for a promised cure. The widow reported that a physician back home had said the case was hopeless and the husband could live only about a year longer.

In 1929 Baker published pictures and stories telling how well five "test" patients had fared under treatment. One patient, however, was already dead before the magazine appeared and the other four died in the next few months.

At the same time, Baker presented testimony in his various trials from patients who said they had been cured or helped. Whether they actually ever had had cancer always was the big question.

One member of Baker's staff was listed as a "specialist" even though he was not a doctor of medicine. He was given that title because he had "special work" to do at the institute.

Baker ran for the Republican nomination for United States senator in Iowa in 1936 and polled a respectable total of 28,162 votes. L. J. Dickinson, then an incumbent senator, won the nomination with 105,000 votes but lost the election.

Amid a tangle of lawsuits and legal actions in many states, Baker in 1938 moved his setup to Eureka Springs, Arkansas. He established a radio station, XENT, across the international border at Nuevo Laredo, Mexico, to escape federal objections to his broadcasting. He returned to Iowa on one occasion in a lavender-hued car with the XENT call-letters gilded on the side.

Then came the blow that put Baker out of business altogether. He was convicted and given a four-year term in 1940 at Little Rock, Arkansas, on a federal charge of using the mails to defraud in advertising his cancer "cure." The district attorney charged the Baker staff "gave the same treatment to everyone, whether for a broken pelvis or a wart on the nose."

After spending from 1941 to 1945 in the federal penitentiary at Leavenworth, Kansas, Baker returned to Iowa and tried to incorporate a "Baker Research Foundation." The state of Iowa said nothing doing.

Baker died at seventy-four years of age in 1958 of jaundice on his ocean-going houseboat at Miami, Florida. He was believed to have been wealthy to the end. But his estate totaled only $10,066.

There was widespread belief that Baker had cached $1 million in cash somewhere in Mexico before he died. The money never was found.

Charles Hanley, Muscatine attorney and executor of the estate, said in 1960: "I wish the [hidden money] report were true. I've spent a year trying to track it down. I've been to Mexico half a dozen times."

Hanley said Baker "probably made $250,000 a year when he was going strong."

"Where did the money go?" the attorney asked. "He had lots of women [but] he died a very lonely man."

M *Great Lumber Baron*

ANY MUSCATINERS predicted that Ben Hershey would go broke.
In 1856 he started building a sawmill that could produce 50,000 feet of lumber in twenty-four hours! There wasn't *ever* going to be that much demand for lumber in the whole state of Iowa, said the scoffers.

He was spending $70,000 of his own money and that of other investors. How reckless can people be!

But never have gossips been more wrong.

Hershey's mill was tremendously successful and he became a millionaire. Those who put money into the project with him realized returns far beyond their wildest dreams.

Hershey, who came to Muscatine from Pennsylvania in 1853, was one of the first great Mississippi River lumber barons. They floated logs down the river in huge rafts from the northern pine forests of Minnesota and Wisconsin. Such raft-logging continued until 1915.

The great bend in the river at Muscatine made that city an excellent location for landing logs.

By 1874, three large lumber mills were in constant operation at Muscatine. They cut 37 million feet of sawed lumber that year, manufactured 20.5 million shingles, 6.9 million laths, and provided jobs for nearly 400 men. Mills in other river cities were similarly busy.

By 1878 Hershey's big mill was capable of producing 100,000 feet of lumber every eleven hours and was providing work for 200 men.

It is understandable why skepticism was widespread in 1856 over Hershey's prospects. A big depression was in the making. Hershey had gotten his new mill "in running order just as the panic of 1857 struck."

One reason for pessimism in the industry at the time was the lack of railroads to carry badly needed lumber west to new settlers far out on the frontier. But a great surge of trans-Mississippi railroad construction was getting under way and the lumber business soon boomed. The railroads themselves became an important market for wood. At one point years later, the Rock Island needed lumber so badly, presumably for ties, that it offered Hershey a large contract "at his own price."

Hershey lived the luxurious life of a nineteenth-century country squire on his farm near Muscatine. He was proud of his fine livestock and horses. He had as many as 500 horses at a time on Iowa and Nebraska farms.

It was believed in those days that feeding geese shelled corn soaked in whisky would make the geese especially tasty for roasting. Farmhand

Dan Finnigan had the task of feeding such corn to the birds on the Hershey farm. Dan, however, was caught soaking the corn in water and drinking the whisky himself. History does not record what happened to Dan.

Hershey himself was killed in 1893 in an accident in Chicago. It is said his expensive gold watch was buried with him at Muscatine. A Muscatine woman who attended the funeral as a little girl said she heard the watch tick as she passed the casket.

Hershey's daughter Mira became a highly successful real estate developer and builder in Los Angeles. She made so much money that she donated an entire hospital to the memory of her father. She also is said to have given $1.8 million to another hospital project and to have made other charitable donations ranging up to $400,000 each.

Graybeard Soldiers

EIGHTY-YEAR-OLD Curtis King of Muscatine volunteered for service in the army—and was accepted. Despite his age, he marched away to war in 1862.

So did Robert Mills, sixty-eight; Samuel Tarr, sixty-six; Enos Mc-Nall, sixty-five; Henry Mockmore, sixty-four; and close to eighty other oldtimers from the Muscatine area, all well past the maximum age limit for military service. They became members of Iowa's famous "Graybeard Regiment" in the Union Army.

The "Graybeards," average age fifty-seven, did garrison and guard duty in various places and thereby freed younger soldiers for field action. The Graybeards numbered 1,041 men. Only Iowa recruited such a a regiment during the war. Says one historian, "No purer patriotism was ever exhibited than that which prompted these men exempt by law to thus serve their country in this great extremity."

Thirteen Muscatine Graybeards died of disease, and probably hardship, during the war, the oldest being Enos McNall, sixty-five. The others were Henry Mockmore, sixty-four; Thomas Greenhow, sixty-three; James Tannehill, sixty-two; Abraham Edwards and William Taylor, both fifty-five; John Kennedy and Daniel Lefever, both forty-nine; William Patterson, forty-eight; John McDonald and George Barnes, both forty-five; and Thomas Mullen and Ben Ninehouse, both forty-four.

Curtis King, the eighty-year-old, did not die in the army but he was not in service long. He enlisted November 9, 1862, and was discharged for disability March 20, 1863. He was a native of Virginia.

What makes the service of the Graybeards particularly remarkable was the fact that they lived in an era when the average length of life probably was under forty years of age.

Colonel and commanding officer of the regiment was George Kincaid, fifty, of Muscatine. Adjutant was David Goodno, fifty-two, also of Muscatine.

The regiment guarded military prisons (including one at Rock Island, Illinois), military installations, supply trains. Guerrillas attacked one such train, wounded four Graybeards. Two fifty-seven-year-old soldiers died. They were Charles Young of Fredonia in Louisa County and Samuel Coburn of Cedar Rapids.

The regiment was relieved of train duty after military authorities found that "riding atop swaying trains proved too strenuous for their aging bodies." The men returned to guarding prisons.

The Graybeards had a reputation of being "more humane" to prisoners than was "common in that day."

The aged soldiers also came from patriotic families. A total of 1,300 sons and grandsons of Graybeards served in the Union Army in 1861–1865.

A *Daily Prayer Vetoed*

N 1844 convention called to draw up a state constitution had scarcely convened in Iowa City when a hot argument broke out.

Elijah Sells of Muscatine proposed that the convention "be opened every morning by prayers to Almighty God." To the dismay of Sells and others, the proposal lost, 44–26. The pioneers were not nearly so religion-minded as many present Iowans believe.

Delegate J. S. Kirkpatrick of Jackson County said that "those who believe in prayer should do their praying at home." Delegate Francis Gehon of Dubuque County said time should not be used in praying when the convention was costing $200 or $300 a day.

Sells, thirty, a native of Ohio, was shocked. He declared he would "regret to have it said of Iowa that she had traveled so far out of Christendom as to deny the duty of prayer." Robert Lucas of Iowa City, a former territorial governor, said rejection of the prayer resolution "would give us a bad name abroad." Jonathan E. Fletcher, also of Muscatine, agreed. He did not want the world to think that Iowa refused to acknowledge a God.

Delegate A. Hooten of Des Moines County humorously recalled a story about Benjamin Franklin who questioned as a boy the necessity of saying grace at every meal. He asked his father why he did not say grace "over the whole barrel of pork at once." Jonathan C. Hall of Henry County said that God should leave the delegates free to proceed with the business of the convention.

One delegate said with fervor, "In the name of Heaven, don't force me to hear prayers!"

That convention, incidentally, produced a constitution that was rejected by the people of Iowa. Another constitution drawn up in 1846 was accepted and used until the adoption of the 1857 constitution, which still is in force.

Sells was one of the founders of the Republican party in Iowa. He twice served in the legislature before beginning three terms as Iowa secretary of state in 1856.

Sells, a protégé of United States Senator James Harlan of Mount Pleasant, held various United States appointments before going to Kansas as federal superintendent of Indian affairs in 1865. Sells served three terms in the Kansas legislature, moved to Salt Lake City in 1878, then served four years as secretary of Utah Territory. He died in Salt Lake City in 1897.

Twain Loved Sunsets

MARK TWAIN loved watching the sun go down at Muscatine.

Twain, one of the greatest of all American writers, lived briefly in Muscatine in the 1850s as a teen-ager. (His brother owned part of the *Muscatine Journal*.)

In his tremendous book *Life on the Mississippi,* Twain wrote:

And I remember Muscatine . . . for its summer sunsets.

I have never seen any, on either side of the ocean, that equaled them. They used the broad smooth river as a canvas, painted on it every imaginable dream of color, from the mottled daintiness and delicacies of the opal, all the way up . . . to blinding purple and crimson conflagrations, which were enchanting to the eye. . . .

All the Upper Mississippi region has these extraordinary sunsets as a familiar spectacle. It is true Sunset Land.

Black Susan Won

THERE WAS NO CLASS in English grammar for Susan Clark in her grade school in Muscatine.

Her father wanted Susan, twelve, to study grammar. He sent her to enroll in Grammar School No. 2.

Susan was not accepted because she was black. Grammar School No. 2 was all white. She had been going to an all-Negro school. The year was 1867.

School officials said public sentiment in Muscatine opposed intermingling white and colored school children. The Civil War had only been over two years.

The school board offered to establish a class in grammar in Susan's old school. Her father said no. He went to court to force the all-white school to accept his daughter.

In a far-reaching 1868 decision, the Iowa Supreme Court ruled that Susan should be permitted to attend an all-white school regardless of what public sentiment might be. This decision handed down more than a century ago came at a time when there was not a whole lot of interest in the civil rights of blacks. (That same year, however, Iowa did amend the state constitution to grant voting rights to Negroes.)

The supreme court ruling in the Susan Clark case said the constitution makes no distinction whatsoever, color or anything else, "as to the right of children between 5 and 21 to attend the common schools." The ruling pointed out that a board could not require "children of Irish parents to attend one school and children of German parents to attend another." The ruling added, "If it should so happen that there be . . . poorly clad or ragged children in the district, and public sentiment was opposed to intermingling such with well-dressed youths, it would not be competent . . . to pander to such false public sentiment and require the poorly clad children to attend a separate school."

To bar Susan from the all-white school, the ruling said, "would tend to perpetuate the national differences of our people and stimulate a constant strife, if not war, of races."

Clamshell Boom

THE BEDS of the Mississippi and its tributary streams were a vast storehouse of clamshells in 1890.

John Boepple, a farm laborer recently arrived from Germany, went swimming in the Mississippi at Muscatine. He cut his foot on a clam. There is no further mention of the injury in reports of the times. But history has plenty to say about Boepple and clamshells.

He had made buttons from animals' horns in the old country. He like the pearly appearance and hardness of clamshells. He took some shells home and cut out a dozen pearl buttons on a foot-power lathe. He sold the buttons to a Muscatine store for a dime. That little sale launched a big industry in Muscatine.

A German immigrant such as Boepple was no rarity in Muscatine. The 1895 state census showed that about 15 percent of the city's population then was German-born. Of the 12,237 inhabitants, 1,848 were natives of Germany.

Boepple tried to interest people in the possibilities of clamshells but they laughed at him. He finally got a cautious individual to invest $10! Some machinery was procured, easterners became intrigued with midwestern freshwater pearl buttons, and the boom was on. One report says: "First, the young men of the town became interested. Then the women and children, the old people—everybody who could get foot-loose—joined the scramble.

"The surface of the Mississippi was dotted with boats for miles, and on its banks at night, the fires of hundreds of clam-boiling outfits glowed."

The clams were boiled to get rid of the meat.

"The rush brought more houseboats, more button shops, more excitement than Muscatine had ever known." Heaps of shells grew "higher and higher" on the riverbank, while "in all the lanes and byways the piles of clamshells littered up" Muscatine.

Clammers realized as much as $30 a week, quite a bit for the times. (Average pay of workers in factories was twenty cents an hour in the United States in 1890 and the average work week was sixty hours.)

Thirty or more factories poured out tons of buttons in Muscatine.

Excitement intensified when one clammer got $2,000 from a Chicago jeweler for a pearl found in a river shell. That brought more prospectors to Muscatine. Fist fights broke out on the river and on the bank over who had the right to harvest clams in certain spots.

Shells sold for $50 a ton.

The big boom really lasted about ten years, although plenty of pearl buttons still were produced in Muscatine until a few years ago. As recently as 1956, seven Muscatine plants turned out one-half billion pearl buttons, 95 percent of all the production in the United States. But plastic buttons, zippers, and the like, have taken over the entire market now.

As clam beds were exhausted, shells were shipped from other areas to Muscatine for processing into buttons. Some 27,000 tons of shells from seventeen states were used to produce 17 million gross of buttons as late as 1937.

There is reason to believe that Boepple, who started it all, did not cash in to any great extent. One report says he was left "a poor and disillusioned man." Another account says that "not even Mr. Boepple had grown rich."

When Bridge Caved In

Two WESTWARD-BOUND TRUCKS rolled up on the Mississippi River bridge at Muscatine in the early morning darkness.

In front was Jim Haynes, thirty, of Streator, Illinois, driving a loaded Coca-Cola truck headed for Des Moines. Not far behind was William Wheatcraft, twenty-six, of Mansfield, Ohio, driving a semi-trailer pulling two dump-truck bodies.

It was 2:30 the morning of June 1, 1956. Both drivers planned to be well into Iowa on Highway 92 by daylight.

Near the middle of the so-called "High" bridge, which is half a mile long, Haynes felt a queer falling sensation.

"I saw the bridge going down," he said later. "I left my truck and ran."

He did so just in time. A middle section 160 feet in length collapsed with a splash into the river. Haynes was uninjured. His truck was left hanging on a section of the bridge which remained upright.

Wheatcraft also escaped with his life but his truck and cargo went down with the bridge. As the structure collapsed, he said, "I could see the girders coming at me. I got out of the truck and climbed over the girders to keep above water."

Ninety minutes before, a motorist fleeing from the police had bounced off a bridge pier while traveling at a high speed. An engineer said the car hit the bridge at a "vital spot" and evidently weakened the structure.

The fact that only two vehicles were on the bridge at the time of the collapse and that both drivers escaped was fortunate. The bridge had been carrying 1,800 cars and trucks every twenty-four hours at the time.

Three Explosions

THE HOME of John Mahin, editor of the *Muscatine Journal,* was quiet at 1:30 in the morning May 11, 1893.

Asleep were Mr. and Mrs. Mahin, their two daughters and son, and a servant girl.

Across the city all was similarly still in the homes of E. M. Kessenger, a retired capitalist, and N. Rosenberger, an attorney.

Suddenly a sharp explosion shook the city, then another, then another.

The Mahin, Kessenger, and Rosenberger homes all had been simultaneously heavily damaged by explosives deliberately planted in the cellars. Miraculously, nobody was killed or even seriously injured. First reports said dynamite or nitroglycerine had been used. Later evidence indicated the explosive may have been gunpowder.

Mahin, Kessenger, and Rosenberger had one common cause: all were drys and all fought vigorously for enforcement of the state's strict law prohibiting the sale of liquor. Consequently, they were hated by the saloon forces which had been growing more powerful politically in this state.

The foundation and first floor of the Mahin home were wrecked; the second floor, where all were sleeping, was not damaged extensively.

Rosenberger had heard a noise and had gotten up to investigate when the blast went off. His wife found herself in the cellar with the baby at her feet, covered with debris. None of the Rosenbergers was injured much. A guest asleep on the second floor suddenly found herself on the ground outdoors. The explosion had left the floor tilted and she slid uninjured to the ground.

The overall loss at the three homes was placed at $10,000 to $15,000, a lot of money in the 1890s.

Mahin, who had been particularly critical toward saloons, said in an editorial, "I am almost dazed to think that there could be in a civilized community any person or persons so dastardly as to seek to take the lives of my innocent wife, daughters and son because of resentment toward me." He pointed out that he, Kessenger, and Rosenberger "have been identified with an effort to enforce the laws against the saloons."

Muscatine was up in arms. The county board of supervisors offered a $2,000 reward and persons who attended a mass meeting subscribed nearly $5,000 for the arrest and conviction of the culprits. The meeting passed a resolution asking the mayor and council to close immediately "all saloons and disorderly houses in the city."

Three men were arrested in 1896, nearly three years later, for the 1893 explosions. Says one account: "One of the wretches, Matt Woods, was proved to have been the person who threw one of the bombs. He was sent to the penitentiary for 10 years."

Woods would not disclose the names of any coconspirators, however, and there were no further convictions.

The blowup attempts did not silence Mahin in his war on the liquor interests. But he was fighting a losing cause. He was identified with the Republican party which was dry. The Republicans unexpectedly lost the governorship in 1889 and 1891 on the liquor issue. Governor Horace Boies, Waterloo Democrat, won election both times on a platform calling for legalizing the sale of liquor under "local option."

The Republicans thereupon adopted the principle of allowing each community to decide whether to allow sale of liquor. Under Republican sponsorship, that local option law was enacted in 1894 and continued in force until 1916.

SUEL FOSTER

A Homely and Gentle Man

HOW UNHAPPY Suel Foster would have been over the recent loss of millions of Iowa elms because of Dutch elm disease!

Foster was a Muscatine horticulturist and tree lover.

He also staged an energetic campaign which helped mightily in mobilizing public support for establishing what is now Iowa State University at Ames.

Foster came from Rochester, New York, in 1836 to Muscatine and joined his brother in buying a one-sixth interest in the townsite for $500. (There were two log cabins on the site.)

It was said that there was only one homelier man in Muscatine than Foster and that was Theodore Parvin. No matter what suit Foster wore, the trousers "always stopped six inches short of the shoetops."

He was a warm believer in the beauty and profit of planting shade, ornamental, and fruit trees. He once said, "The sugar maple and the elm, I am glad to find, are about equally thrifty and beautiful in our broad prairie state."

He was especially disturbed by destruction of the natural forests for lumbering purposes. He was one of Iowa's earliest conservationists.

In 1856 Foster started urging in magazine articles the establishment of an Iowa college to educate those who till the soil.

"The day is coming—soon coming—when every farmer's son and daughter must be educated for the science of farming, the greatest of all sciences," he wrote. "We must have a farmers' college with a large experimental farm attached to it."

He pushed his campaign in a number of succeeding articles. He promoted a petition urging the legislature to appropriate the money to buy a section of land for a model farm and to build college buildings. He sought to recruit urban support by pointing out that cities need "stout, robust and healthy" persons from the farms.

"If our cities are not thus supplied with men and women," he commented, "we should see them fast going into decline, like the once-powerful nations that reached their climax of wealth, luxury and profligacy, like Rome and Greece and Spain."

Pressure from Foster and others, including legislators, such as B. F. Gue, finally resulted in passage of a bill in 1858 to set up an agricultural college and farm. Foster served on the original board of trustees and was its president and chairman of the executive committee for four years. He left the board in 1866. The college was formally opened in 1869.

He is credited with having cast the deciding board vote which fixed the location of the college near the village of Ames in Story County.

Foster wanted students at the college to perform "a certain amount of daily labor." He is said to have favored "labor for health, for economy, for practical illustrations of studies and for the great moral principles of the dignity of labor."

For a gentle man, Foster had his share of thrills. He was a brother-in-law of Serannus Hastings, Iowa congressman and supreme court judge. Hastings moved to California in the gold rush days and arranged for Foster to escort Mrs. Hastings and three children to the west coast in early 1850.

They traveled by steamer to the Isthmus of Panama, crossed the isthmus by horseback (there was no Panama Canal then), waited four weeks for a ship to round Cape Horn, and finally reached San Francisco in April 1850, after a trip of three months.

Foster worked in 1850 as a California census taker in the Feather River area where he listed 2,500 men digging for gold. He found some miners getting $20 to $100 a day but the average man realizing only $1.50. Living costs averaged $1 a day. Foster decided he would be better off back on the farm than to stay and dig gold. He returned to Iowa for good in the winter of 1850–1851.

Foster introduced the "Wealthy" apple into the Muscatine area. He grew a lot of apples—and that led to problems. He was an ardent temperance man. Although he was "compelled to make cider from his waste apples, he never permitted the cider to get hard." He hastened to turn the excess cider into vinegar.

THEODORE PARVIN

Heaviest Rainfall

THANKS to a notable amateur, an officially accepted record was obtained at Muscatine of the heaviest known annual rainfall in Iowa history.

Theodore Parvin was the amateur weather observer and he measured 74.5 inches of moisture at Muscatine in 1851. That was almost 2½ times the normal rainfall now for such cities as Muscatine and Des Moines. Recent average for Muscatine has been 31.88 inches a year, while that of Des Moines has been 31.06 inches.

Parvin came to Muscatine in 1838 when he was secretary to Robert Lucas, Iowa's new territorial governor. Parvin immediately began making weather observations three times a day—temperature, rainfall, wind.

"Parvin was a young unmarried man," commented one writer, "and what induced him to keep a weather record is more than one can imagine at the present time."

Parvin kept painstaking records for twenty-two years at Muscatine, or until 1860. The reports of Parvin and those who followed have been called the "oldest continuous weather record in the midwest."

Parvin did the measuring August 10, 1851, when Muscatine was hit by a downpour of 10.71 inches, the second heaviest twenty-four hour rainfall in the official Iowa weather records. (Heaviest official fall was 12.99 inches at Larrabee, Iowa, June 24, 1891.)

On that fateful August day in 1851, Papoose Creek went on a wild rampage in Muscatine. Bridges over Second, Third, and Cedar streets were washed away. Worse yet, one Mrs. Lafferty and her three children were drowned as they tried to escape from their little house.

Des Moines was just as hard hit with excessive rain that same summer. The Des Moines River was a raging torrent, reportedly three miles wide in places. This was the Des Moines River flood which hit a warehouse filled with wooden shoes from Holland at Croton, Iowa. The "thousand wooden shoes were washed down the river."

Parvin's faithful observations show that Muscatine was soaked with six consecutive excessively wet years in that era, from 1848 through 1853. Here are his moisture readings for the years: 1848–39.62 inches; 1849–59.16 inches; 1850–49.08 inches; 1851–74.5 inches; 1852–59.39 inches; 1853–44.92 inches.

Smithsonian Institution in Washington accepted Parvin's early Muscatine weather records as valid.

As the Civil War approached, the federal government decided to locate a base for war supplies in interior United States. An island between Rock Island, Illinois, and Davenport, Iowa, was proposed as a site for the base.

Opponents in Congress declared the location was unsuitable because the Mississippi River there was frozen shut to traffic nine months of the year. Somebody in Congress remembered Parvin's weather observations and obtained the records from Smithsonian.

The Parvin figures gave a lie to the nine-month freezeover report. The Rock Island site was approved and the arsenal is there yet, more than a century later.

Parvin moved in 1860 to Iowa City where he became a professor of natural science at the University of Iowa.

Overall, few men have made so many contributions to Iowa as did Parvin. He was a librarian, historian, and lawyer. He was a founder of the state historical society and of the Masonic order in Iowa. He established the Masonic Library in Cedar Rapids. He served as editor of the *Annals*, state history publication.

MARSHALLTOWN

BILLY SUNDAY

Preached To 100 Million

ADRIAN ANSON's eyes popped.

Never had he seen a baseball player run so fast as Billy Sunday.

Anson, a great player himself, happened to see Sunday play in a sandlot game at Marshalltown. Anson, a native of Marshalltown, was managing the major league team now known as the Chicago Cubs. He promptly took twenty-year-old Sunday to Chicago.

The young player became the sensation of baseball with his running. He dashed around the bases in fourteen seconds flat. He easily beat the champion runner of a rival league. The year was 1883.

Sunday played major league baseball for seven years. His speed is still a legend of the game.

Sunday is best known in history, however, for the way he chased the Devil and the Demon Liquor. He became perhaps the greatest of all the nation's hell-and-brimstone evangelists. He once estimated that he preached his fiery brand of gospel to 100 million persons in his lifetime.

Marshalltown was a city of 13,300 population in 1909. But nearly 200,000 people came to hear Billy deliver seventy-four sermons in a six-week religious revival there. They came from long distances by train, by buggy, and even in a few automobiles, which were starting to be popular. Many of the faithful came a number of times.

He gave his audiences a real show in the color and vigor of his sermons. He smashed chairs, pounded the pulpit, challenged the devil, even made a baseball slide right on the platform. His old-time Bible preaching was straight to the point.

"I know no more about theology than a rabbit does about ping pong or golf," he once said. "I want to preach the gospel so plainly that men can come from the factories and not have to bring along a dictionary."

He shouted, "I know there is a Devil for two reasons; first, the Bible declares it, and, second, I have done business with him!" His digs at hypocritical church members delighted crowds. He predicted that hell "will be so full of church members their feet will be sticking out the windows."

Religious sources credited him with converting hundreds of thousands of Americans to active Christianity. One report published in 1914

120

listed 167,000 conversions by Sunday in eighteen large cities, including 26,000 in Pittsburgh and 18,000 in Columbus, Ohio. A 1909 report said Sunday won nearly 2,000 converts during the Marshalltown revival. The reports said many students, college and high school, loved Billy Sunday.

He might have been a tremendous force on television today.

> *Sunday is one of many lively and significant persons who have sparked community life of Marshalltown for generations.*
> *A Marshalltown man taught coin tricks to European royalty. A Marshalltown woman devoted a lifetime to working with ghetto children in Chicago. A Marshalltown man similarly devoted his life to educating backward blacks in Mississippi.*

Billy Sunday had been working for a Marshalltown furniture store for four years when he went into professional baseball. (He did not set the world on fire with his bat. He struck out the first thirteen times he batted in the National League but did much better later.)

Billy was born in 1862 near Ames. His father, a Civil War soldier, died of disease in the army one month after the child was born. Billy and one of his brothers spent part of their childhood in orphanages in Glenwood and Davenport because their widowed mother could not always support them.

Sunday liked his liquor before he got religion. He and other ballplayers dropped into a downtown Chicago saloon one Sunday afternoon in 1887 and "got tanked up." They came out and sat on a curb at State and Madison streets. Across the street a gospel meeting was in progress. Groggy Billy found himself listening. He recognized "the gospel hymns I used to hear my mother sing back in the log cabin in Iowa."

"I sobbed and sobbed," he said later. He left his companions and went into a nearby gospel mission where he "staggered out of sin and into the arms of the Savior."

He continued to play big league baseball although not on Sunday. Once when a batter smashed a ball over his head in the outfield, Sunday prayed as he raced back. He said, "God, if you ever helped mortal man, help me get that ball and you haven't got much time to make up your mind either."

The Lord must have been on his side. Sunday leaped and caught the ball in a spectacular play.

In 1890 he could have continued playing major league baseball for a salary of $500 a month, big money in those days. Instead he chose to embark in religious work with the Chicago YMCA at $83 a month. That job was a stepping stone in Sunday's development as an uproarious (but sincere) evangelist.

"Some of [his] platform activities make the spectators gasp," said one writer. "He races to and fro across the platform. . . . Like a jack-knife he fairly doubles up. . . . One hand smites the other. . . . Once I saw him bring his clenched fist down so hard on the seat of a chair that I feared blood would flow, and the bones broken. . . .

"Yet, it all seems natural. Like his speech, it is an integral part of the man. Every muscle of his body preaches in accord with his voice."

Billy broke at least one chair on the platform in Marshalltown where he went after liquor sellers and liquor users with hammer and tongs. His 1909 goal in Marshalltown was to close the saloons. There had been as many as twenty-one licensed saloons (now called taverns) in Marshalltown.

"I'll fight this hellish liquor traffic to the last ditch!" he shouted. "You can't look through a beer glass and have compassion for men on their way to hell." (Beer was sold only in saloons in those days, as was hard liquor.)

Many times and in many places Billy said, "I'm going to make this place so dry they'll have to prime a man to spit."

He declared that "we have plenty of whisky [and] booze in our politics but no God." He charged: "The wets are the worst gang of cutthroats this side of hell. . . . If I were God for 15 minutes, they wouldn't be on this side of hell either!" He told his listeners, "If you are a lowdown, filthy, drunken, whisky-soaked bum, you will affect all with whom you come in contact."

In those days, saloons could sell liquor only if their owners could obtain permission in the form of the signatures of a majority of the voters of a community on a petition. The permission was good for five years. Then a new set of petitions had to be circulated.

A reported 5,000 men stood up in one of Sunday's meetings at Marshalltown and pledged they never would sign any saloon petitions.

The drys tried after the Sunday revival to get the voters to withdraw the permission that had been granted to Marshalltown saloons in 1906. The drys were balked, however, by a technicality. They then waited until July 1, 1911, when they did succeed in driving the saloons out of business. One saloon keeper reopened the next day selling only pop, buttermilk, and "Holy Roller cocktails," which were nonalcoholic of course.

But, as everyone knows, Marshalltown did not stay dry indefinitely.

One of Billy Sunday's most dramatic announcements was this, "And now, Devil, you have been walking these streets long enough." Then, as Sunday knocked slowly in cadence on the pulpit, he said to his audience, "The Lord . . . has been . . . knocking . . . at the door . . . of your life . . . but you won't . . . let him in . . . you won't . . . let him in."

He did not like deathbed confessions which he said are like "burning a candle at both ends and then blowing the smoke in the face of Jesus." He did an authentic headfirst slide on the platform in describing how an old-time ballplayer attempted to become a Christian as he was dying. Such an attempt, Billy said, is "just like trying to stretch a triple into a home run." He made a diving slide along the platform to illustrate his point. "But the Umpire said 'You're out!'" Billy reported. The slide and the deathbed effort both were too late.

Billy Sunday appeared at many religious meetings in his home state of Iowa over the years. He drew 550,000 at a Des Moines revival series in 1914. He came to Des Moines a final time in 1933 but got sick. He died soon afterward in Chicago at the age of seventy-one. He ordered: "No sad stuff when I go. No black, no crepe, no tears. But have them sing the 'Glory Song.' " Which they did. Here is one verse:

> Oh, that will be glory for me,
> Glory for me, glory for me,
> When by His Grace I shall look on His face,
> That will be glory yet glory for me.

E. A. CONLEY

Fist Fight in Cow War

THE TROOPS slowly advanced, their bayonets pressing back the crowd of irate farmers near New London, Iowa.

The year was 1931. Iowa's "cow war" was in progress.

A number of southeast Iowa farmers had refused to allow state veterinarians to test their cattle for tuberculosis, as required by law. Some veterinarians had been roughed up.

Iowa Governor Dan Turner called out 1,900 National Guardsmen to protect the veterinarians while the testing proceeded.

The farmers being forced back at New London bitterly assailed the oncoming troops. Shouted one farmer, "Why don't you drop your guns and fight fair?"

The challenge was accepted for a fist fight between a farmer and a guardsman.

Who the farmer was is not known. He was a big fellow, however. The guardsman selected for the match was Major E. A. Conley of Marshalltown.

The contestants squared off. Conley hit his opponent once and down he went. He courageously got up. Conley flattened him again. The fight was over. The troops had no more trouble.

Not generally known at the time was that Conley was an excellent boxer. He had fought Gene Tunney in a soldiers' tournament in France during World War I. Tunney later became heavyweight champion of the world. Tunney won the fight in France, but did not knock Conley out.

Originally a Marshalltown baker, Conley became assistant chief of the Iowa Highway Patrol. Later he served as acting chief. He attained the army rank of colonel during World War II and presently is a brigadier general, retired, in the Iowa National Guard. Now past eighty, he lives in Tucson, Arizona.

The County Seat Conflict

A STREAM of dirty water squirted from a big sausage stuffer failed to slow the troops advancing from Marshall to Marietta.

A volley of eggs and decayed vegetables did not hinder the marching soldiers either, nor did the shouts of women using unladylike language.

Warfare—of a sort—had broken out between the neighboring towns of Marietta and Marshall (which later would be renamed Marshalltown). The conflict was over the location of the Marshall County Courthouse. Marietta had it. Marshall wanted it.

The struggle went on for seven years before Marshall emerged the victor in 1859 and Marietta faded into insignificance.

Henry Anson, founder of Marshall, maintained later that his town might have become the state capital of Iowa if all the energy expended on capturing the county seat could have been devoted to a drive to winning the Statehouse. There was some validity to Anson's viewpoint. The location of Marshall near the geographical center of the state might have been a good argument for placing the Statehouse there.

Also, the state capital battle was waged in the 1850s at about the same time that Marshall and Marietta were locked in combat. Transfer of the state government from Iowa City to Des Moines was completed in 1857, only two years before final settlement of the Marshall County Courthouse struggle.

The first major clash between Marietta and Marshall took place at the ballot box. A countywide election in 1856 resulted in a victory for Marietta, with 482 voters favoring continuing Marietta as the county seat and 348 backing Marshall.

Another election was held in 1858. Before the election, Marshall constructed within its boundaries a building designed to be a courthouse and donated it to the county. Marshall also was accused, perhaps correctly, of bribing voters with "bottles of whisky, packages of tea, dried apples and plugs of tobacco."

This time Marshall apparently won on a vote of 667 to 562. But Marietta was far from defeated. Election officials found an excuse to throw out the votes of three pro-Marshall precincts. The excuse: There was no record of the judges and clerks of election having been properly sworn! The "correct" election totals were: Marietta 519, Marshall 462.

Marietta again was declared the official winner. But her string was beginning to run out. The battle went to the courts which held for Marshall.

Marietta, however, made no move after the court rulings to surrender the county government.

The sheriff thereupon summoned the Bowen Guards, a local military organization, to march upon Marietta. Warned of the forthcoming invasion, Marietta frantically mobilized.

As the guards approached, one Mr. Daly of Marietta appeared with a "huge sausage stuffer from which he sent streams of muddy water upon the invading hosts." Angry women likewise went into action: A minister serving as chaplain of the guards had his clerical robes "badly soiled with eggs thrown by the fair hands of Marietta ladies." The women also hurled comments "more suited to outdoor exercises than to parlor conversation." Old vegetables struck some troopers. (Throwing things at guardsmen is not strictly a modern development.)

Only slightly impeded, the armed guards moved into the Marietta public square and confronted the defiant crowd. "For God's sake, don't shoot!" implored William P. Hepburn, a young attorney. Nobody did. The guardsmen had no intention of hurting anybody. Their purpose was to intimidate Marietta into giving up the county offices and records, not to take any violent action.

The military unit might not have gotten anything anyway had the issue been forced. Marietta people reportedly had placed a keg of gunpowder under the county safe. The defenders reportedly had vowed that day to blow the county records to smithereens rather than to yield to the Marshall "army."

A final showdown was averted when an official came out and read a district court injunction forbidding the seizure of the county records by the Marshall contingent. The Bowen Guards shamefacedly went home empty-handed.

That injunction was Marietta's final small triumph. A new canvass of the second election was held and the votes of the three disputed precincts were included in the official totals. A settlement designating Marshall as the county seat was signed December 29, 1859. Two days later the county offices were moved to Marshall. The "war" was over.

Hepburn, the peacemaker at the confrontation in the Marietta square, developed into one of the big men in Iowa history. A native of Ohio, he came to Iowa in the mid-1850s and was elected Marshall County prosecuting attorney in 1856 at the age of twenty-three.

Hepburn served with distinction in the Civil War and attained the rank of lieutenant colonel. He first settled in Memphis, Tennessee, after the war and moved to Clarinda, Iowa, in 1867. He was elected nine times to Congress by southwest Iowa voters in the period from 1880 to 1906. The important "Hepburn Act," which placed railroads under workable federal regulation, bears his name. He was chairman of the House committee on interstate and foreign commerce at the time of the act's passage in 1906.

Hepburn died in 1916 at Clarinda at the age of eighty-two. Iowa Governor George W. Clarke said in a euology that Hepburn was "a man of forceful character, strong in his convictions, a lawyer of ability, a splendid soldier, a great debater, devoted to his country."

JAMES W. WILLETT

T *"You're Dang Right I Ran"*

HE 141 Civil War veterans present were all in their eighties and nineties. Nevertheless, many of them marched, a few blocks at least, in their 1931 state convention parade in Marshalltown.

Iowa sent nearly 76,000 men to the Union Army in the Civil War and 13,000 died. The toll was almost equal to the combined number of Iowa lives lost in all wars since, including World War I, World War II, the Korean War, and the Vietnam War.

The Civil War had ended sixty-six years before the 1931 state convention of the Grand Army of the Republic (GAR), which was the name of the Union Army veterans organization.

One grizzled veteran at the convention told how he had been at the Battle of Bull Run where the defeated Union troops ran from the victorious Southerners.

"Did you run?" the veteran was asked. "You're dang right I ran," he replied with emphasis. "Did all of your buddies run?" "No, some didn't and they're still down there." Buried on the battlefield, he explained.

A deeply reverent part of the convention program was a "campfire" held by the old soldiers one warm June evening on the grounds of the Iowa Soldiers Home. A large crowd of spectators gathered under the trees with the veterans in the flickering firelight. Nearby were more than 1,000 graves in the Soldiers Home cemetery, all marked with identical headstones arranged in serried ranks.

Old, middle-aged, and young sang old songs that balmy night, the stirring "Battle Hymn of the Republic," the quick "Marching through Georgia," the haunting "Tenting Tonight on the Old Campground." The end of the era of the Civil War veteran was nearing and all present knew it. (The last Iowa Civil War veteran died in 1949.)

The mournful notes of "taps" sounded over the hushed crowd as the campfire ended. Then James W. Willett of Tama, a doughty veteran and a district court judge, lifted his hand and said in a stentorian voice that carried far, "Quiet! The lights are out—and the soldier sleeps."

Judge Willett had been national commander of the GAR. He was a man of strong opinions. He constantly told historians: "Don't *ever* call it the Civil War. The correct name is 'The War between the States.'" Alas! Judge Willett lost that battle. The "Civil War" has come to be an accepted name.

Fire Inspired Invention

F OR TWENTY-FOUR HOURS William Fisher struggled to keep up the water pressure in the city mains during a big Marshalltown fire.

Fisher was superintendent of the waterworks, which he had helped complete in 1876.

While he was working around the clock to maintain needed pressure in the city mains, Fisher got the idea for his constant-pressure pump governor. That invention marked the beginning of the Fisher Governor Company, which started business in 1880. (This major Marshalltown industry now is known as the Fisher Controls Company, a division of Monsanto.)

Fisher had been a pioneer engineer in the North Western Railroad shops at Clinton and had helped design and build waterworks in Clinton, Muscatine, and Anamosa before coming to Marshalltown.

It is hard to tell now what fire was burning when Fisher first devised the pump governor. Early Marshalltown had some spectacular fires, particularly before the waterworks were built.

The biggest conflagration started May 2, 1872, in an elevator on the southeast side. Fanned by a strong southeast wind, the flames spread with ruthless speed and destroyed five elevators, three lumberyards, two hotels, two factories, a railroad depot, and a number of stores and homes.

The burned-out area totaled 15 acres, a major blow to a city of 3,500 population.

Wind-borne sparks dropped as far north as Main Street and raised fears for a time that the city would be totally destroyed. Cinders and half-burned letters were blown as far north as the town of Albion, six miles away. The heat was so intense that two fire fighters had to pour every other bucket of water on each other in order to survive.

Profiteers hurried into the stricken area with horses and wagons and charged the "exhorbitant price" of $2 to $5 per trip to haul household goods to safety.

A fire company rushed by fast train from Grinnell to Marshalltown in thirty-four minutes, blinding speed for a twenty-three-mile trip in those days. Fire fighters in Des Moines and Cedar Rapids also were mobilized but canceled train trips when word came that the fire was under control.

The total loss was fixed at $300,000, which now does not seem to have been any great amount as fires go. But $100,000 were treated with more respect in those days than $1 million are now.

Mayor Ticketed Self

MAYOR AARON C. CONAWAY gave himself a traffic ticket in 1928 for an illegal left turn on Main Street.

The energetic mayor did so to show that nobody was exempt from prosecution. He paid a fine of $1.

That unimportant incident took place at about the beginning of what was, for the times, a wild era of law enforcement problems in Marshalltown. In the next couple of years the city experienced the arrest and conviction of the first apprehended aerial bootleggers in Iowa history; the embezzlement of some $3,000 in public funds by a municipal court clerk; the disclosure that cans of drinking alcohol seized in liquor enforcement had unaccountably "turned" to water while in possession of the police department; the indictment of a police chief and a policeman on liquor conspiracy charges.

Police Captain Frank West looked up at a plane high over the city and commented, "I can smell the liquor clear down here."

Prohibition was still the law of the land. Manufacture and sale of alcoholic beverages were illegal. But bootlegging (illicit sale of liquor) was at its height all over the United States.

The fanciest liquor reaching Marshalltown was being flown in by Milo Hilton of Des Moines. The liquor was smuggled by boat from Canada and loaded in Hilton's Stinson-Detroiter plane near Detroit.

Hilton and a fellow flyer landed at Marshalltown in November 1928 with 360 pints of bourbon whisky and 48 pints of champagne for the holiday trade.

None of the liquor ever reached Hilton's customers. When the plane taxied to a stop, a contingent of officers dashed from a hiding place, arrested the flyers, and seized the plane and the cargo.

Hilton was convicted of bootlegging and spent some time in jail. The plane was confiscated but apparently a mortgage accounted for most of its value. The liquor was distributed to hospitals for medical use under a court order.

Not long afterwards, Marshalltown's municipal court clerk was convicted of embezzling money collected in court fines, including Mayor Conaway's $1. The clerk served a penitentiary sentence.

The most popular hard liquor in those days was not whisky or wine but alcohol, perhaps because of necessity. Whisky of any quality was particularly hard to get.

Bootleggers did a thriving trade selling alcohol in amounts ranging from half a pint to a gallon. Marshalltown, a city of 17,373 in 1930, was reputed to be supporting approximately thirty bootleggers at that time. Seizures of liquor and alcohol by the police were frequent.

Marshalltown police on one occasion confiscated a small barrel of moonshine whisky on a farm north of the city. The farmer pleaded guilty and was fined. The liquor disappeared into official channels but only briefly.

The police held a party a few weeks later. Guests were served moonshine, the same whisky that had been taken from the farmer! Somehow, the police never were required to account for that liquor.

Alcohol seized by the police was kept in a vault of the city building for safekeeping. The keeping did not prove to be very safe.

A court order was issued to Marshall County Sheriff Charles E. Wicklund to get a number of cans of alcohol from the vault for distribution to the hospitals. Wicklund was suspicious and arranged for a chemical test of the contents of the cans. He was not surprised when several of the cans were found to contain pure water. Townspeople believed, probably correctly, that officers had been nipping away at the cans.

Incidentally, the favorite drink in prohibition Iowa was so-called "spiked" beer. The drinker filled the empty space at the top of a bottle of "near beer" (practically nonalcoholic) with alcohol. Then the drinker placed his thumb over the opening and held the bottle upside down to permit the alcohol to mix with the beer.

It was in this era that Marshalltown landed what it believed to be a real prize in J. F. Glassco, the new chief of police. Glassco said he was a former member of the Royal Northwest Mounted Police in Canada. He told of once being sent into the Arctic after two desperadoes, one of whom he had to kill. (He brought back the body on a dogsled.)

Glassco displayed a picture of himself in a Mountie uniform. He told of chasing a murderer worth $4 million all over the United States and of finally getting his man in St. Petersburg, Florida. He also told of being wounded in action five times in France during World War I.

Skeptics checked with the mounted police who said they never heard of Glassco. They said the Mountie uniform in the picture was a fake. Further, the chief's war record was found to be much less stirring than he had related.

Glassco was indicted in 1930 on the testimony of Cedar Rapids bootleggers who said they had been paying the chief $1-a-can "protection money" on illegal alcohol shipped into Marshalltown. A number of police officers who did not like what had been going on testified against the chief. Glassco, who had been deposed as chief, flatly denied all charges, however, and was acquitted by a district court jury.

Legal beer came back in 1933 and Iowa's first state liquor stores opened in 1934. The day of the alcohol bootlegger waned.

Laid Rails at Night

AN ANGRY MAYOR of Marshalltown is said to have waved a pistol at a crew of workmen and to have thereby halted temporarily the building of a railroad.

In 1883 property owners opposed construction in the Nevada Street neighborhood of what is now the Great Western Railroad. Residents sent for Mayor J. H. H. Frisbie. He climbed up on a boxcar and threatened the tracklayers with his pistol. They stopped work.

Opponents of the railroad planned to go to court the following Monday for an injunction. The railroad, however, brought in rails and ties at night. When Monday came, the railroad had been completed through Marshalltown. The property owners, and the mayor, had been defeated.

LAURENCE JONES

$700,000 in Gifts

A BOY nailed a shoe on a mule at graduation exercises.

He did so to demonstrate he was entitled to a diploma from a most unusual school which was founded by Laurence Jones of Marshalltown.

The institution is Piney Woods Industrial School in Mississippi.

Laurence Jones, a gentle black man, traveled slowly around Mississippi in 1907 wondering, "What can I do with my education?" He had just obtained his degree from the University of Iowa. He also had been the first Negro to graduate from Marshalltown High School (class of 1903) in the history of that school.

He sat down one day in the heart of Mississippi near an abandoned Negro cabin and a "beautiful cedar tree." He read, wrote, meditated. He returned to that spot again and again. Black children started coming there to talk with him.

He gave a sixteen-year-old boy something to read. The boy handed it back. He was unable to read. Jones told the lad, "So long as I am in this part of Mississippi, I'll come to this old tree every day and I'll help you learn to read."

Jones never got away from that spot the rest of his life.

He found himself with a never-ending project on his hands. Other black children also wanted to learn to read. Soon Jones had an informal class of thirty. He decided to start a school there.

A former slave willingly contributed the old cabin and forty acres of surrounding land as a school site. Jones returned to Iowa where he received contributions from residents of Marshalltown, Des Moines, and elsewhere. The former Finkbine Lumber Company of Des Moines contributed 800 acres of land.

Jones put the students to work making bricks out of sand and cement. They used the bricks to erect gray-colored buildings.

A 1955 report said the Piney Woods campus then totaled 1,600 acres and the school had an enrollment of 500 black students from twelve Mississippi counties and twelve other states.

Some 5,000 students had graduated from Piney Woods by 1955. Most of the graduates had gone into teaching.

"Piney Woods is a work-your-way school entirely," Jones once said. "Everybody works and they graduate prepared to make a living."

Contributions, many from Iowa and elsewhere in the North, averaged about $65,000 a year in the 1950s (much more now). Then came a big windfall in 1954. Jones appeared on Ralph Edwards's TV program, "This Is Your Life."

Edwards asked the TV audience to send contributions of $1 each to Piney Woods. More than $700,000 poured in and was placed in the school's endowment fund.

Jones was born in St. Joseph, Missouri, and came to Marshalltown after his first year in high school. He earned his board and room working in a hotel in Marshalltown and as a club doorman for $1 a night.

Another Marshalltown black, Herbert R. Wright, served in the diplomatic corps in the early years of the century. He was a 1901 law graduate of the University of Iowa and he practiced law in Des Moines for a time before he was appointed United States consul at Utilla, Honduras, in 1903. In 1908 he was transferred to Puerto Cabello, Venezuela, where he served until 1918.

STEPHEN PACKARD

Carpetbag Governor

ONLY THE GLEAMING bayonets of federal troops enabled Stephen Packard to serve as governor of Louisiana for three and one-half months. Without the military support he would have been thrown out of office in five minutes.

Packard was one of the South's famous "carpetbagger" governors. They were Northerners who moved into the defeated South after the Civil War and got themselves elected to office by questionable means. They got the carpetbagger nickname because they reportedly brought their few belongings in suitcases then known as carpetbags.

Packard's lively experiences in Louisiana politics in the 1870s preceded his career as a major breeder of fine livestock at Marshalltown. His beautiful nineteenth-century home west of Marshalltown is still one

of the showplaces of the Iowa countryside. The home, which was taste-
fully refurbished in the 1940s by David Wine, is believed to be more
than 100 years old.

Packard served with valor in a Vermont regiment during the 1861–
1865 Civil War. When peace came, he moved to New Orleans where
he practiced law. He was a Republican. He was appointed United
States marshal for Louisiana in 1869.

In 1876 Packard was declared elected governor of Louisiana on
the Republican ticket even though Louisiana was heavily Democratic.
Francis Nichols, the Democratic nominee, insisted that he had been
elected, and not Packard. Nichols was probably right.

Even though no state ever is supposed to have more than one governor at a time, both Packard and Nichols were inaugurated on January
18, 1877.

Packard opened his office in New Orleans's St. Louis Hotel which
was being used as a Statehouse. Nichols established his rival state government in an Odd Fellows lodge building. A Republican legislature
met in one place, a Democratic legislature in another. There were even
two competing state supreme courts.

President Rutherford Hayes ended the ridiculous situation April 24
by withdrawing the federal troops. Packard immediately lost his job,
as did the other Republicans.

The president appointed Packard American consul in Liverpool in
1878. Packard returned to this country in 1885, bought 1,100 acres of
land near Marshalltown, and spent nearly twenty-five years there as a
notable livestock breeder. In 1909 he moved to Seattle, Washington,
where he died in 1922 at the age of eighty-three.

M *"Not out for Dollars"*

Y FRIENDS all think I'm nuts," said millionaire David Wine
when he moved from Chicago to an Iowa farm.

Wine was sixty-five when he and his wife settled on the 1,100-acre
Governor Packard farm west of Marshalltown in 1946.

Wine spent $28,000 remodeling the grand old home (three bath-
rooms), another $18,000 for an Aberdeen-Angus bull, many thousands
more for other fancy cattle. His total expenditures exceeded $300,000
in less than two years.

Asked if he was breaking even on his cattle operation, he replied,
"I am not out for the dollars." He did not need to be. He owned the
Kewanee Iron & Metal Company, a big Illinois scrap metal firm, a chain
of Chicago furniture stores, a laundry company, a linen supply firm, and
valuable Chicago real estate. He acquired the farm in 1930 on a mortgage foreclosure.

He installed indoor plumbing in five tenant farmhouses on his
land. He said, "I'm a great believer in John the Baptist. Cleanliness, a
clean body, means a clean soul."

The Wines did not stay around Marshall County in the winter. They went to Palm Springs, California. And in 1947 they moved back to Chicago. Wine felt that he had not been accepted by the other cattle breeders in the area.

He had not always been rich. He was a German-Jewish immigrant who came to America from East Germany in the 1890s when he was seventeen years old. He had thirty-five cents in his pocket when he landed. His first job, repairing organs, paid him ten cents an hour. He said eighteen of his relatives were burned to death by the Nazis in Warsaw, Poland, during World War II.

"I am a full-blooded American citizen," he once said with fervor. "I can appreciate citizenship. Every man in the United States should get down on his knees at least once a day and pray for the flag and for the privilege of living here."

A *Taught King Tricks*

FUTURE KING of England learned coin tricks from T. Nelson Downs of Marshalltown.

Downs was a famed sleight-of-hand expert who performed for a full season in London's Palace Theater around 1900.

Among those who enjoyed Downs's show was the Prince of Wales, heir apparent to the English throne. The prince went backstage where Downs taught him a few stunts with coins. Downs was invited to the royal palace by the prince, who became King Edward VII in 1901 upon the death of his mother, Queen Victoria.

Downs originally was a railroad telegrapher. He spent his spare time in railroad stations practicing slipping half-dollars from the palm to the back of the hand and return, quicker than the eye could follow.

Downs first appeared in the smaller American vaudeville houses, soon graduated to big-time show business. He and Thurston, the famed magician, were close friends. Said Thurston, "In his prime, Tommy Downs was the best coin manipulator in the United States." Thurston added, "There was a great demand for American acts in Europe and for several years we two were featured in the leading cities in Europe."

Downs was so highly regarded in the field of magic and hokum that the widow of the famous escape artist Harry Houdini came to Marshalltown to visit the old coin artist in his declining days.

In 1935 some forty of the top magicians in the nation gathered in Marshalltown for a testimonial dinner honoring the venerable Downs. It was a show long to be remembered.

There was one unfortunate accident. A crystal glass set was presented to Mr. and Mrs. Downs. The person doing the presenting stumbled and smashed the glassware. Not even the combined skill of all forty magicians could put the glassware together again.

Downs died in 1938 at the age of seventy-two in Marshalltown, which he always called home, no matter where he might be.

JESSIE BINFORD

T *Slums Appalled Her*

HE SLUMS in Chicago appalled Jessie Binford.

"When I saw and smelled all the dirt and filth, I wondered if I could take it," she said. "I wondered if I had made a mistake."

She could take it, and did for more than sixty years, helping miserably poor and underprivileged children.

Miss Binford, daughter of a prominent Marshalltown attorney, got her first look at Chicago squalor in August 1902 when she was twenty-six years old.

She rode in a horse-drawn cab down unpaved South Halsted Street, amid the sights and smells of uncollected garbage, of stables and outhouses, of trash-filled alleys. Drunks staggered out the swinging doors of saloons. Swarms of ragged children chattered in Yiddish, Italian, and English as they played in the street. The heavy odor of the stockyards hung over the city.

Miss Binford was born to a life of culture. She attended Smith College in Northampton, Massachusetts, and was a graduate of Rockford, Illinois, College.

Her outlook on life underwent a profound change when she heard the great Jane Addams deliver a lecture in the Methodist Church in Marshalltown. Miss Addams was the foremost fighter of her time against the poverty and wretchedness of life in the Chicago tenements.

Jessie was shaken by the lecture. She and her brother previously had organized a Marshalltown club for underprivileged boys. The club met in a log cabin in the Binford backyard.

Miss Addams visited in the Binford home a couple of hours before boarding a midnight train back to Chicago. Jessie peppered the notable guest with questions.

Jessie went to Chicago to see for herself. She came home but did not stay. She returned to Chicago in 1904 and began her long career of unselfish service to downtrodden human beings, particularly children.

Miss Binford founded the Juvenile Protective Association in Chicago and served as its director for decades. She became closely identified with Miss Addams's Hull House at 800 South Halsted Street, which did so much for generations of Chicago's poor. Miss Addams founded that famed settlement house in 1889.

Jessie Binford said of Jane Addams: "She was one of the greatest persons who ever lived. Nobody ever forgot her. Everyone always felt that Jane Addams understood him, understood what made him what he was." Miss Addams died in 1935.

Miss Binford lived in Hull House the latter part of her long life. At eighty-five years of age, she was still hard at work—and far from senile. But she lost her last big battle in Chicago.

Plans were announced in the early 1960s for location of a $200 million campus of the University of Illinois in the Hull House neighborhood.

A protest group headed by Miss Binford denounced the project. She objected strenuously to the razing of thousands of "homes, stores, and churches" to provide space for the campus. She said the loss of homes would worsen the Chicago housing shortage, particularly for families below the middle income level. She called the program "a heartless assault upon thousands of little people."

Her efforts were in vain. The university was built. Only the Hull House building was preserved as a memento of the long struggle against ignorance, dirt, poverty, illness, liquor, drabness, and corruption in Chicago's slums.

Miss Binford returned in her final years to Marshalltown where she died at the age of ninety in 1966.

The depth of her interest in problems of children was demonstrated in a committee report she presented in a National Probation Association session in Minneapolis in 1931.

She told of a talented boy at Hull House who "drew a picture of a man representing his father, and a woman representing his mother, defiantly facing each other in a bitter quarrel."

"On both he drew asses' ears," she said. "His home, like so many others, has become the scene of constant misunderstanding and quarrels."

She said the guardians of children "have the duty" to live lives "of honesty, sincerity, and courage" as examples to youngsters. She concluded, "If we would understand the delinquent, we must know the members of his family; their needs and visions, especially in relation to the child and his to them. If his family fails him, then he is handicapped indeed, for all his larger and less intimate social relationships."

Perhaps Jessie Binford had an insight into young people that would help adults understand to some degree the unrest among students. In the 1931 report, Miss Binford said that families "are the conservers of the past and therefore are essentially conservative."

"The child," she added, "is the builder of the future and is essentially progressive. Therefore, there will always be conflict between the child and the family."

"America Will Pass Away..."

Is our civilization ever going to collapse?

Will Durant, the noted historian and philosopher, was asked that question in Marshalltown in the early 1930s.

Durant's answer was that western civilization undoubtedly will decline but it is difficult to predict when.

Such a decline, he said, might develop from these "weaknesses" in American life:

1. "Overurbanization." Cities were getting too large and life too congested.

2. Too great a "division of labor" in production. No single individual or small group of individuals builds a house or a car or provides food for a family. Thousands of persons are involved in many production processes. The production and distribution of goods have become too vulnerable to interruptions that can and do halt the flow of supplies to people.

3. "Loss of religious faith" which has been a stabilizing influence on life in the past.

Durant's observations of forty years ago seem disquietingly appropriate in the 1970s.

He had come to Marshalltown to deliver an evening lecture in the Congregational Church in Marshalltown. He had coffee afterward with the Reverend William Leen, a Catholic priest; the Reverend Willis K. Williams, the Congregational minister; and a newspaper reporter. During a far-ranging discussion, Durant said there was nothing any individual could do to prevent any collapse of civilization if that was in the cards, and there was no use worrying about it.

Durant, who has written *The Story of Civilization* and other noted works, since has been quoted as saying that "America will pass away as states such as Greece and Rome have passed away" but American genius "will live as Greek and Roman genius are living."

COUNCIL BLUFFS

$3.5 Million Train Robbery

THE BIG STEAM LOCOMOTIVE pulling the fast mail train puffed to a stop in the chilly November evening darkness.

An automobile that had been traveling alongside the train halted also. Two teen-age youths jumped out of the auto and smashed a window in an unguarded but sealed railroad car.

They clambered inside, quickly tossed ten mail sacks out onto the ground. A third young man lounged around the locomotive up ahead as a lookout.

The auto driver piled five bags into his vehicle and sped away. One of the teen-agers grabbed four mailbags and ran.

The whole process was over in a hurry, perhaps as little as four minutes.

But one mailbag was inadvertently left beside the train.

Thus was staged a $3.5 million train robbery at Council Bluffs, one of the most spectacular crimes of its kind in American annals. The time was 6:40 on a Saturday evening in November 1920.

The seven-car train was traveling east on the Burlington Railroad. The rifled car contained a rich store of government bonds, securities, and cash, bound from the San Francisco Federal Reserve and perhaps elsewhere in the west to New York and Chicago.

The robbers were Fred Poffenberger, nineteen, and Orville Phillips, seventeen, Council Bluffs youths who broke into the car; Merl Phillips, twenty, the lookout, and Keith Collins, twenty-six, who drove the getaway automobile.

All they realized from their exploit was an unhappy type of fame in Council Bluffs history and swift punishment at the hands of the law.

The train had come to a stop for a railroad crossing after passing over Indian Creek. When the train started up again, a conductor saw the lone mailbag that had been left behind. Thirty minutes later postal inspectors and other law officers were hot on the trail.

Within five days both Phillips boys had confessed and Poffenberger's confession followed shortly thereafter. Authorities disclosed they were looking for Collins. He was arrested at Westville, Oklahoma, fifteen days after the robbery.

Most shocking were the reports by Collins and Poffenberger on what they did with the stolen bonds. Collins said his share of the loot was $25,000 cash and $500,000 in United States government bonds.

He believed he never could sell the bonds. He said he dropped a suitcase containing all $500,000 in bonds off the Douglas Street bridge into the Missouri River. Officers dragged the river a whole day without finding the suitcase which was weighted with bricks.

"What did you do with your loot?" Poffenberger was asked. "I burned $800,000 in bonds because I could not dispose of them," he replied. "You did what?" asked the startled official. "I took them home and burned them in the kitchen stove."

Some of the bonds appear to have been canceled anyway.

One report said the mailbag left behind contained $426,000. Whether this amount was in cash or securities was not disclosed.

A later report listed $1,351,000 taken in the robbery. This appears to have been incomplete. At least news reports of court actions years later still referred to the crime as the $3.5 million Council Bluffs train robbery. But the list told of $500,000 in government bond coupons being shipped from San Francisco Federal Reserve to Chicago and $423,600 in canceled government bonds.

Other securities in the list included 100 shares of General Motors stock and 50 shares of Kennecott Copper for which no value was given. Anyone today owning the 1920 equivalent of either 100 shares of General Motors or 50 shares of Kennecott would be rich indeed. Such stocks have increased many times over in value in the last half-century.

Collins received a total of thirty years in sentences. Poffenberger got eighteen years and Orville Phillips thirteen years. The disposition of Merl Phillips's case is not known.

All appeared before Federal Judge Martin Wade. The judge commented: "I wish Sunday Schools would set a week apart for teaching young men of this country the Ten Commandments and I would like to see an extra week given to the Commandment 'Thou shalt not steal.' The trouble nowadays is to get young men to take life seriously. They must be told that movies, bright lights and idleness are not everything."

The judge's movie comment probably was in reply to a statement earlier by Collins. He had remarked: "They say this is the biggest mail train robbery ever staged. If that is true, I believe I am worth $100,000 a year to a movie company."

Sixteen years later, Collins tried unsuccessfully through a legal maneuver to get out of prison where he had been serving time continuously since the robbery.

Poffenberger was a dropout who quit school before he finished eighth grade even though he had been "the brightest boy in the class." While in custody, he gave this advice to boys: "Obey your mother no matter what she says. Complete your schooling no matter what sacrifice is needed. Stay at home. Let the street gangs get along without you. Get into the kind of work that you like."

One report says that "the very magnitude of the loot was the undoing of the robbers." They expected thousands and got millions. They probably expected to be pursued by a few postal inspectors. Instead, they found themselves being chased by an army of secret service agents, detectives, police officers, and a big contingent of postal officers.

The robust past of Council Bluffs includes many other exciting persons as widely varied as Abraham Lincoln, Generals Grenville Dodge and Mat Tinley, Mormon Brigham Young, and penitentiary warden Percy Lainson. Nor should Amelia Bloomer be forgotten.

Abe's Stories Not for Ladies

A THRILL of anticipation ran through Council Bluffs, population 1,300. Abraham Lincoln was in town and had agreed to speak! The year was 1859.

Lincoln was still two years away from the presidency of the United States but nevertheless was well known because of the famous Lincoln-Douglas debates in Illinois in 1858.

The Council Bluffs hall was full for the address by the tall and gaunt Springfield, Illinois, lawyer. Sawdust had been sprinkled on the floor to deaden sounds. The only light came from candles placed along the walls.

Not much of what he said has been preserved. He was a Republican and the Republican Council Bluffs weekly said he "applied the political scalpel to the Democratic carcass." The Democratic weekly in sarcastic vein said he discussed the "Eternal Negro."

In any event, the speech could not have been obnoxiously political because a reception was given for Lincoln later at the home of W. H. M. Pusey, Council Bluffs banker and a Democrat. Pusey had been a friend and business associate of Lincoln at Springfield before moving to Iowa.

One guest at the reception recalled later that "along about 11 o'clock they shooed out the women and the preachers so Abe could tell some of his favorite stories." His slightly ribald stories probably would be looked upon as quite harmless to women and preachers now.

Lincoln spent three days in Council Bluffs but not by choice. In fact, he had not planned to come at all. He had been in Kansas to deliver some political speeches. At St. Joseph, Missouri, he was invited to go along on a trip up the Missouri River to Council Bluffs.

He accepted the invitation for rest and relaxation and to inspect seventeen city lots and ten acres of prairie at Council Bluffs. The properties were owned by Norman Judd, Chicago attorney and Lincoln's campaign manager. Judd put up the real estate as security for a $3,000 loan from Lincoln.

The riverboat was scheduled to turn around after a stop at Omaha and return to St. Joseph. The boat, however, got stuck on a sandbar and Lincoln was marooned in Council Bluffs for three days.

The time ultimately proved to have been well spent. Lincoln met and talked with Grenville Dodge, a Council Bluffs engineer and surveyor who was an enthusiastic promoter of a transcontinental railway to the Pacific. Dodge had been engaged in surveys of possible rail routes through the western wilderness. He wanted Council Bluffs to be the eastern terminal of such a railroad. He found Lincoln deeply interested in the possibilities.

Lincoln and Dodge walked up onto a bluff and looked out over the Missouri. There is a tall granite shaft on the bluff now to commemorate that occasion.

In 1863, when Dodge was serving as a top-flight general in the Civil

War, he got a summons from President Lincoln to come to Washington. Dodge was somewhat uneasy that he might be slated for a reprimand. Instead, Lincoln wanted to talk about railroad matters. Dodge later wrote: "He [Lincoln] recalled our conversation in Council Bluffs. On the report I made to him, he fixed the eastern terminal [of a transcontinental railroad] on the western boundary of Iowa, in the townships that Council Bluffs is located in." Thus was Council Bluffs designated as the eastern end of the Union Pacific Railroad which was completed in 1869.

Incidentally, while Lincoln was in Council Bluffs in 1859, the Republican newspaper described him as the "distinguished Sucker." That term was not an insult. Illinois had been nicknamed the "Sucker" state. Illinoisians long were called "Suckers," but that was before the term got to mean a person easily deceived.

Collier's encyclopedia says a number of Illinois zinc and lead miners went north to work the mines in the spring and returned south to their homes in the fall. Their travels were compared to the migrations of sucker fish, hence the nickname.

GRENVILLE DODGE

"Saddest Day of My Life"

I s it possible for you to do anything for this poor woman who is in so much trouble?"

That was the plea which President Lincoln directed to Major General Grenville Dodge in 1865. Dodge, who had had a brilliant war career, was Union Army commander in Missouri at the time.

A guerrilla fighter harassing Union forces had been convicted of murder. He was scheduled to hang. The doomed man's mother begged Lincoln to save her son's life. The president in turn asked Dodge to spare the guerrilla if he could. Dodge, a tough soldier, was cool to the request. He was afraid that showing mercy to one guerrilla might encourage others to become bolder and more ruthless. Dodge decided to execute the man.

Then Dodge reported, "That night about midnight, I received a dispatch from the war department notifying me of Mr. Lincoln being shot." The president was dead.

The shocked Dodge did not have the heart to proceed with the execution. He commuted the sentence to life imprisonment.

Dodge and his staff were ordered to go to Springfield for the Lincoln funeral.

"It was the saddest day of my life," he wrote later. "The streets were lined with thousands and thousands of people in great distress and sorrow. At every step we could hear the sobs of the sorrowing crowd. . . . There was hardly a person not in tears and when I looked around at my troops I saw many of them in tears."

Few Iowans have left so indelible an imprint on their times as did Dodge. He was chief engineer of the Union Pacific during the epochal construction of that railroad across the continent.

One authority says: "He [Dodge] surveyed and built more than 10,000 miles of railroad and established Dodge City, Kansas, and Cheyenne and Laramie, Wyoming. . . . He was the friend and adviser of every Republican President between the Civil War and World War I. . . . In politics he was the leader of Iowa's ruling faction. . . . He made and unmade senators and congressmen. . . . He had solid financial talents as well, which earned him the respect of such financiers as Jay Gould."

In addition he was a highly competent Civil War major general who was wounded in action. A great deal of his military value during the war stemmed from his expertness as an engineer.

General Ulysses S. Grant, later president, described the tremendous job that Dodge did in Tennessee in 1863 in rebuilding 182 bridges and repairing 102 miles of railroad within forty days. All this was accomplished even though he had to detail blacksmiths to make the necessary tools, axemen to cut timber for bridges and fuel, and car builders to fix locomotives and cars.

When Dodge died in 1916, James Clarkson, nineteenth-century editor of the *Des Moines Register*, said, "He was the American of yesterday who deserves constant study at the hands of the Americans of today."

JACOB R. PERKINS

A *Warden-Novelist-Pastor*

COUNCIL BLUFFS WARDEN attained nationwide popularity as a novelist and was a beloved pastor besides.

He was the Reverend Jacob R. Perkins, minister at First Congregational Church at Council Bluffs for twenty-five years (1922–1947).

He wrote *The Emperor's Physician,* a biblical novel that sold 400,000 copies, and *Antioch Actress,* another biblical story that sold 200,000 copies.

He typed 2,500 words a day while serving as pastor. "I don't go ringing doorbells," he once said. "My people don't want me to."

Before going to Council Bluffs, he served four years as Fort Madison penitentiary warden, from 1916 to 1920. He was a Sioux City minister when appointed to the penitentiary post. He may be the only clergyman ever to have served as a prison warden in Iowa.

The pastor found the going rough at Fort Madison. He had hoped to change many prisoners into good citizens. Instead, he said ruefully, "all that you do is snatch a few brands from the burning."

Six weeks after he took over at the penitentiary, a riot resulted in the death of a prisoner. A short time later, another prisoner was killed in another battle. All of which was "very unlovely," Mr. Perkins said. "I came up against a great deal of realism," he commented.

His book *The Emperor's Physician* is told in the first person by the evangelist Luke. The doctor in the story is Roman Emperor Tiberius's physician. Mr. Perkins first read the book in installments on Sunday evenings to his parishioners in a San Francisco, California, church. Not until he had been in Council Bluffs for twenty years, however, was the book published.

His other writings included a biblical novel titled *Pontius Pilate's Wife* and a biography of General Grenville Dodge.

A magazine once called the preacher-writer the "pool champ" of Council Bluffs. He liked to play bottle pool at noon in the Council Bluffs Elks Club. He died in 1959.

MAT TINLEY

General Gave Up His Pants

A GREAT SOLDIER cited often for bravery that was demonstrated repeatedly under fire. . . . A practicing physician with a kindly touch in treating little children, and adult patients as well. . . .

That was the kind of man Lieutenant General Mat Tinley of Council Bluffs was. He served his country with distinction in the Spanish-American War and in World War I. He was granted numerous military awards for wartime service. He used good judgment in the way he commanded Iowa National Guard troops called into service during farm and labor troubles in the 1930s.

Yet, perhaps recalled more than anything else about Tinley is the story of Sergeant Pugsley and his pants.

Pugsley came out of the famed Argonne battle in France in World War I with his pants "wrecks after the fighting." He was ticketed for a promotion and he was ordered to report to an officer training camp back of the lines. He expressed doubt that his pants could hold together long enough for him to reach camp.

Tinley was a colonel at the time and he was wearing a good pair of pants. He said to Pugsley: "You and I are about the same build. It doesn't look as if I am going to have to worry about my clothes for a while. You and I will just trade pants." Which the commanding officer and the sergeant did, on the spot.

On another occasion, with German shells bursting around him at Badonvillers in France, Tinley shouted over a field telephone to a French general back of the lines, "No, the Germans haven't broken through, and they are not going to." It was his birthday, March 5, 1918, and he received the Croix de Guerre from the French for his valor that day.

When peace came the following November, Tinley took his regiment, the 168th Infantry, into Germany as part of the army of occupation. He received an order saying that the American troops should not be polite in dealing with the Germans. The order added, "The [German] children are particularly ill-behaved and pestiferous; they must be repulsed when endeavoring to curry favor."

A captain serving under Tinley said he never before had seen him "quite so mad." The captain said Tinley sarcastically observed that the order "must have been written by the guy who won the war." Added Tinley: "Now he wants the army of occupation to start spanking little children. Let him do his own spanking."

The Tinleys of Council Bluffs have been one of Iowa's most remarkable families. Mat's sister Mary also was a physician widely known for her skill in treating diseases of women and children. A brother Hubert was a bank president, another brother Emmet a president of the state bar association, and still another brother John was a district court judge. Other members of the family also attained positions of distinction.

Mat Tinley had a sufficiently large following to claim 230 pledged votes of delegates for the Democratic nomination for vice-president at the party's national convention in 1932. Franklin Roosevelt, the presidential nominee, decided, however, that he wanted John Nance Garner of Texas for the nomination. The Democratic National Convention accepted that decision, as did Tinley. The Roosevelt-Garner ticket was elected.

Mat Tinley practiced medicine for fifty-one years in Council Bluffs, not counting the periods spent on active military duty. At the time of his death in 1956, he was described as the first Iowan to attain the rank of lieutenant general, a promotion granted at the time of his military retirement in 1940.

He served in a number of civic capacities also. In 1933 he was chairman of the state commission named by Governor Clyde L. Herring to draw up recommendations for a new state liquor law. Out of those recommendations came the law which established the present Iowa state liquor store system.

Polygamy in Iowa

A NEWS STORY from Council Bluffs in 1873 said "Mrs. Stenhoufe, the ex-Mormon, told an audience how she felt when she used to see her husband fixing himself up nobly to go out and spend the evening with another wife."

The Mormons were a dramatic and often resented religious sect in the 1840s and later. They were chased out of Nauvoo, Illinois, in 1846 and began in Iowa one of the great religious treks in history. They flowed westward. A reported 15,000 were on the march by July of that year with 3,000 wagons; 30,000 head of cattle, horses, and mules; and "a vast number of sheep."

Some Mormons practiced polygamy (having more than one wife). They founded Salt Lake City in Utah where a Mormon civilization has prospered ever since. Polygamy was formally abandoned in 1890.

But polygamy was practiced among some Mormons from 1848 to 1852 in the Council Bluffs area, which was a major Mormon center for several years. So was "winter quarters" at Florence, Nebraska, across the Missouri River. Florence is now part of Omaha.

Brigham Young and other Mormon leaders always were fearful (with considerable reason) of outside interference with their way of life and their religion. That is why they sought to gain favor in 1846 by agreeing at Council Bluffs to enlist 500 Mormon men for service in the army. The United States was at war with Mexico. The agreement said the men were not to be sent to Mexico for combat duty but were to march to California, which they did. Evidently the idea was to secure California against possible seizure by the Mexicans. The Mormons saw no military action.

In explaining the enlistment agreement, Young said at Council Bluffs, "If we want the privilege of going where we can worship God according to the dictates of our consciences, we must raise the battalion."

Young also talked to the Mormon recruits at Council Bluffs before they left. He advised them to be chaste, humane, and not to take life unnecessarily.

The Council Bluffs area continued for a time to be of importance to the Mormons who settled there in sizable numbers. The name of the community then was not Council Bluffs. The settlement first was called Hart's Bluff. Miller's Hollow and Kanesville followed as early names of the town.

The number of Mormons in the area totaled 7,828 in 1850. Brigham Young sent orders two years later for all Mormons to come to Utah right away. They sold their Iowa properties and left. The remaining 1,000 people organized a new town government and renamed their municipality Council Bluffs. The name stemmed from the fact that Indians had used Missouri River Bluffs as places for holding tribal councils.

PERCY A. LAINSON

I "We Are Deserting These People..."

I AM AGAINST the death penalty no matter what the crime," said Percy A. Lainson, warden at Fort Madison penitentiary. "It doesn't make up for murder no matter how terrible.

"You can't do anything with revenge in your heart and be right."

The gravel-voiced Lainson, warden from 1943 until his retirement in 1958, previously served nine years as Pottawattamie County sheriff at Council Bluffs. He is generally regarded as having done a good job at Fort Madison. He was a longtime Council Bluffs resident.

As did many others, Lainson urged abolition of the death penalty in Iowa. That penalty was abolished in 1965, one year after his death at Council Bluffs.

Lainson had been a company commander in the Rainbow Division in France in World War I and saw plenty of military action.

As long ago as 1946, Lainson was pushing for prison reforms. He wrote: "We are leaving the job half done in not providing supervision, counsel and guidance to those persons whom we release daily from our prisons. To be brutally frank, we are deserting these people at a time when we could help them the most."

He was moved by the plight of men sentenced to spend the rest of their lives in prison. In 1956 he said, "We have 46 lifers here who in my opinion could be let out the front gate and we would never hear any more about them." He added, "Surely there must be some alternative to placing men behind high walls for 34 and even 50 years in one unbroken span, with death their only tangible hope for freedom."

AMELIA BLOOMER

The Original Bloomer Girl

A MELIA BLOOMER caused more of a sensation in the 1850s wearing bloomers at Council Bluffs than the scantiest miniskirted girl does today.

Amelia wrongfully is immortalized in history as having invented that horrible feminine garment known as "bloomers." She did no such thing, but she publicized bloomers as part of her campaign for equal rights for women.

For a woman to appear in public wearing pants in any form was incredible a century or more ago. Mrs. Bloomer showed up in an outlandish costume featuring a skirt that stopped just below the knee, but also wearing underneath full Turkish trousers that ended in "ruffles at the tops of her high shoes." By today's standards, her body and legs were extraordinarily well covered.

Two other women wore bloomers first, beginning in 1851. Mrs. Bloomer lived in Seneca Falls, New York, at that time and was editor of the *Lily,* a publication devoted to fighting for women's rights. Mrs. Bloomer learned of the pants costume and started wearing it. Her appearance in bloomers became a big story in the New York newspapers which named the garment for her. She protested but the name stuck.

Amelia and her husband, D. C. Bloomer, settled in Council Bluffs in 1855. She wrote upon her arrival, "I found the high winds that prevail here much of the time played sad work with short skirts when I went out." She added that she was "greatly mortified by having my skirts turned over my head and shoulders on the streets." She need not have been embarrassed, however. She had plenty else on.

Mrs. Bloomer wore bloomers until hoop skirts, which she liked, came in. She said such skirts were "light and pleasant to wear" and did not require heavy underclothes.

She helped establish in 1870 the Iowa Equal Suffrage Association which was devoted to winning for women the right to vote. She became second president of that organization but did not live to see the association goal realized. She died in 1894 after thirty-nine years residence in Council Bluffs. Women finally got the right to vote in 1920.

The Equal Suffrage Association merged into the League of Women Voters many years ago.

Mrs. Bloomer was described as a forceful and vigorous speaker. But she was small and dainty physically. She was described as being as delicate as "Dresden china."

JAMES D. EDMUNDSON

T *Long Life Inherited?*

HE JENNIE EDMUNDSON HOSPITAL in Council Bluffs, the Art Center in Des Moines, and an Indian statue in Oskaloosa all came into being because of sizable gifts by James D. Edmundson, a Council Bluffs banker and lawyer.

When his first wife died in 1890, Edmundson established the hospital as a memorial to her.

He paid for the statue of Indian Chief Mahaska in the city square at Oskaloosa as a memorial to his father William Edmundson, who was one of the commissioners appointed in the early days to organize Mahaska County.

When James Edmundson died at ninety-four years of age in 1933, he left $600,000 to establish the Art Center in Des Moines where he lived his final years. He did not credit clean living as being the reason for long life. He believed that a person's "vital spark" inherited from his ancestors usually determines how long he lives.

Edmundson explained, "It isn't the food you eat or the life you lead that makes for longevity." If a person's ancestors lived to be 100, he would have a chance to live that long also, "barring accidents."

IOWA CITY

JOHN IRISH

Body in a Haystack

T HE CITY was shocked. The body of Mrs. Mary Herrick had been stolen from her grave!

She was a respected elderly Iowa City lady. Her funeral had been held on a cold December Thursday afternoon in 1870.

Somebody took the body from the grave that night.

Suspicion pointed to the new medical college at the University of Iowa. The suspicion was well founded.

The Johnson County sheriff got a warrant to search the place. He found nothing.

John Irish had seen to it that the body had been removed before the sheriff got there. At the direction of Irish, the body was passed out a window to a horseman. He took the corpse to a haystack out in the country.

John Irish was a notable Iowa City newspaper editor. He also was a trustee of the university. He took prompt action because he feared enraged public opinion would force abolition of the medical school if the body were found there.

> *Irish was one of many vigorous and exciting persons Iowa City has had in its long existence as a university city and onetime state capital.*
>
> *The list includes Michael Hummer, who was foiled when he tried to seize a church bell; Robert Finkbine, who built the Statehouse in Des Moines to the highest standards of workmanship; and Samuel Kirkwood, Iowa's untidy but great Civil War governor.*

John Irish had been instrumental in getting the medical school established at the university. The school had opened in September 1870, only three months before the body theft.

All medical schools were handicapped in those days by the lack of sufficient bodies which students dissected in learning to be doctors. Few families would permit the use of a body of a deceased relative for such a purpose. Also, many well-meaning persons raised storms of protests against assigning the bodies of paupers and tramps to such use.

150

Yet, the skill of a surgeon begins with dissection. Said Irish, "The surgeon must dissect the dead or mangle the living."

Since medical schools simply had to have bodies, thefts from graves were not uncommon. Some people made a profession of it. Frequently medical students dug up bodies themselves. Nobody knows who was responsible for the Iowa City theft.

Irish said he was awakened by medical students on Saturday night, December 31, 1870. They told of the sheriff applying for the search warrant. Irish immediately arranged for the horseman to take away the body.

Irish evidently did not leave his house that night. He said he opened the window at midnight. In the "keen winter air," he heard "the horse leave his stable . . . and in due time heard his hoof beats on the hard road west of the river."

Twenty minutes later, Irish said, the sheriff and a crowd came down Clinton Street to the medical college rooms in old South Hall. Irish knew they would find nothing. He went back to bed, he said.

Iowa City was in a turmoil the next day. Critics leveled bitter blasts at Irish.

Relatives of Mrs. Herrick came pleading for return of the body, no questions asked. Irish disclaimed all knowledge of the case but promised to see what he could do. He wrote a letter to all students promising immunity if the body were returned. He then talked to undertakers Nixon and Doe, located on the present site of the Jefferson Hotel. He requested that an empty coffin be placed in back of their establishment at twenty minutes before midnight and then taken in at twenty minutes after midnight.

The plan worked. The body was found in the coffin and duly reburied. Irish does not say so but another report said the face already had been partly dissected.

The reburial did not halt the clamor. Newspapers over the state demanded that the medical college be discontinued. Irish was a member of the Iowa House of Representatives at the time. He had served two terms, was a candidate for a third term. His opponents had him arrested for body-snatching. He never was convicted. And he was reelected.

At his urging, the legislature legalized the use of human bodies for dissection. That act, of course, did not increase the supply of needed bodies. Lack of bodies has been a recurring problem at times for medical schools.

The dean of the new university medical college expressed deep regret over the body theft and said the action was totally unauthorized. He said the approved procedure used by the college was to get bodies from other states. The chances are, however, that such bodies were similarly stolen.

His enemies kept after Irish. The legislature finally passed a bill that knocked him off the university board of trustees. He may have known a lot more about the grave theft than he ever admitted. The night of December 31 was New Year's Eve. Irish was twenty-seven years old.

He said he had gone to bed. That does not sound like the kind of a
New Year's Eve a relatively young Irishman would have spent; even in
1870. But that was his story. He was, however, bothered by the fact
that the body involved was that of Mrs. Herrick. He was a friend of
the Herrick family.

Irish continued a firm friend of the university and a vigorous editor.
He was Democratic nominee for governor in 1877 but lost to Republican
John Gear, 121,000 to 79,000.

M *Trapped in Belfry*

ICHAEL HUMMER claimed the First Presbyterian Church in Iowa
City owed him $600 back pay.

He tried to get even by taking the church bell. He did not get the
bell. Instead he found himself marooned in the belfry.

The 1848 story of Hummer's bell is a hilarious footnote in Iowa
history.

Hummer had been pastor of the church which was hampered by
financial troubles. Somewhere along the line he became interested in
spiritualism. He moved to Keokuk.

When he failed to get his claimed back salary, he and a friend came
to Iowa City in a wagon. Hummer went up into the Presbyterian
church belfry. Using a block and tackle, he lowered the church bell to
the ground. A crowd gathered.

Hummer stayed up in the belfry to remove the block and tackle.
The friend left to fetch the horses and wagon. Somebody took away the
bell and hid it by sinking it in the Iowa River near the mouth of Rapid
Creek.

When the friend returned, the bell was gone and the ladder had
been taken down. Hummer was stuck up in the belfry "raving and
scolding and gesticulating like a madman, at which the boys and loafers
below were laughing and hurrahing."

The friend put up the ladder and rescued Hummer but the bell
was forever out of his reach.

The plan in Iowa City was to return the bell to the church when
Hummer was safely out of sight. Some Iowa Cityans going to California,
however, pilfered the bell from the river and took it with them in the
hope of selling it along the way. They did peddle the bell to the
Mormons in Salt Lake City.

The whereabouts of the bell meanwhile had become a mystery in
Iowa City. Hummer consulted the spirits who told him the bell was
hidden under the state capitol (now Old Capitol). The spirits were
wrong, of course. Some years later, returning California gold hunters
told of the Salt Lake City transaction.

Presbyterian church officials got word in 1868 from Brigham Young that the bell indeed was in Salt Lake City but was not being used and would be shipped back to Iowa City upon payment of shipping charges. But apparently the bell never was sent for. For all anyone knows, the bell is still in Salt Lake City.

NILE KINNICK

N *Might Have Been Governor*

ILE KINNICK might have become governor of Iowa or a United States senator by this time. He died at twenty-four years of age in 1943 when his naval plane crashed into the Caribbean Sea during a training exercise.

Kinnick is remembered best for the great record he established as a football player and top student at the University of Iowa.

Political reporters also remember him as a tremendous potentiality in politics.

He was a twenty-two-year-old law student at the university in 1940 when he introduced Wendell Willkie, Republican nominee for president, at an Iowa Falls meeting. The Kinnick introduction was well done. His talk was gracious, poised, short, in good taste. His performance was impressive.

He might have followed in the footsteps of his grandfather George W. Clarke of Adel who was a courageous and constructive governor of Iowa from 1913 to 1917.

Kinnick's accomplishments as an all-American halfback on Iowa's famed "ironmen" team of 1939 earned him the Heisman trophy awarded annually to the nation's outstanding football player. In accepting the award, he said, "I thank God I was born to the gridirons of the midwest and not to the battlefields of Europe."

But his fate was otherwise. He died a naval flyer in wartime. One writer said of his Heisman speech in New York: "He made a tremendous hit, did the lad from Iowa City and you couldn't help but think that here was the typical American boy . . . [his talk] was modest without being obnoxiously so. . . . Why does war have to take such really human beings? It doesn't seem fair. It doesn't seem fair."

Major John Griffith, the Big Ten commissioner, said, "Kinnick was one of the greatest little guys we ever had in the conference."

A Suddenly Went Tongue-Tied

A SUDDEN QUIET took over the 1860 Republican National Convention in Chicago when William Penn Clarke of Iowa City arose to announce the Iowa vote.

Clarke was chairman of the Iowa delegation. The question in the 11,000 minds in the hall was, Would Iowa go for Abe Lincoln? The Republican presidential nomination was by no means assured for Lincoln before the balloting began.

Clarke, an attorney, opened his mouth to speak. But no words came out. He was so excited he was unable to talk. Tension mounted.

Clarke stood helpless "in a vain stammer or stutter." The astonished Iowa delegates soon realized that he was "suffering from an impediment of speech that was serious only when he was laboring under great excitement."

Another Iowa delegate rescued Clarke by announcing the Iowa vote, which was widely split on that first ballot. The thirty-two Iowa delegates, with eight votes among them, gave Lincoln and William Seward of New York two full votes each and the rest scattered. Lincoln was nominated on the third ballot. On the final ballot, he got 5½ Iowa votes, to two for Seward and one-half for Salmon Chase of Ohio.

Clarke also took a big financial loss at the convention. He was in charge of the Iowa headquarters in the delegates' hotel. Some Iowa delegates "liked wines and Kentucky Bourbon more than was good for them." They ordered lots of liquor which was charged to headquarters. Clarke was stuck with the liquor bill after the convention adjourned.

E Barred from Campus

EVEN MAJOR presidential candidates were prohibited from speaking on the University of Iowa campus as recently as 1948.

Iowa's Henry A. Wallace was the most notable victim of that rule, now long since abolished. Wallace, a former vice-president, was the Progressive "third party" candidate for president in 1948. He was barred from holding a meeting on the university campus, had to go to the city park instead.

The state board of regents had put the no-candidates rule into effect. Wallace asked his mostly student audience of 4,000, "Is it the desire of the board that you graduate without ever having met a practical political fact at any time?"

Two eggs were thrown at Wallace in the park. Both went wide of their mark. One egg bounced off a little girl and landed on a reporter. Wallace had these further annoyances that day in Iowa City: the car in which he was riding was ticketed for parking in a prohibited area, and when he went to his room in the Hotel Jefferson the bed was not made.

Johnson County was not very good to Henry in that 1948 election either. He got only 359 votes for president there, compared with 8,600 for President Truman and 7,100 for Thomas Dewey.

SAMUEL KIRKWOOD

S *"A Modest and Majestic Man"*

AM KIRKWOOD'S CLOTHES were white with flour from head to foot.

He came to the convention in his work clothes. He did not dream he would be called upon to speak. But he was. The speech launched one of the most brilliant political careers in Iowa history.

The convention was held in Iowa City in 1856 to organize the new Republican party in Iowa.

Kirkwood operated a flour mill on the Iowa River near Iowa City. He also farmed. He had moved to Iowa from Ohio the year before.

At first he sat quietly at the convention and listened. There were other former Ohioans present. They knew Kirkwood and his ability. Several kept calling for Kirkwood to speak.

Somebody in the audience asked in a loud voice, "Who the hell is Kirkwood?"

He unwillingly arose. The speech that followed made such a deep impression that Kirkwood was nominated and elected an Iowa state senator that same year.

Three years later, in 1859, he was elected governor. He served four rugged years as Iowa's great governor of the Civil War period. Later he served twice in the United States Senate, once more as governor and finally as secretary of the interior in President Garfield's cabinet.

Kirkwood's carelessness in dress was legendary. But he probably was not as unpresentable as his political enemies charged. He once was described as not wearing socks and another time as having "a big head and long hair hanging down like an Indian's."

When a messenger brought a telegram from Washington in 1861, he found the governor "in boots and overalls caring for his stock" on the farm. A *Davenport Democrat* editor once said he opposed electing a man governor who didn't "know enough to keep himself clean." That

riled Kirkwood's friends who admitted he was no fashion plate but
said he could not be accused of a "want of cleanliness." A later historian
described Kirkwood as "a quiet man . . . a modest and majestic man."

Kirkwood was a bitter foe of slavery. He pounded at that issue in
the 1859 campaign when he opposed Augustus Dodge of Burlington for
governor. Dodge was the Democratic nominee. In a debate at Bloomfield, Kirkwood pictured a mythical slave mother fleeing to freedom
with a baby in her arms and pursued by bloodhounds.

Kirkwood asked Dodge, "Would you turn such a mother back to
her master?"

"I would obey the law," replied Dodge, meaning that he would
follow the fugitive slave law which required runaway slaves to be returned to their owners.

Shouted Kirkwood, "So help me God, I would suffer my right arm
to be torn from its socket before I would do such a monstrous thing!"

The crowd "broke into a frenzy that resembled the sweep of a cy-
clone through a forest."

Kirkwood defeated Dodge but it was no walkaway. The vote was
56,500 to 53,300. There were a lot of southern sympathizers in Iowa.
Dodge also was a good candidate. The Republicans picked up some
support among ordinary people from Kirkwood's casual appearance.

Fighting the Civil War beginning in 1861 proved to be a desperate
undertaking for Iowa and for Governor Kirkwood. The state treasury
was empty. Constant calls came for additional regiments which were
supposed to be financed by the state. Kirkwood and a number of banker
friends pledged their own resources for soldier uniforms, equipment,
and food. They got back the money ultimately, but Kirkwood once was
in hock for more than he was worth and his creditors were pounding on
the door. He reported at one point that uniforms worn by three Iowa
regiments already in service "today have not been paid for."

All told, while Kirkwood was governor, Iowa sent 60,000 men into
the armed forces, an enormous number for a state whose 1860 population was under 700,000. The total number of Iowans who served before
the war ended reached nearly 76,000, of whom 13,000 died.

Kirkwood was a strong backer of President Lincoln. Kirkwood once
advised Lincoln to fire General George McClellan as commander in
chief of Union forces in the East. The president replied: "Governor
Kirkwood, if I believed our cause would be benefitted by removing
McClellan tomorrow, I would remove him tomorrow. I do not believe
today. . . ." But Lincoln later did remove McClellan.

The Kirkwoods had no children of their own but adopted and
reared a nephew, Samuel Kirkwood Clark. He was fatally wounded in
action in the Union Army. He died in a hospital in St. Louis, with the
Kirkwoods at his bedside much of the time in his final days. The grieving
Kirkwood said of the young man, "He was as noble, as true-hearted, as
brave a boy as has lost his life in this struggle."

Then, as now, the hazards of travel plagued governors. Kirkwood twice was thrown out on the ground in 1863 when stagecoaches upset between Grinnell and Des Moines. He escaped both times with bruises.

Late in life Kirkwood's portrait was painted by George Yewell, a nationally known artist whose home had been in Iowa City. The large Kirkwood portrait, and others of notable Iowans by Yewell, are to be seen in the State Historical Building in Des Moines.

Kirkwood was eighty-one years old in 1894 when he said: "I am an old man now. My race is nearly run." He died the next day, a man beloved by Iowa.

ROBERT S. FINKBINE

Perfectionist Builder

IOWA SPENT $2.6 million between 1873 and 1886 building the golden-domed capitol in Des Moines.

The state got its money's worth, thanks to Robert S. Finkbine of Iowa City. He was the superintendent of construction. He was scrupulously honest and a perfectionist.

"His eagle eye was on every part of the work from start to finish," said one historian. "The state never lost a dollar . . . expended under his supervision. No contractor was able to deceive him in the quality of work furnished."

A speaker at the Statehouse dedication ceremonies in 1886 said there was "not a dishonest dollar" in the building from the foundation "to the crown of the dome." Governor Buren Sherman said in 1884, "It is no doubt a fact that no other public building in the United States has been constructed with more rigid economy."

Finkbine's own reports also carry hints of his exactness. He said in 1884, for example, "Portions of the work in the library [in the Statehouse] and part of the rail on the grand stairs are badly done and will not be accepted until made good." His salary as superintendent, in the last two years at least, averaged $333 a month, not much now but good money in those days.

Finkbine, an Iowa City contractor, first came to Des Moines as a state representative. He served two terms. He moved to Des Moines where he died in 1901.

WILBUR TEETERS

A Souvenir Pie

A BAKED PIE was kept for years as a souvenir by Dean Wilbur Teeters.

He got the pie from a man whose wife had unexpectedly baked it for him. The man wrote, "Since she has not been in the habit of baking me pies, I wonder if you would mind finding out what is in this one."

Analysis showed the pie to contain sufficient strychnine to kill ten persons.

Teeters said he reported what he had found to the letter writer and heard no more about the case. Teeters, tongue-in-cheek, said he presumed they "lived happily ever after."

Teeters was dean of pharmacy at the University of Iowa from 1904 to 1937 and was an Iowa faculty member a record sixty-four years. He was widely known as the "poison expert" of his times. He testified many times in murder cases where the victim died of poisoning.

A farm wife died in one south Iowa triangle case. Teeters's tests showed strychnine in the victim's vital organs. The "other woman" confessed.

But analysis on another occasion showed that "blood" on an ice pick really was barn paint, and an innocent man was saved from possible conviction.

Dean Teeters died in 1959 at ninety-three years of age.

"We Must Have a School"

FATHER BLEW stood up in the wagon and observed to the listening crowd that there were many children in the community.

"They are like prairie chickens in a buckwheat patch in fall," he said, "and yet so far they are learning nothing. They are ignorant children.

"They know nothing except the wild freedom of these great meadows and the skills for the little daily tasks which you assign them.

"How shall these children become citizens of the great Republic unless they learn its history and can read its law? We must have a school. All you who are in favor of a school for this community raise your hands."

Every hand went up except that of Peter Mitchell, the Englishman; but he was deaf and could hardly have been expected to give assent to the proposition until it was explained to him.

Such charming passages are the writing of Thomas Macbride in his Iowa historical book, *In Cabins and Sod-houses,* a gentle picture of pioneer life in Iowa prior to 1860.

Macbride was president of the University of Iowa from 1914 to 1917. He also was an excellent botanist and a scientist in other fields. But he will be longest remembered for his interest in promoting parks in Iowa. (Macbride Lake and state park near Iowa City are named for him.) He once said, "Indeed, a fine, well-planned park is not unlike a great cathedral; a great solemnity seems to attend both; the grove rather better, I think, because it has a higher ceiling, is cleaner and has far finer ventilation; it is all outdoors."

The public park also must be quiet, he said.

"There shall be no noise; nor dog nor boy with gun; nor klaxon, nor calliope nor trumpet call. In the park all voices shall be musical; birds undisturbed and happy as they flash in sunshine across the meadow, or dive in safety in some thicket; music of running water, the joyous cries of children playing in safety along the graveled roads, safe from speeding car; the music of the voices of happy people, for whom beauty and quiet and leisure, shall for once exist together."

GEORGE KELLER

Key Man in Work Relief

U NEMPLOYMENT was desperately heavy in 1933 in Iowa and elsewhere in the nation. A worker could not buy a job.

The federal government launched several programs designed to create work. Professor George Keller of the University of Iowa in Iowa City was named Iowa state engineer of the setup known as CWA (Civil Works Adminstration). He officed in Des Moines.

CWA preceded such programs as PWA (Public Works Administration) and WPA (Works Progress Administration). The ultimate goal of all such programs was to meet the employment emergency by providing worthwhile jobs. The programs overlapped to some extent.

Within several weeks the CWA "crash" program had more than 60,000 Iowans at work on roads, airports, and in factories.

Keller, a professor of mechanical engineering, was drafted for the relief post by Governor Clyde L. Herring. Keller had been a railroad blacksmith when he got a job teaching forging at the university in 1908. He decided to enroll in university classes. He graduated in 1913.

Keller remained in charge of the work-relief setup after CWA ended. Expenditures in work-relief programs totaled $130 million during his 1933–1941 career battling unemployment. Among other things, he directed the Iowa WPA program a number of years.

Workers on WPA projects did not get very big paychecks by today's standards. The average Iowa WPA employe was paid $48 for ninety-six hours of work each month in 1939. The minimum wage was thirty cents an hour. A dollar, however, did buy a lot more in the 1930s than now. Pork chops were ten cents a pound in Des Moines in 1934, top beef roasts fifteen cents a pound.

In 1938 Keller listed these public improvements realized from three years of work-relief programs in Iowa: 9,500 miles of roads surfaced or resurfaced; 2,500 miles of roads graded; 600 miles of streets improved; 170 public buildings constructed or improved; 55 recreation fields constructed; 150 miles of water or sewer pipe installed, 21 sewage plants built or improved; 6,500 sanitary toilets constructed; and 2 million garments made.

Keller, who also was president of the Iowa City Water Company, never got back to full-time university teaching. He was fatally injured in 1941 in an auto accident on Highway 6 west of Grinnell.

A *Delightful Stutterer*

A MOST DELIGHTFUL STUTTERER was Dr. Wendell Johnson, speech pathologist at the University of Iowa. Once, at the beginning of a speech, he said: "My n-n-n-name is W-w-wendell J-j-johnson. The n-n-name doesn't have as many syllables in it as that sounds."

He was a horrible stutterer until he was thirty-seven years old. He came to the University of Iowa from his native Kansas because he heard Iowa was doing something about stuttering. He remained the rest of his life at Iowa and became foremost in the speech pathology field.

He said he used to be "one of the most speechless guys you ever saw." He told of being introduced to somebody after climbing into a car.

"We had gone a mile before I could say 'pleased to meet you,'" Johnson recalled. He had all but overcome his stuttering completely in later years.

He maintained that it isn't the way that children talk which makes them stutterers but the way grownups listen. A small child's hesitation and repetition in talking is normal, Johnson said. Parents hear such hesitation and immediately begin to worry that the child is a stutterer.

"The kid doesn't know he is doing anything wrong—until he sees the reaction," Johnson said. "Then he'll try hard to do what's wanted, and he'll show effort and tension. The harder he tries the worse he does and the worse he does the worse the listener reacts. Pretty soon the child has a real problem."

Johnson would stutter now and then in an interview, maybe to prove that he still could do it. He died in 1965 at fifty-nine years of age.

Collector of Magazines

AN AMAZING COLLECTION of old magazines accumulated in the early 1900s in the office of the *Republican,* weekly newspaper at Audubon.

Editor of the paper was David Mott. He was an avid reader and he received a lot of free magazines in return for the publicity he gave magazine articles.

He had a sixteen-year-old son, Frank Luther Mott. The lad decided to arrange and index the magazines. He read as he worked and he became absorbed in the magazine as a mirror of American life.

After college and a newspaper career, Frank Luther Mott became dean of the University of Iowa school of journalism in 1927. He continued working on magazines and won a Pulitzer Prize in 1939 for volumes two and three of his *History of American Magazines.* He was working on the fifth volume in 1964 when he entered the hospital at Columbia, Missouri, where he was dean of the University of Missouri school of journalism. Death came to Frank Luther Mott that year at Columbia at the age of seventy-eight.

Salary Cut of 44 Percent

THE SALARY of a University of Iowa president once was cut 44 percent, from $18,000 to $10,000 a year.

The Iowa legislature voted that whopping salary reduction for Dr. Walter Jessup in the depression year of 1933. He resigned in 1934 and and became president of the Carnegie Foundation for the Advancement of Teaching.

Dr. Jessup had a turbulent but constructive career in his 1916–1934 years as the university president. During his administration were established the Iowa child welfare station, the school of religion, the college of commerce, and the schools of letters and fine arts. The university hospital also was built, in 1924. The Rockefeller Foundation donated $2,250,000 for the hospital and the legislature appropriated an equal amount.

The Jessup regime also experienced some major adversities. Iowa was ousted from the Big Ten athletic conference in 1929 for a temporary period because athletes had accepted aid from a so-called trust fund. The

1931 legislature held an investigation into charges of mismanagement at the university. The investigating committee absolved Jessup and found no basis for criminal charges against anyone, although some changes were recommended in handling university finances.

The total university enrollment was 3,523 when Jessup became president and had risen to 9,903 when he left. (The enrollment exceeds 20,000 now.)

B *Mr. History of Iowa*

ENJAMIN SHAMBAUGH was Mr. History of Iowa in his time in Iowa City. It has been estimated that his contributions to history and political science literature total more than 50,000 pages.

He established the university department of political science and also the *Palimpsest* and *Iowa Journal of History,* both historical publications.

Few persons have had so much reverence for Iowa's past. In the late 1930s he said that the centennial to look forward to was the 100th anniversary of Iowa's statehood in 1946. He very much wanted to be around for that observance. But it was not to be. He died in 1940 at sixty-nine, six years before the statehood centennial.

DES MOINES

D WAC Did Striptease

E-EMPHASIZE glamor and sex!

That was the order given to army officers assigned to the first WAC training center at Fort Des Moines.

The order was fairly well enforced. Then a WAC stripteaser spoiled it all.

The WACs (Women's Army Corps) came into being in 1942 at Fort Des Moines on the south edge of Des Moines. World War II was raging. The United States desperately needed fighting men.

The WAC center was set up to train women to handle army jobs back of the lines and thereby free soldiers for combat duty.

Some 72,000 women went through training at Fort Des Moines between 1942 and early 1946.

> *The WACs are an exciting and important part of Des Moines's past. Many other individuals and groups, both good and bad, have enlivened the history of Iowa's capital city the last 125 years. For example: Mercenary men successfully used corruption to get the Statehouse located on the east side; Des Moines reformers fought unsuccessfully to retain a longtime Iowa law forbidding the sale of cigarettes; a notable president brought his peace campaign to Des Moines; a Des Moines diplomat and his wife were lucky to escape from China with their lives (they subsisted on horse and mule meat).*

The nation was not certain in 1942 that the WACs were a good idea. Some people did not believe the army was a place for decent women.

Ribald stories were common. Here was one of the mildest:

A WAC recruit asked, "Where do I eat?" "You mess with the officers," she was told. She replied, "Yes, I know, but where do I eat?"

Army officers assigned to Fort Des Moines took a lot of kidding about "training the skirts."

Strict conduct rules were put into force. Army men were forbidden to look at WAC legs. The men were warned against letting their language become "too picturesque."

The WACs themselves were placed under rules described as strict as those of a girls' boarding school. Among other things, weekend leaves were to be granted only on formal application. A girl could not leave the Des Moines area except for "extra special reasons."

The application for leave had to be accompanied by a letter of invitation from the family with which the WAC planned to spend the time. The WAC also had to say whether she was related to the host family. Weekend leaves began Saturday noon and ended Sunday night.

Posing for sexy pictures for newspapers and magazines was forbidden. Colonel Don Faith, commandant at the center, warned that

Fort Des Moines was to be "no glamor girls' playhouse." But sex was hard to tone down.

First feminine commanding officer of the WACs was Colonel Oveta Culp Hobby, thirty-seven, of Houston, Texas. She was an attractive woman. Associated Press editors in New York requested a picture of Colonel Hobby posing in a bathing suit at the Fort Des Moines pool.

"We told you there would be no girlie pictures," an army officer angrily told an Associated Press reporter. "Right away you want cheesecake of the boss."

"Cheesecake" was a slang term used to describe a photograph that emphasized the feminine leg. The AP did not get that picture.

One grizzled old regular army sergeant at the Fort got into big trouble. He was assigned to handing out feminine clothing to the WACs and how he detested it! He was warned not to talk for publication about the clothing. A news reporter wheedled the sergeant into disclosing the clothing list.

The resulting story, which was printed all over the nation, began: "There will be little excuse for the uniforms of WACs bulging in the wrong places. The army is going to issue two girdles apiece to the girls."

The sergeant immediately lost that job. He disappeared from sight. He probably was transferred elsewhere. Which was what he wanted. He had no stomach for the "women's army."

Sex reared its head in a different way July 20, 1942, when the WAC center formally opened. The dedication drew girl reporters as well as men from around the nation. The male reporters on the scene found themselves badly handicapped. Some girl scribes were not above nuzzling up to male army officers at the post. There were no female officers yet. Women reporters thus got the stories and scooped the men all over the place.

Nevertheless, the army kept the lid on sex pretty well at Fort Des Moines—until WAC "Amber d'Georg" cut loose. Her real name was Catherine Gregory. She went AWOL from the WACs late in November 1942. She was very pretty. She had reddish brown hair and a Shape.

One of her troubles was that she did not go AWOL far enough away.

She was found doing a striptease in the Casino Theater in downtown Des Moines. She also performed a "Samoan love dance" to the accompaniment of music and soft lights.

She was hauled back into the army, quickly discharged from the service.

Capitol Bribery

THE IOWA STATE CAPITOL might be located today on the west side of the Des Moines River in Des Moines if one or more state commissioners had not been bribed with property and perhaps money.

One historian said flatly that four commissioners "received real estate worth over $50,000" for placing the Statehouse where it is now on the east side.

It is certain that one commissioner got fifty lots as a payoff.

The juicy capitol location scandal in the late 1850s created wild excitement around the Iowa legislature and started an eastside-westside feud that lasted for generations in Des Moines.

Involved was Grenville M. Dodge, later a revered Civil War hero and famed railroad builder.

The state capital was moved in 1857 from Iowa City to Des Moines. Two years earlier, a capitol location commission was named to investigate possible sites in Des Moines. The law required that the new capitol in Des Moines be placed "within two miles of the junction of the Des Moines and Raccoon rivers."

The westside, which was the principal part of town, was confident of getting the capitol. An 1854 Des Moines map identifies as "capitol hill" an area from Second Avenue to Fifth Avenue and north of the present Keosauqua Way, immediately north of downtown Des Moines. Eastsiders had other ideas. They made a vigorous bid for the capitol. The group included Alexander Scott, Harrison Lyon, and John S. Dean, after whom Des Moines streets are named.

The capitol commission came to Des Moines in 1855 and for a second and final time in April 1856. Benjamin Pegram of Council Bluffs, a business associate of Grenville Dodge, was one of the five commissioners.

John Baldwin of Council Bluffs, a Dodge partner, scurried around Des Moines. His sole goal was to make some money from the situation, by corrupting commissioners and others. He did not have to work on Pegram who was part of the conspiracy.

"The air was full of plots and schemes," says one report. "There were wheels within wheels. . . . Excitement was intense."

The westside offered the state at least ten acres of land for a site and $200,000 in other real estate if the capitol were placed west of the river. The eastsiders offered forty acres of land, nearly all owned by Scott, and to construct a capitol without expense to the state.

When the eastsiders did win out, they built a three-story brick capitol at a cost of only $35,000. Construction costs were low then. The new capitol was located where the Iowa soldiers' and sailors' monument is now, south of the present golden-domed Statehouse.

The Iowa House launched a full-scale investigation of the location conflict. The probe demonstrated that not all pioneers were angels. Said the investigators' report: "It appears from the testimony that 250 lots were set apart on the east side of the river to influence the location of the capitol; that town lots, or interests in town lots, were given to affect the location; that Pegram was bribed; that Baldwin was the go-between with Pegram, if not more of the commissioners, and the proprietors of land on both sides of the river; that he appeared to have Pegram, if not a majority of the commissioners, for sale to the highest bidder."

Baldwin also was described as offering to obtain the location for the westside for a payment of $50,000. Baldwin refused to answer when asked if some commissioners were given an interest in eastside lots. James A. Williamson, eastside attorney and later a notable Civil War soldier, said Pegram received "about 50" lots. Williamson declined to say whether Baldwin got any money or property during the negotiations.

Lyon testified he gave Baldwin ten lots. Scott refused to answer when asked if he had conveyed, or agreed to hold in trust, property for commissioners. (Witnesses "took the Fifth Amendment" in those days also.)

The investigating committee absolved Stewart Goodrell, one of the commissioners, of being involved in any wrongdoing.

Pegram and Baldwin were not punished. Nor were any of the other commissioners.

Grenville Dodge possessed considerable power in the legislature and it was lucky for Baldwin and Pegram that he did. Dodge succeeded in having defeated a legislative resolution demanding that Pegram pay the state $10,000.

Dodge also "saved his partners—and his firm—from disgrace" by seeing to it that no action was taken on the investigating committee's report. A historian termed the case "one of the most unsavory episodes" in Dodge's life.

Scott and other eastsiders borrowed money from the state permanent school fund to build the capitol as promised. They expected to be in position to pay off the loan shortly. Instead, they went broke.

The nationwide financial crash of 1857 was partly responsible for the plight of the eastsiders. More important, however, was the fact that eastside property did not suddenly turn highly valuable. The main Des Moines business district did not move from the westside to the capitol area as the eastsiders hoped.

They had borrowed a lot of money in various loans and had posted property as security. When they could not meet those obligations, they lost the property. But they did not have to pay what they owed the school fund on construction of the capitol. The legislature took action releasing the eastside group from that debt.

Scott had been an early operator of ferry boats (there were no bridges then) across the Des Moines River. After going bankrupt on the Statehouse venture, Scott went West, hoping to recoup in the "Pike's Peak" gold rush of 1859 in Colorado. He never got there. He died en route in Nebraska.

Many years before, Scott stood on a bluff southeast of the present Statehouse "overlooking a grand view of the Des Moines River valley." He said, "When I die, I want to be buried here, where I stand."

He was brought back and buried there, although the area was private property at the time. Later the Statehouse grounds were enlarged to include the Scott grave which is in the southeast part of the grounds.

How sinful was the acceptance of bribes for locating the capitol on the eastside? Not very, in the opinion of one early historian.

"It was generally understood and believed at the time that at least some of the commissioners made a very good thing, financially considered," the historian wrote. "In those days, many countyseats were to be located. . . . It was generally considered right and proper for locating commissioners to 'make something' for their own private pockets. If the rule was good when applied to location of countyseats, why should it not also be good when applied to the location of a state capitol?"

President Visited Cemetery

W HEN ULYSSES S. GRANT came to Des Moines as president of the United States in 1875, he wanted above all else to visit the grave of Brigadier General Marcellus N. Crocker in Woodland Cemetery.

As he stood by the grave, the president said with a touch of reverence, "General Crocker was fit to command an independent army."

Those words were carved later on a memorial stone for Crocker in the cemetery.

Crocker was one of Iowa's most illustrious soldiers in the Civil War. He was a brilliant lawyer, fervent patriot, and a completely fearless and highly competent soldier. He fought under Grant at Shiloh, Corinth, and elsewhere. His brigade was known as the "Crocker Greyhounds." Although he came under fire many times, Crocker never was wounded. He died of tuberculosis in 1865.

President Grant attended, in Des Moines, the 1875 reunion of the "Army of the Tennessee," which he once commanded.

One of the most significant presidential visits to Des Moines was that of Woodrow Wilson in 1919. President Wilson was on a nationwide tour seeking support of the American people for the old League of Nations and for the World War I peace treaty.

He said in Des Moines that the league would secure future peace "in the only way it can be secured," by international cooperation. The president delivered thirty-six speeches before his health broke under the strain. The United States Senate refused to go along with the president and the United States did not join the league. There are those who believe the league might have had some success in staving off later conflicts (World War II, the Korean War, the Vietnam War) had the United States become a league member in 1919.

In 1936 a Democratic president and his Republican opponent met face to face in the Statehouse. The president was Franklin D. Roosevelt. The Republican was Governor Alfred M. Landon of Kansas, who had been selected as the GOP presidential nominee some weeks before. The meeting in the office of Iowa Governor Clyde L. Herring was nonpolitical and cordial.

Roosevelt had called the conference to discuss what steps should be taken to combat the drought which wrought such havoc in the Midwest. The summer of 1936 was the hottest on record for Iowa. The crops took a real beating.

A number of United States Senators (including Harry Truman of Missouri) and other governors took part in the conference. But all eyes centered on Roosevelt and Landon. Less than three months later, Roosevelt was reelected over his Republican opponent by a landslide margin. Landon carried only two of the forty-eight states.

Roosevelt, however, did not seem that far ahead on the day of the drought conference. Landon "sunflower" buttons were numerous in the crowd of 160,000 which gathered in Des Moines. The "sunflowers," however, had practically vanished by election day.

Roosevelt told Landon: "Don't work too hard. These campaigns are trying."

Roosevelt, a polio victim, was transported through the Statehouse in a wheelchair, but the spectators did not see that. They saw only his cheery smile and the wave of his hat as he rode in a convertible through crowded downtown Des Moines. He was taken by wheelchair through curtained corridors to and from Herring's office in the Statehouse.

Aided by a cane, Roosevelt walked slowly from the ground-floor door to the car parked on the west side of the Statehouse. Franklin D. Roosevelt, Jr., preceded his father and ordered, "No pictures." The cameramen obeyed. The president got into the car by first seating himself on the car floor and then boosting himself by his strong arms up into the back seat.

Iowa fields did not look too parched that day. There had been some rain. Herring drolly observed to Roosevelt, "I was almost afraid the drought conference would be rained out."

After the conference, the federal government took a number of steps to aid drought-stricken farmers.

IDA B. WISE SMITH

S *Cigarettes Illegal*

ALE OF CIGARETTES was illegal everywhere in Iowa for twenty-five years from 1896 to 1921.

Iowa was ridiculed as a "hick state" because of that law.

Debate in the legislature during passage of the anticigarette measure was lively. Senator W. H. Berry of Indianola said a court witness was unable to testify on one occasion because smoking two cigarettes had "unbalanced him." Senator L. A. Ellis of Clinton, however, said the measure "undertakes to regulate habits of individuals and can never be enforced."

The law was widely violated almost from the time of passage. The situation got worse when smoking cigarettes increased spectacularly among servicemen in World War I. The 1921 legislature repealed the ban on sales.

Ida B. Wise Smith of Des Moines, noted foe of liquor, staged a strenuous drive to keep the anticigarette law on the books. She asked Governor Nate Kendall to veto the 1921 repeal bill. She said that to legalize the sale of cigarettes would be "contrary to the wishes of a great majority of the women of the state." But the governor signed the measure.

Mrs. Smith experienced many more defeats in subsequent years. A onetime Des Moines school teacher, she was national president for eleven years of the Women's Christian Temperance Union (WCTU). She lived to see national Prohibition come and go and to see Iowa move from a "dry" to a "wet" state, which made her most unhappy.

Ida B. Wise Smith was respected by the wets and by the drys alike. She advised her fellow drys to "be sweet and kind—and don't scold" in promoting their cause. In addition to her never-ending battle against liquor, Mrs. Smith worked hard for laws to improve the welfare of children. She died in 1952 at eighty-one years of age.

Cigarettes figure in a delightful story about Mary Huncke of Des Moines, longtime state welfare chairman and official.

Mrs. Huncke was returning to Iowa by train from a national welfare meeting. An elderly woman sat beside her. Some young women came into the car, sat down, lighted cigarettes. Mrs. Huncke's offended seatmate commented, "We never did such things in *our* day, did we?" Mrs. Huncke, also well on in years, retorted, "Lady, *this* is my day." Mrs. Huncke, incidentally, did not smoke.

FRANCIS M. DRAKE

Governor Injured

I OWA'S OLDEST GOVERNOR at the time of his inauguration was Brigadier General Francis M. Drake, after whom Drake University is named.

He was sixty-six years old when he took office in 1896. He was the last of the old Civil War "soldier-governors." He served but one term as the state's chief executive. He did not seek the Republican nomination for a second term in 1898.

Drake suffered a severe leg wound in a Civil War battle. The wound never really healed.

While he was governor, he went by streetcar one day from downtown Des Moines to the Statehouse. Rain was falling as he hurried up the north steps of the capitol. He slipped and fell. An edge or point of stone penetrated the wound. He was in such pain the next few weeks that he was not able to do anything, including running for office. He retired from politics. He died in 1903.

Drake University was named for him after he gave the institution $20,000. One historian says that he gave the university more than $230,000 in a twenty-year period and bequeathed the institution another $50,000 in his will. His wealth stemmed from railroad building and banking. He lived in Centerville.

EDWIN H. CONGER

"China Belongs to Chinese"

CHINA was aflame with rebellion while Edwin H. Conger of Des Moines was United States minister to Peking at the turn of the century.

Conger and his wife were besieged in the Chinese capital during the bloody Boxer revolt of 1900. The Iowans were fortunate they were not killed. The German minister was murdered and his secretary was wounded during the uprising. A Japanese legation official also was slain.

For weeks all foreigners including the Congers were penned up in the British legation. As the siege lengthened, food grew scarce. Eighty horses and mules had to be slaughtered and eaten. Only a few such animals were left when Allied troops arrived and relieved the trapped diplomats and their families.

The Boxers were a secret antiforeign society in China. Their name in Chinese meant "the first of righteous harmony." Shouting "down with the foreign devils," they attacked westerners. Says one account: "Making the night awful with their yells, countless thousands of Chinese would swarm forward. Only their compact masses made continued defense possible. The marines would fire as fast as they could load . . . the defenders' machineguns carried wholesale death to the assailants. Yet such courage did the Chinese display that it seemed impossible to keep them much longer at a distance." But hold them the defenders did.

"The anxiety of the people of Iowa [for the Congers] was intense," said one report, "and one morning the news came that all the foreign ministers and their families . . . had been slaughtered." That news, thankfully, was not correct.

"All through the terrible ordeal," a report said, "Major Conger was one of the bravest of the defenders. His wise counsel was acknowledged by all to have aided materially in saving the little garrison from extermination."

Conger continued as minister to China until 1905 when he was appointed minister to Mexico. He resigned soon after and moved to Pasadena, California, where he died in 1907. He previously had served as minister to Brazil and two terms in Congress. He also served two terms as state treasurer.

Mrs. Conger expressed great sympathy for the Chinese. Discussing the "unequal treaties" and other foreign-imposed limitations, she wrote: "Poor China! Why can not foreigners let her alone with her own? . . . China belongs to the Chinese and she never wanted the foreigner on her soil." Some historians believe the long Chinese hatred of western nations stems in part from the Boxer era.

Farmers Jammed Capitol

U PWARDS of 2,000 farmers marched grimly into the Statehouse and halted proceedings in the Iowa House of Representatives.

The invaders were members of the Iowa Farm Holiday Association. That organization was formed to demand guaranteed "cost of production" and other aids for poverty-stricken farmers.

What the farmers did that day was out of line. Interrupting the deliberations of a legislative body is inexcusable. But nobody was punished. The date was March 13, 1933. The nation was in the throes of a deep depression. Farmers were caught in a squeeze of disastrously low prices for their products and high debts and taxes.

Top hogs brought only $4.10 per 100 pounds that day in Chicago and prime cattle were $7.25. Chickens were 4 cents to 6 cents a pound in Iowa, corn 10 cents to 13 cents a bushel, oats 9 cents a bushel, eggs 6 cents to 9 cents a dozen.

Stores were selling eggs at retail as low as three dozen for 29 cents, pork roasts for 5½ cents a pound, beef roasts for 6½ cents, round steak 11½ cents, butter 18 cents.

Average value of Iowa farmland dropped from $227 an acre in 1920 to $65 in 1933. Landowners saw one farm in every nine sold at sheriffs' sales in that period.

The farmers jammed the main floor and galleries of the Iowa House chamber that day and there was an overflow crowd in the Statehouse rotunda. It was said that a few demonstrators carried such items as pickaxe handles and ropes.

Several farmers announced they wanted to find State Senator Mike Fisch (Democrat, Le Mars) for the purpose of hanging him by the neck over the rotunda bannister in the Statehouse. That may, or may not, have been only talk. In any event, the senator reportedly discreetly went far up into the golden dome and thus kept out of harm's way.

The farmers offered a resolution saying that if Congress did not act soon to "provide justice for the American farmer, we shall prepare to strike and hold our products from the market." Then, they said, they would want Iowa Governor Clyde L. Herring "to declare an embargo upon shipments of all food products out of Iowa."

John Chalmers of Madrid, Holiday Association president, got up to the Speaker's rostrum in the House chamber and addressed the crowd. He was not gentle. He said maybe farmers and organized labor should forcibly adjourn the legislature "if you are going to continue to let this suffering go on." He predicted such forcible adjournment might "happen next Monday." But it did not.

Herring came to the House chamber to talk to the farmers. He had lost a fortune himself in the decline of real estate values. At the time of his election as governor a few months before, it was said that he did not have sufficient ready cash to buy coal to heat his big Des Moines home. He told the crowd, "We are all having the same trouble and we are going to iron it out together."

Numerous federal measures, such as corn loans and "corn-hog contracts," served to alleviate farm troubles somewhat. Also, two severe droughts in 1934 and 1936 boosted grain prices. What finally "solved" the "farm problem," however, was the inflation of World War II which started in 1939.

HENRY A. WALLACE

Questions Progress

T HE AUTOMOBILE, good roads and electricity destroyed the United States I had come to love and understand," Henry A. Wallace said in a 1962 speech in Des Moines.

Wallace, former vice-president and longtime Des Moines resident, added: "I still tend to distrust the values and systems thrust upon us since World War I. Electricity and a thousand and one gadgets are no final answer.

"I suspect the pioneers of eighty years ago were perhaps just as close or even closer to that answer than we. It may be more difficult to live virtuously and wisely with abundance than with scarcity."

Wallace was secretary of agriculture under Roosevelt from 1933 to 1941 and then was vice-president in the Roosevelt administration from 1941 to 1945. Wallace was secretary of commerce under President Truman in 1945–1946 and then ran a poor race as Progressive third-party candidate for president in 1948.

Wallace lived the final years of his life at South Salem, New York, where he pursued his scientific interest in hybrid development of chickens, strawberries, and gladioli. He was among the first and foremost experimenters in development of hybrid corn which increased yields of that crop so spectacularly beginning in the 1930s. Ever the scientist, Wallace kept track of his own symptoms and reactions while he was dying in 1965. Death came at seventy-seven years of age from a rare paralyzing disease called lateral sclerosis.

His father before him, Henry C. Wallace, was secretary of agriculture under Presidents Harding and Coolidge before his death in 1924. Henry C. was a Republican. Henry A. also was a Republican to begin with but switched to the Democratic party and later was a Progressive.

G *Retreat from Railroads*

ETTING the United States government out of the railroad business in the 1920s was a colossal task that was expertly performed by James C. Davis.

He was a Des Moines attorney who was appointed director general of American railroads in 1921 by President Harding.

The government had taken over operation of all railroads during World War I as part of the war effort. Washington agreed to pay annual rentals of some $900 million to rail owners for use of the lines.

When peace came, the lines were returned to their owners. Davis got the job of settling the endless claims and disputes between rail and federal officials.

The railroads filed claims exceeding $1 billion against the government, a tremendous figure then. Federal officials submitted counter claims of $438 million.

Under Davis's careful management, the railroads finally got $244 million from Washington which in turn collected $195 million. In other words, the government was out of pocket a net of less than $49 million. In addition, Davis collected "some $500 million which the railroads were indebted to the government on account of advances made" to buy equipment and property.

When Davis resigned in 1926, President Coolidge was in the White House. In a letter of appreciation, the president complimented the Des Moines attorney for a difficult job done "in a most satisfactory manner, due to your energy, ability and tact." Coolidge said "the thanks of the country should be extended to you in most generous measure."

Davis returned to his railroad law firm in Des Moines. He died in 1937 at eighty years of age.

ALBERT B. CUMMINS

The Barbed-Wire Trust

A NATIONWIDE TRUST jacked up the price of barbed wire from 7 and 8 cents to 10 and 11 cents a pound in the 1880s era.

Furious Iowans organized the Farmers Protective Association to fight the trust. The farmers badly needed the newly invented barbed wire at lowest possible prices. Cattle, which had caused all kinds of trouble breaking through old-time fences, learned immediately to stay away from the sharp barbs.

The association arranged with a Des Moines factory to manufacture barbed wire in defiance of the trust. The factory began selling to farmers at 7½ cents a pound and was able later to cut the price to 4½ and 5½ cents a pound.

The trust and the farmers soon were locked in angry court battles. Albert B. Cummins, a Des Moines attorney, led the legal battle for the farmers. For five years the bitter struggle continued. The trust used bribery with considerable success and even succeeded in alienating one of the association's prominent attorneys. Nevertheless, the association refused to give in and the power of the trust finally was broken. A dozen leading Iowans, including Cummins, were acclaimed for their stubborn and triumphant resistance.

The barbed-wire battle gave Cummins a statewide reputation and paved the way to his brilliant achievements in political leadership.

Cummins wanted to be a United States senator. The ruling forces of Iowa Republican politics—Nathaniel M. Hubbard of the North Western Railroad and Joseph Blythe of the Burlington Railroad—thwarted Cummins for years. But he successfully challenged their power in 1901 and won election as governor. He said in his 1902 inaugural address, "Corporations have and ought to have many privileges; but among them is not the right to sit in political conventions or occupy seats in legislative chambers."

He bitterly attacked lobbyists, presumably including those of the railroads.

"The professional lobbyist, I regret to say, has become one of the features of legislative assemblies," Cummins said. "He has become a stench in the nostrils of a decent community and ought to be driven out with the lash of scorn, pursued by the penalties of the law from the presence of every official and from the precincts of every legislative body in the Republic."

Cummins was elected governor three times, to the extreme distaste of the railroads. They bribed politicians in those days with passes good for free rides on trains. In one drive against Cummins, passes were reported "as thick as flies in midsummer." In 1906 Cummins termed the free pass "a vicious practice." The legislature thereupon enacted a law forbidding such passes.

Cummins finally achieved his goal of winning a seat in the United States Senate, where he served three terms. The Esch-Cummins law enacted in 1920 provided for creation of a national railway labor board and for eventual consolidation of railroads into several large systems.

SIOUX CITY

Took Hens off Nest

T HE MOST wildly imaginative swindler in Iowa history came to grief in federal court in Sioux City.

He was Oscar Hartzell who bilked perhaps 40,000 suckers out of an amount estimated as high as $1.3 million. Thousands were Iowans.

For years Hartzell duped investors into believing he was on the verge of getting billions of dollars from the "estate" of Sir Francis Drake, piratical English sea captain of four centuries ago. A gullible Iowa farmer said of the estate, "I'm taking my settin' hens right off the nest to put everything I've got into this thing." But there was no Drake estate.

> *Hartzell was one of a lot of spectacular people who have flashed across the Sioux City horizon in past decades. There was famed Eddie Rickenbacker who won a major 1913 auto race in Sioux City while wearing a bat's heart around his finger. Harry Hopkins, who spent nearly $10 billion in federal money during New Deal days, was the son of a Sioux City harness maker.*
>
> *William Harding of Sioux City, Iowa's World War I governor, ordered Iowans not to use a foreign language while speaking over the telephone, or anywhere else.*
>
> *A Negro hotel owner once drove railroad builders off his Sioux City property with a shotgun.*
>
> *Henry Clay Work, who composed the Civil War song "Marching through Georgia," once lived in Sioux City. So did Frederick M. Hubbell, who later became Iowa's richest man at Des Moines. As a youth Hubbell was jilted by a Sioux City schoolteacher.*

"The King Is with Us"

I NVEST $50 and get a return of $100,000 on your investment. Maybe more. Put in $1 and you might get $5,000 back.

That was the kind of pitch which Oscar Hartzell and his agents used in their "Drake estate" scheme.

An aged Plover, Iowa, couple contributed $1,000 on the promise of getting $1 million in return. They never recovered even a dime of their own money.

The victims were told the Drake estate value in England might reach $22 billion. The British government "is afraid there will be a revolution if all that money is taken out of the country," Hartzell said, then added: "But the King is with us and he's going to see that we get what's coming to us. I have been in touch with London and I hear the estate is going to be settled and distributed before the next harvest."

Hartzell never saw the king or anyone else in the British government. His story was the product of his own fertile imagination. But he did live in luxury in London for ten years on the never-ending flow of money he received from foolish Americans.

Hartzell once said his share of the forthcoming Drake estate would be enough to buy all the land in Iowa, all the railroads and city property, absorb all the bank deposits in the state, "and then have more money left over than I ever thought of." He peddled that line from 1920 until he was convicted in 1933 in Sioux City.

What Hartzell told the contributors was that he needed their money to help pay expenses of the highly secret process of final settlement of the estate in England. They eagerly supplied the cash, usually at the rate of $2,500 a week while he lived in London.

Hartzell was a onetime Madison County farm boy and a former Polk County deputy sheriff. His racket was outlined in detail to a 1933 federal court jury in Sioux City. He received a ten-year sentence which he began serving in 1935 at Leavenworth. He died of cancer in prison in 1943.

The Drake estate fraud existed before and since Hartzell but never on such a grand scale.

With the blessing of the first Queen Elizabeth, Sir Francis Drake plundered Spanish ships in the 1570s. Drake brought home a lot of treasure to England. Drake died in 1596. His valid will went through the courts and his property was distributed among relatives. He had married twice but left no children. The estate was closed forever.

Hartzell mysteriously told of a third unknown Drake wife who he said had a son. Hartzell claimed the wife and son were cheated in the final settlement of the Drake estate. The Iowan said he had located a descendant of that son. Hartzell said he and the descendant entered into an agreement whereby Hartzell would get one-fourth of the estate for his efforts and he would give half of that fourth to contributors. Hartzell added to the mystery later by refusing to divulge whether he himself was the heir.

Hartzell spiced up the story still more by saying that Queen Elizabeth had taken vast treasures from Drake and had hidden the wealth in famed London Tower.

The Iowan first listed J. P. Morgan, the New York banking magnate, among the top Americans who were strenuously fighting the whole Drake estate project. Later Hartzell told this story with a straight face,

"You can tell them that Morgan isn't fighting us any more because Morgan himself is contributing."

At Sioux City, court goers listened to three weeks of testimony by victims of the hoax, by Hartzell agents, by a London detective, and a London barrister. But Hartzell never took the stand in his own defense.

Regarding Hartzell hints that he hobnobbed with the king and high-up British officials, the London detective testified that the Iowan did no such thing. The detective said that all Hartzell did in London was to receive the money, send cables about imagined "developments" to the United States (and complaints when the remittances were not as large as expected), and spend long hours drinking in a plush club.

The British government deported Hartzell as an undesirable alien. He was arrested when he landed in New York and was taken to Sioux City for his last trial.

EDDIE RICKENBACKER

Rickenbacker Won $10,000

Eddie Rickenbacker, a hero of both world wars and a major airlines official afterward, competed in a 300-mile auto race in Sioux City in 1913. He drove a Duesenberg. The top prize was $10,000. Rickenbacker and his crew were broke. Never has such a group needed more to win.

At Eddie's request, his mother consulted a book on Swiss lore on how to get lucky. She recommended that he cut the heart out of a bat and tie the heart to a middle finger with red silk thread. Eddie obtained a bat at Sioux City.

"I hated to kill the little creature," he said in his autobiography, "but I had convinced myself that it was our only hope. Not being up on bat anatomy, I may have removed the gizzard rather than its heart, but whatever it was, I tied it to my middle finger. I was invincible. Let the race begin!"

He was invincible. He won the $10,000. (The race was marred by the fact that another competitor bounced off Rickenbacker's car and crashed. The other driver and his mechanic were killed.) After the event, Rickenbacker "took the team to the best hotel in Sioux City." They all enjoyed "brimming tubs of hot water" and then "went out to buy the best food in town."

HARRY HOPKINS

"*Tax ... Tax ... Elect ... Elect*"

H UNGER is not debatable," Harry Hopkins said when asked to explain his vast federal expenditures. He was known as the greatest spender of all time in the 1930s. He was far removed from his native Sioux City when he spent $9,600,000,000 during the depression. He was national head of the federal Works Progress Administration (WPA) at the time.

The money was used to provide badly needed work for millions of jobless Americans.

Hopkins never apologized. On a visit to Des Moines in 1939, he told the heavily Republican legislature, "If I had the whole business to do over again, I would do everything to get more for the people than they got."

He was accused of using WPA money to build support for candidates on the Democratic ticket. A columnist once quoted him as saying, "We will spend and spend, tax and tax, elect and elect." He never admitted making that remark. But he did say on one occasion: "I am feeding the hungry, clothing the naked and sheltering the destitute regardless of their age, creed, color, race or place of residence. If that be politics, I plead guilty."

The Hopkins family moved from Sioux City to Grinnell when Harry was eleven. He was graduated from Grinnell College before becoming a social worker and then finally an assistant to President

Franklin D. Roosevelt. He was closest to the president of all Roosevelt's advisers. Hopkins hoped to succeed Roosevelt in the presidency but health forbade such a candidacy. Hopkins died in 1946.

Roosevelt himself came to Sioux City in 1932 to deliver one of his major farm addresses of that depression-period campaign. Republican President Herbert Hoover was running for reelection. Roosevelt was the Democratic nominee. Speaking to a crowd of 25,000 in the Sioux City baseball park, Roosevelt said Hoover's was "the greatest spending administration in peacetimes in all our history—one that has piled bureau on bureau, commission on commission and has failed to meet the dire needs or reduced earning power of the people."

Roosevelt won a landslide victory but then went on to become a much bigger spender than Hoover.

Roosevelt drew loud applause in his Sioux City speech when he said, "I will continue to preach the plight of the farmer who is losing his home, and when the authority of administration is placed in my hands, I will do everything in my power to bring relief that is so long overdue."

Roosevelt did launch an extensive federal farm relief program when he became president in 1933.

President Grover Cleveland also visited Sioux City and its huge "corn palace" in 1887. Cleveland called the corn building "the first new thing that has been shown me." He was given a many-colored ear of squaw corn which he put into his presidential pocket. The "corn palace" was the center of Sioux City's annual corn festival which attracted nationwide attention in the late 1800s.

WILLIAM HARDING

Foreign Language Row

F EELINGS RAN HIGH against the Germans in parts of Iowa and elsewhere during World War I. Germany was the enemy in that 1917–1918 conflict. Tens of thousands of Iowans were German-born and many used the German language regularly.

William Harding of Sioux City, governor of Iowa from 1917–1921, issued a proclamation during the war forbidding the use of any foreign language over the phone. Also prohibited was the use of foreign languages in churches and schools. Many Iowa churches conducted services in German and some used other foreign languages.

Harding's proclamation, which was not a law, probably did not have much effect. The governor next recommended to the 1919 legislature an act to require all children in public or private schools to be instructed in the English language. The legislature passed such a measure and also approved another act to require "the teaching of American citizenship in the public and private schools."

Harding was a great campaigner and his was an exciting administration. Concerning liquor, he was a "wet," unusual for a Republican in those times. The Democrats were the party of the "wets." The 1916 race for governor of Iowa was a strange occasion in that "wet" Republican Harding was pitted against Edwin T. Meredith, who was a "dry" Democrat from Des Moines.

Harding got a laugh all over the state by a remark during a campaign speech on a hot summer day in New Hampton. Indicating with his hands, he said, "Boys, wouldn't a stein about so high go awful good right now?"

Meredith, who later was national secretary of agriculture and a 1924 presidential possibility, made some innocent remark about Harding having had to mortgage his home. Harding retorted, "Ed, you take all the voters who are not in debt and I'll take all who, like me, have given mortgages and I'll beat you hands down." Harding did, by 127,000 votes.

Whether Iowa's mud roads should be paved was a major issue in the Harding administration. Much of his strength in the 1916 victory came from farmers opposed to "hard roads." Harding was against issuing bonds to pave highways. He also strongly opposed federal aid to states for highway building. Then, as now, states had to match federal highway grants. Said Harding: "Federal aid is a form of lottery for extraction of money from pockets of people under conditions only temporarily painless. It is a sedative administered to the taxpayer under the influence of which he pays for the prize out of his own pocket." But he came around to acceptance of federal aid. The system of Iowa primary and secondary roads was set up under his administration.

Much earlier, a Negro hotel operator named Henry Riding created a stir in Sioux City by threatening with a shotgun a crew of workers laying a railroad track. They tried to cross his property without first getting his consent. They didn't intrude. He knew how to use a gun if he had to. He was a Civil War veteran.

Later the railroad paid Riding $21,000 to cross his land. He attracted further attention when he had a tombstone put up in preparation of his death. He was in excellent health at the time.

Another historical footnote: Pearl Street in Sioux City originally was named for a Negro cook on a Missouri River boat which docked at the end of that street.

A "Sing It As We Used to Sing It..."

QUIET twenty-four-year-old printer settled in Sioux City in 1856. He arrived by stagecoach from Council Bluffs and built his own cabin, stuffing the cracks with moss and bark.

The printer was Henry Clay Work and work was something he did not find much of in his trade on the frontier. After a time he sold his property at a profit and moved to Chicago where he became a famous songwriter.

He wrote "Grandfather's Clock," "Lily Dale," and "Babylon is Fallen," all in the Stephen Foster style. But Work's best known composition, one that lasted for generations, was "Marching through Georgia," a great Civil War song. Every school child in the northern states knew that song. Here is the first verse:

> Bring the good old bugle, boys,
>   We'll sing another song,
> Sing it with the spirit that
>   Will start the world along,
> Sing it as we used to sing it
>   Fifty-thousand strong,
> While we were marching through Georgia.

FREDERICK M. HUBBELL

F Disappointed in Love

REDERICK M. HUBBELL had a fabulously successful business career. He founded the Equitable Life Insurance Company of Iowa in Des Moines. All the stock of that company still is held within the family. He did business with the great railroad barons of the nineteenth century. He was a public utilities magnate and probably the keenest real estate investor Iowa has ever seen.

Yet as a teen-ager in Sioux City, Hubbell could not get the girl he wanted. She was Mary Wilkins, Sioux City's first schoolteacher. She arrived on a river steamer in 1857. Her home had been in Keosauqua.

Mary was twenty years old and had "flashing eyes and a vivacious manner." Hubbell was less than nineteen but already had a reputation for knowing how to make money. He served as deputy district court clerk for Woodbury County and he was admitted before long to the practice of law. He immediately became smitten with Mary.

First entries in Hubbell's diary indicated he was making progress and had high hopes of marrying Miss Wilkins. They even read Latin together on dates! But the romance did not prosper. She left Frederick and married Charles Rustin, an energetic individual who had been Hubbell's partner in some speculative ventures. Mourned Hubbell in his diary, "I have learned something and experienced a great deal of happiness with Mary and it is all over and I must begin again." He went to Des Moines in a few years and married Fanny Cooper.

MURIEL HANFORD

The Peacock Girl

"Y OU CAN'T BEAT FUN."

Muriel Hanford coined that slogan for her nightclub, "The Peacock Inn," at Sioux City.

She got the money to open the club in 1934 by hocking a "big square diamond" she long had worn. The club operated in the Jackson Hotel during the 1930s.

Muriel, a woman with a lot of zip, originally gained fame before World War I as the "Peacock Girl" in the Ziegfeld Follies in New York.

In her fast-moving and flamboyant life, she traveled the old RKO vaudeville circuit, married and divorced a Sioux City millionaire, was an opera singer briefly, played bit parts in Hollywood, drove an ambulance in London during wartime, and operated another "Peacock Inn" at Arnolds Park, Iowa, for many years.

She was born in Burlingame, Kansas, and was on the New York stage when Arthur Hanford of Sioux City started giving her the rush in 1914. He had been a prominent Yale University football player and was from a wealthy Sioux City produce family. She divorced actor Robert Keane and married Hanford in 1920. She said Hanford "made me get a divorce." She became a socialite in Sioux City. The Hanford marriage broke up in 1929 and she got a divorce in 1932. Hanford was killed in a plane crash in 1935.

Muriel returned to vaudeville for a time, then went back to Sioux

City to launch a night club. She declined in a court hearing in 1935 to say whether she sold liquor-by-the-drink, then contrary to Iowa law. She said answering that question "might tend to incriminate me." But she did tell the grand jury in Sioux City that she sold liquor. The ban against selling liquor was widely violated in those days, not only in Sioux City but most other larger Iowa cities.

Muriel made her stage debut at the age of three as an angel in "Uncle Tom's Cabin." But she said of that angel role, "I want to be remembered as anything but that." She died at seventy-five years of age in 1965 at Fort Lauderdale, Florida, where, almost to the end, she sang and even danced a bit nightly in a restaurant she owned.

Dawn, Blazing Cloud

Theophile Bruguier wound up with not one wife but two, simultaneously. They were Indians and sisters. Their names were Dawn and Blazing Cloud. He was a French-Canadian trader.

Bruguier, his wives and their father, Sioux Chief War Eagle, settled in the Sioux City area in 1849, five years before the town was laid out by Dr. John Cook.

War Eagle's presence probably saved the white settlers from being harried by the Indians. War Eagle long had been known as a sincere friend of the whites. He was taken in 1837 to Washington where President Martin Van Buren presented him with a medal.

Bruguier owned 160 acres of land in what is now Sioux City. The tract extended from the Missouri River to what is now Seventh Street and from Perry Creek to Jones Street. He sold the land to a trapper for $100.

Tradition said that War Eagle was buried astride a horse on top of a bluff near the confluence of the Big Sioux and Missouri rivers. He is buried there all right but not on a horse. Investigation showed his body to have been placed in a reclining position.

Buried on another bluff on the other side of Sioux City is Sergeant Charles Floyd who died in 1804. He was a member of the famed Lewis and Clark exploratory expedition which came up the Missouri and which paved the way to settlement of the Far West.

Both the War Eagle and Floyd burial sites are well marked with memorials. But there is nothing to recall the memory of General Nathaniel Lyon, once of Sioux City, a brave Civil War officer who was killed in action at the Battle of Wilson's Creek in Missouri in 1861. That was the first of many large engagements involving Iowa troops during the war. Lyon was considered likely to have become one of the top Union Army generals of the war had he lived.

Also not generally remembered is the fact that Herbert Quick, famous early Iowa author (*Vandemark's Folly, The Hawkeye*) was mayor of Sioux City from 1898 to 1900. Quick wrote some of his earlier successful fiction in Sioux City where he had gone to practice law after he was admitted to the bar in 1890.

A contemporary of Quick in the period of the 1890s was William I. Buchanan of Sioux City who served as American minister to the Argentine Republic from 1894 to 1900 and later was first United States minister to Panama.

WALLACE M. SHORT

T *Won with "Wobbly" Help*

HE "WOBBLIES" helped elect a preacher to the office of mayor of Sioux City.

"Wobblies" was the name given to members of Industrial Workers of the World (IWW), an organization of agitators dedicated to the overthrow of capitalism.

They came into Sioux City beginning in 1914. Their big nightly meetings in early 1915 stirred up the city. The authorities arrested many of the transients in an effort to get them to leave. The jails became overcrowded. The city had a lot of granite shipped in and put the prisoners to work breaking big stones into little ones.

Wallace M. Short, a tall and scholarly onetime Congregational minister, took up the cause of the workers. He ran for mayor on a platform opposed to "persecution" of the transients. With strong labor support, he became mayor in 1918 and held the office until 1924. He ran three times for governor of Iowa in the 1930s, once as a Republican and twice as a Farmer-Labor candidate. He never got anywhere in statewide politics.

One of the most dramatic agitators to use Sioux City as a base of operations was a wrinkled old Communist named "Mother Bloor." She went forth daily from her Sioux City apartment in the 1930s to preach revolution against a government "of, by and for the trusts." She originally had been a New Yorker. She urged farmers to take part in the farm strike movement then upsetting Iowa and the Midwest. She urged direct action to prevent the sale of farms through foreclosure of mortgages. Plenty of direct action did take place, whether due to her urging or not. In the most notorious case, a district court judge was dragged off the bench at Le Mars and almost hanged. "Mother Bloor's" real name at the time was Mrs. Andrew Omholt.

Major General Park Findley, Iowa National Guard officer who was called into service during the troubles, termed Sioux City "a hotbed of Communistic activity." He said that some of those participating "are not aware of Red backing in the troubles but it is there nevertheless."

Most of the farmers involved, however, were not Communists by any definition. They were objecting to the disastrously low prices of farm produce. (Hogs three cents a pound, cattle a nickel.)

Farmers established picket lines along highways leading into Sioux City in a vain effort to boost prices by preventing farm produce from reaching market. This was called the "farm holiday" movement. Farmers signed agreements not to haul any farm products to market while the farm holiday was on.

R. D. Markell, sixty-seven, persisted in continuing to haul milk into Sioux City from South Dakota. A car filled with Iowa farm pickets approached the milk convoy. A fusillade of bullets riddled the front end of the pickets' car. They left in a hurry.

The next time Markell came, a force of seventy farmers awaited on the road and in the ditches. Markell was bringing 1,000 gallons of milk into Sioux City. Two telephone poles and a spiked plank blocked the highway and forced the South Dakota man to stop. He got out of the truck and rolled a pole off the road.

Somebody fired a shot. Guns blazed on both sides. Markell's two sons stood among milk cans and fired at the pickets who were shooting from the weeds and behind telephone poles.

The elder Markell was wounded in the abdomen but he removed the other pole and the plank. He died later. Harry Markell, one son, was hit in the head. Keats Markell, the other son, was struck in the head and his left thumb was shot away. Both sons recovered, as did Nile Cochran, a Moville, Iowa, farm picket who was shot in the neck and head. Cochran was found guilty of manslaughter and given a three-year term in the South Dakota penitentiary.

In another incident, pickets gathered north of Sioux City to prevent passage of trucks en route to markets in late winter of 1933. A truck carrying 1,000 one-pound prints of butter was stopped. The driver "got smart," the pickets said. They thereupon dumped his butter into the Floyd River and sent him home.

"It's a shame to waste that butter," said a picket. "Let's fish it out." The butter was recovered from the river. Some of it had landed on the river ice. The butter was loaded into a truck. Two youngsters in the group, Lawrence Krause and John Sokolovske, started down the road. They put from two pounds to five pounds of butter in each farmer's mailbox until the supply was gone.

OTTUMWA

A   *Ate Green Corn Eighteen Days*

STURDY OTTUMWA SOLDIER survived an exhausting 700-mile walk from prison to freedom, but the ordeal brought death to his two comrade Iowans.

Major Augustus Hamilton somehow escaped from a Confederate prison at Tyler, Texas, in 1864 during the Civil War. He had been an Ottumwa attorney in the prewar days.

He and 340 other Iowans were captured in April of that year when overwhelmed by a much larger Confederate force during the battle of Mark's Mill in Arkansas.

Hamilton and Captains Allen Miller of Unionville, Iowa, and John Lambert of Albia, Iowa, slipped out of the prison in the heat of a Texas July.

For the next thirty-three days they lived a life of literal hell as they fled toward the Yankee lines far to the east. For eighteen days they subsisted entirely on raw green corn. For weeks their clothes were wet through. Not once were they able to sleep under cover. They hid in thickets in the daytime and traveled at night. Their only direction guide was the North Star.

After the bottoms of their boots wore out, they used the tops to make moccasins which gave some protection to their bleeding feet.

On August 24 they staggered into a federal camp at Pine Bluff, Arkansas, 700 miles from Tyler.

Hamilton withstood the hardships well and was able to return to his command in the 36th Iowa Infantry. He was promoted to lieutenant colonel. But Captain Miller was in such poor health that he had to be sent home to Unionville. He died less than a month later during a "slow fever that produced insanity."

Captain Lambert tried to return to service but proved unfit for duty and he died the following January 6 "from the effects of the exposure and hardships endured while making his escape."

Death did not come to Hamilton until he was ninety-one years old in 1918. He returned to the practice of law in Ottumwa after the war and was editor and publisher of the *Ottumwa Courier* for many years.

Severely wounded and also taken prisoner in the Mark's Mill battle was Lieutenant Colonel Francis Drake of Centerville, later governor of Iowa and a founder of Drake University of Des Moines. Colonel Drake was paroled by the Confederates because of his wound.

C   *A Pipe of Peace*

HIEF WAPELLO of the Fox tribe and Joseph Street are reputed to have smoked a pipe of peace within what is now Ottumwa.

The Indian chief and Street, who was a federal Indian agent, were close personal friends. They really had no need to smoke a peace pipe to get along with each other.

190

Wapello and many other early Indians greatly admired Street, who was known all over the Midwest as the paleface who treated the red men with consideration and fairness.

Street died in 1840 and is buried in a small cemetery near the railroad in the town of Agency east of Ottumwa. Before his death in 1842, Wapello requested that he be buried next to Street, and he was.

Ottumwa is rich in Indian tradition. Wapello put up his tepee at the corner of what now is Main and College streets. The present site of Ottumwa High School once was an Indian camping ground. Chief Appanoose located his village in what is now south Ottumwa.

The town originally was named Louisville in 1844 but became Ottumwa in 1845. The name Ottumwa has been interpreted to mean different things, including "rippling waters" or "place of swift water," "place of perseverance or self-will," or "place of the lone chief."

EDNA FERBER

O *A Bitter Little Girlhood*

OTTUMWA of the 1890s did not present a very pretty picture when seen through the eyes of a little Jewish girl. But that would have been true of many cities of the times.

The child was Edna Ferber, who became one of the great American writers of the twentieth century. She was born in Kalamazoo, Michigan, in 1887 and lived from 1890 to 1897 in Ottumwa where her father was an unsuccessful merchant. The family moved to Appleton, Wisconsin, when Edna was ten.

She won the 1924 Pulitzer Prize with her novel, *So Big*. She wrote such other top books as *Cimarron* and *Show Boat* and she collaborated in writing such widely known plays as *Dinner at Eight* and *Stage Door*.

Her biography talks of the "brutality and ignorance" of a drab Ottumwa of her childhood and the sense of persecution under which Jewish families lived there. She saw things somewhat differently, however, when she returned on a visit as a middle-aged adult in the late 1920s.

"I found Ottumwa a tree-shaded, sightly, modern American town of its size; clean and progressive," she wrote. "I had planned to stay overnight [but] memory was too strong."

Instead, she drove back to Des Moines alone that evening, and weighed her thoughts en route.

"For the first time in my life," she said, "out of the deep well of depression where they had so long festered, I dragged those seven years of my bitter little girlhood and looked at them.

"And the cool, clean Iowa air cleansed them, and I saw them, not as bitter and corroding years but as astringent, strengthening years; years whose adversity has given me and mine a solid foundation of stamina, determination and a profound love of justice."

She was a most perceptive youngster. The high water she observed as a child in the Des Moines River at Ottumwa, and in the Mississippi elsewhere, formed the basis for her flood description in *Show Boat*.

"I knew how rivers behaved," she wrote in the biography. "I saw bridges as they swayed, crackled, then, with screams of despair, were swept downstream. . . . I saw houses tossing like toys in midstream. . . . People . . . marooned on housetops."

She saw a mob hang one Frank Johnson in 1893 at Main and Market streets in Ottumwa. She was six. Johnson was accused of raping a five-year-old girl. The mob dragged Johnson from the office of a justice of the peace and took his life despite the pleas of Dr. LaForce, the Ottumwa mayor.

Miss Ferber wrote of the swinging body: "It had legs and arms that waved like those of an insect. Then they ceased to wave. The thing straightened itself and became decorous and limp, its head drooping as though in contrition.

"The animal sounds from the crowd swelled, then ceased. Suddenly, they [the people] melted away, seeming to flow up and down the streets in all directions. I heard the clang of the police patrol wagon."

Whether Johnson was guilty was a matter of considerable argument at the time. Some declared "positively he was not the guilty one while others are equally certain that he was guilty." The mob hanging angered many Ottumwans who decided there never would be any more of that. It was said that public sentiment would not "tolerate such violence and contempt for law."

Edna saw "Kelly's Army" of jobless men float down the Des Moines River on rafts in 1894, bound for Washington to demand work. They were "hungry, penniless, desperate."

She marveled at the shrieks and hysteria at the old-time religious revivals. She was almost trampled in the throng when she was taken to the Ottumwa Opera House to hear the famous "Cross of Gold Speech" in 1896 by William Jennings Bryan, the Democratic nominee for president. She became separated from her father but another man hoisted her on his shoulder and she heard the speech, "not a word of which I can recall." She was only nine.

Concerning her years in Ottumwa, she commented: "It is not for me to say whether all this was good or bad for me. Probably bad and good. Certainly it made for an interesting childhood."

Miss Ferber, who never married, died in New York in 1968 at the age of eighty-one.

HERSCHEL LOVELESS

He Reduced Sales Tax

H ERSCHEL LOVELESS cut the Iowa sales tax from 2½ percent to 2 percent in 1957. The next year he successfully opposed raising the same tax from 2 percent to 3 percent.

Loveless, an Ottumwa Democrat, twice was elected governor of Iowa, largely on the tax issue. He was a good vote getter for the Democrats—until he got ambitious to be vice-president of the United States.

He first attracted attention in 1947 when, as streets superintendent, he took charge of Ottumwa's battle against disastrous flooding along the Des Moines River. The voters elected Loveless mayor in 1949, a post he held until 1953.

Loveless was the Democratic nominee for governor of Iowa three times. He ran a strong race in 1952 and lost only because President Eisenhower carried Iowa in a Republican landslide.

In 1956 Loveless defeated Republican Governor Leo Hoegh whom he called "High Tax Hoegh." Loveless won in part because the sales tax had been boosted during the Hoegh administration from 2 percent to 2½ percent. Said Loveless, "Our progressively increasing tax burden is not being reflected in accomplishments." The next year Loveless through a veto forced the 2½ percent sales tax back to 2 percent. And he was reelected in 1958 on a platform of not increasing the tax again.

In 1960 Loveless supported John F. Kennedy for the Democratic nomination for president. The Kennedy forces convinced him that he might be selected as the vice-presidential nominee. Political observers, however, never believed Loveless had a chance. In the end Kennedy selected Lyndon Johnson as his running mate.

Governor and Mrs. Loveless were eating lunch in a Los Angeles hotel when a reporter brought word that Kennedy had named Johnson. Mrs. Loveless reacted angrily. She told the reporter his statement could not be true and "you should not go around saying such things." She did not comment further after the reporter explained he had heard the announcement from Kennedy himself a few minutes before.

Loveless also sought election to the United States Senate in 1960 and was beaten by Jack Miller, Sioux City Republican. The Loveless loss was believed to have been due partly to his preoccupation with pursuing the vice-presidency and partly to Miller's energetic campaigning. Miller also was helped by the fact that Richard Nixon carried Iowa for president by a large margin.

Kennedy was reported to have said after winning the presidency in 1960: "One surprise to me in this election was the defeat of Herschel Loveless for senator in Iowa. He's one guy I never expected to have to find a job for."

Kennedy appointed Loveless to the federal renegotiation board in Washington, a position the Iowan held until Republican President Nixon took office in 1969. Loveless subsequently got a job as corporate vice-president of Chromalloy American Corporation.

Loveless sometimes got very irritated by what his opponents said about him in political campaigns. In 1958 he defeated William G. Murray, Ames Republican, in the race for governor. Loveless and Murray spoke in a joint appearance that year before the Greater Des Moines Chamber of Commerce. Loveless got so burned up at Murray's comments that he refused at the end of the program to shake Murray's outstretched hand.

RICHARD NIXON

Pat Worked in Bank

P AT NIXON may have had more impact on Ottumwa than did her husband Dick.

President and Mrs. Nixon lived in Ottumwa for seven months during World War II.

The president was a lieutenant (j.g.) at the Ottumwa naval air base. He was sent to the Pacific May 7, 1943.

Pat worked as a teller in the Union Bank & Trust Company. She called her salary, said to have been $80 or $85 a month, "scandalously low."

The Nixons were called a quiet and well-behaved couple by their acquaintances. His office duties included opening the mail and assigning typing work to employees. He was said to have been "very reserved . . . a nice fellow to talk to but one who didn't go out of his way to mix . . . very conscientious . . . a good Joe . . . a little on the meek side . . . he didn't let his hair down and have fun."

Nixon's superior officer said Dick came to the officers' club occasionally to have a few drinks and to play the piano. The Nixons had a $55-a-month apartment at the Hillside, East Fourth and Green streets.

One feminine bank employee said of Pat: "She was a bit glamorous. . . . One thing I remember was that she colored her hair. That was years before we all did that. . . . She was a very ambitious person, very interested in fixing up the apartment."

Nixon's superior officer said he never heard Nixon talk politics. Said the officer, "I was surprised when he ran for Congress." That successful candidacy was the first step in Nixon's rise to the presidency.

A *Criticized Heroes*

N OTTUMWAN'S Civil War history, *Iowa Colonels and Regiments,* irritated a lot of people because of its caustic appraisals of some men.

The author was Addison Stuart, a lawyer who was severely wounded in the war.

Stuart praised the fighting Iowans of the war most of the time, but inserted occasional other comments that were termed "scathingly sarcastic."

For example, he said of Colonel Samuel Summers of Ottumwa: "He is sociable and agreeable and would be generous and liberal if he loved money less. 'Keep what you get' is his motto."

Stuart called Colonel Edward Winslow of Mount Pleasant "a splendid officer" but possessing "self conceit which sometimes discovers itself immodestly."

Of Colonel Daniel Anderson of Albia he wrote, "He is a fair public speaker but too prolix to be entertaining." Of Colonel Henry J. B. Cummings of Winterset, Stuart said, "He was a good tactician but beyond that possessed little merit as a soldier."

Stuart praised Colonel James B. Weaver of Bloomfield but said Weaver "has some vanity" and an "affectation in delivery" of a speech. Stuart quoted a fellow officer as saying that "from Weaver's walk you could tell he was Colonel of the Second Iowa."

T *". . . Let Me Sow Love . . ."*

HE CHEERFUL WORKERS dug a stove out of the mud-filled kitchen. They dragged a mattress heavy with water and mud from a bedroom. They excavated furniture buried in living rooms.

The workers came to Ottumwa in the summer of 1947 from all over the United States to do what they could for 150 unfortunate families who had been living on flood-stricken lowlands near the Des Moines River.

Most of the seventeen volunteers were students. They ranged in age from eighteen to thirty years. Nine were women. They spent their warm vacation months working in the stench and mud left by the devastating floods.

They not only were unpaid, they also footed their own bills while they labored. One student turned down a yacht trip to work in the Ottumwa mud. They were members of an American Friends Service Committee volunteer camp.

As much as one-third of the city of Ottumwa was under water during the spring that year. The lowland area known as "Central Addition" was under twelve feet of water.

None of the volunteers was an Iowan. One was a Finnish girl student visiting this country to observe work camps in operation. In charge of the project was Franz E. Hohn, a mathematics professor from the University of Maine. Only two of the group were Quakers. Sectarian religious ties did not mean much. Everybody got up at 5:30 in the mornings. They sang as they worked.

The muck was so thick that it was hard even to find the streets at first. The workers had to shovel a path to the front door before they could enter a house. They shoveled tons of mud, opened windows, scraped walls, salvaged bedsprings and other equipment. They did not attempt to make the modest little homes livable, only to get them ready for repair work. They cleaned out twenty-five homes a month. Many other volunteers assisted in the work.

Such a crisis cannot happen again in the area. For one thing, the big dam upstream at Red Rock apparently will prevent future major floods on the lower Des Moines River. Also, only a few families moved back into the addition after the 1947 flood. The city procured all the property in the 1950s and used the area to establish a park. The river channel has been relocated and two main highways intersect in the old addition.

But some Ottumwans long will remember the unselfish service of those young volunteers who worked in the spirit of this prayer of St. Francis of Assisi: "Lord, make me an instrument of Your Peace; where there is hatred let me sow love; where there is injury, pardon; where there is doubt, faith; where there is despair, hope; where there is sadness, joy."

Industrial Development

WHAT PROFOUND RESULTS sometimes flow from chance meetings! Joseph G. Hutchison, an Ottumwa lawyer and industrialist, went to England on a business trip in the 1870s.

On his way home he became acquainted with Thomas D. Foster who was bound for the United States to find a location for a packing plant. Foster was a nephew of John Morrell, English meat-packer.

Hutchison urged Foster to visit Ottumwa which Hutchison described as an excellent site for such a plant. Foster agreed after looking over the city. The big Morrell plant, a vital part of the Ottumwa economy, began operations in 1876 and is still going.

Hutchison later became an important member of the state legislature and is credited with being author of the law under which Iowans must first register in order to vote. He was another Ottumwan who was selected as a major party candidate for governor of Iowa. In 1889 he was nominated by the Republicans and he campaigned on a platform of strict enforcement of the state's antiliquor laws of that era.

Republicans in the "wet" counties along the Mississippi River deserted the ticket, however, and Hutchison was beaten by Democrat Horace Boies of Waterloo. Boies ran on a "wet" platform. Hutchison attained the dubious distinction of being the first Republican nominee to lose a race for governor of Iowa since the party was founded in 1856. But the contest was close. Boies's margin of victory was only 7,000. He got 180,000 votes, Hutchison 173,000.

Thomas Foster was the patriarch of the noted Foster family in Ottumwa. He died in 1915.

She Wrote about Lincoln

WIDELY KNOWN for her writings about Abraham Lincoln and in the field of romantic history was novelist Honore Willsie Morrow (1880–1940), born in Ottumwa. She was editor of the old *Delineator* magazine from 1914 to 1919.

She wrote *With Malice Toward None, Mary Todd Lincoln, Forever Free, The Splendor of God, Yonder Sails the Mayflower, Beyond the Blue Sierra, Argonaut* (a story of gold rush days), and many other books.

Mrs. Morrow was the widow of a New York publisher. She was living in England and was visiting a sister in New Haven, Connecticut, when death came.

FORT MADISON

They Tried to Forget

THE TAPROOM in the Hotel Anthes was filled with visiting newsmen trying to have a gay time. They did their best that night to try to forget why they had come to Fort Madison.

At dawn on the morrow in the penitentiary, they were to see two men hanged by the neck until dead.

It was the job of the reporters to witness that grim event and to send out news stories telling the state and the world what happens when men are formally put to death.

But tonight . . . let's have another beer . . . why go to bed? . . . How can a guy possibly go to sleep? . . . Does anybody ever get so hardened that he does not dread seeing human lives brought to a violent end? . . .

Hollow music from the juke box pervades the room. . . . "Beer Barrel Polka" . . . "Indian Love Call" . . . "A-Tisket A-Tasket." . . . Some couples dance. . . . "Ramona, I hear those mission bells above." . . .

Did those two guys eat anything on their last night? I hope not. The warden told me they shunned food and I put that in my story. Now if they change their minds the story will be wrong. . . . Yeah, it is wrong but only a little. I just came back from the Fort. They nibbled at some pork sandwiches and that was all. . . .

They've said their goodbyes to the warden. Marlo again told the warden he didn't do it, didn't kill his nephew. Franz didn't say anything. . . .

The talk goes on . . . a lot is said but the overwhelming thought in every mind is that two men will be put to death in four hours . . . PUT TO DEATH! . . .

Finally, at 3:30, you get to bed. . . . Forty-five minutes to sleep. . . . Others have gone to their rooms ahead of you. You wonder if they have gone to sleep. . . . You stay wide awake . . . thinking. . . . Why didn't you ask the boss to send somebody else? . . . The phone rings . . . 4:15 sir. . . . Thank you. . . . You haven't even shut your eyes. . . . Up in death row, Franz hasn't either. They say that Marlo slept some. . . .

It is still dark out the window. Dawn does not come until 5:22 on April 19 at Fort Madison. . . .

The crowd gathers in front of the turnkey's office outside the wall. Many are official witnesses who will sign statements verifying that the executions were carried out. In addition to the newsmen, the others include the sheriffs who will spring the traps sending the men to their deaths, county attorneys, prison officials. . . . At least one witness is a woman. . . .

Once inside the prison, where the tall and forbidding walls seem to bear down heavily on everyone, the group gathers in the half-twilight of the coming dawn in front of a certain cellhouse. . . .

The two men, wearing carnations in their lapels, emerge from the cellhouse with their clergymen. . . . Franz is wearing a half-frozen smile on his face. . . . Both are small men physically. . . . Franz, thirty, was convicted of slaying a girl friend. . . . Marlo is thirty-two, was found guilty of killing a nephew. . . . Marlo is married, has three small children. . . .

There is a brief pause. Flash bulbs pop. Marlo stands back to avoid having his picture taken. . . .

The final 500-foot walk to the gallows begins, with Warden Glenn Haynes leading in his straight military stride. . . . The crowd goes around a corner . . . down some steps . . . into the stockade. . . . The two men walk firmly up the gallows steps. . . . A minister and priest go up with them. . . .

The doomed men look down upon the 150 witnesses, the largest crowd up to that time ever to see an execution in the penitentiary. . . . Any final statements? Franz says no, Marlo shakes his head. . . . The clergymen shake hands with the two. . . .

Guards fasten straps around the legs and arms, fix the nooses around the necks, pull black hoods over the heads. . . . All is ready. . . .

The warden drops his arm in signal. . . . The sheriffs pull the levers. . . . The bodies fall, come to a quick stop with a sickening wrench. . . . Franz's body shudders. . . . Both sway like a pendulum as the seconds tick away. . . .

One witness runs and hides his head against the wall. . . . I didn't see it! I didn't see it! he sobs defensively. . . .

Physicians apply stethoscopes to both chests. Marlo is pronounced dead in nine minutes, Franz in 11 minutes. . . . Preparations are made for quick removal of the bodies. . . .

"That will be all, gentlemen," the warden announces. . . .

All, except that the families and friends of the men will never be the same. And the witnesses, newsmen included, never will be the same again either. Something profoundly permanent happens to a person's soul when he sees men die on the gallows. . . .

That's how it was on April 19, 1938, when Franz Jacobsen of Ottumwa and Marlo Heinz of Dubuque were executed. There have been forty-one legal hangings in Iowa history, the last in 1963. The state's death penalty law was repealed in 1965.

Fined for Contempt

JESSE BROWNE was six feet seven inches tall, a huge man for pioneer times. He was a colorful community leader in Fort Madison and a politician who liked liquor.

Browne came into a Fort Madison courtroom "tight as a brick" in 1838 to listen to the trial of a farmer trying to avoid being evicted from his land. Browne wore a turban and a blanket wrapped Indian-fashion around his tall body.

He was impressed by the argument presented by the farmer's attorney. Browne turned around to the other spectators and roared: "Hear him! Hear him!" His yell could be "heard a mile."

"General Browne," said the judge sternly, "I fine you $5 for contempt."

"Fine and be damned!" shouted Browne. "You owe me $200 and this is the only way I'll ever get it!" He roared again.

The roars were repeated and so were the fines until the sum reached $40. That amount was duly credited on the note Browne held against the judge. The farmer, incidentally, won the case and was not evicted.

Physical prowess was much respected on the frontier, and Browne packed a punch that downed most opponents with one blow. He was a poor businessman but highly capable in other ways. He was elected president of the first Iowa territorial council (predecessor of the state senate) in 1838 and Speaker of the first Iowa House of Representatives in 1846.

He once bought several rounds of whisky for the crowd in a Rushville, Illinois, tavern. He decided to disperse the crowd. He swore loudly that all present had lived long enough and with that threw a powder keg into the stove.

Everybody dashed for the doors. Browne just sauntered out, mounted his horse, and rode slowly away. There was no explosion. Browne knew the keg was empty.

He died at a daughter's home in Kentucky in 1864 at the age of sixty-six.

HALE HAMILTON

The Notable Hamiltons

FOR TWO YEARS large audiences in the Gaiety Theater on New York's Broadway enjoyed *Get Rich Quick Wallingford,* a comedy that starred Hale Hamilton, a native of Fort Madison, Iowa.

One reviewer said shortly after the opening in September 1910 that Hamilton played the role of Wallingford "breezily and delightfully." He was a topflight actor on the New York stage and in the movies in Hollywood for more than a generation.

Hamilton, from a notable Fort Madison family, was born in 1880 in the 600 block of Avenue G and grew up there. He played important roles in amateur theatricals as a youth and he made the stage a life career after attending the University of Kansas.

The Wallingford play was written by George M. Cohan and had to do with two New York sharpies who come to a small Iowa town to fleece the hicks. The sharpies float all kinds of enterprises, the town booms, the sharpies become rich and marry two charming young women.

Hamilton first appeared on the professional stage in Shakespeare's *Midsummer Night's Dream* in New Jersey in 1899. He played in such dramas as *The Pit, The Fortune Hunter, Society and the Bulldog, Good Night Nurse, It Pays to Advertise, Divorce à la Carte, Dear Me,* and *What's Your Husband Doing?*

He entered the silent films in 1921. He appeared in two Garbo pictures and with Wallace Beery and Jackie Coogan in *The Champ.* He died in Hollywood in 1942.

John D. M. Hamilton, a brother of Hale, was national chairman of the Republican party in the late 1930s. He headed the GOP in the party's disastrous 1936 presidential campaign. Alfred M. Landon, the Republican nominee, carried only two states. Democratic President Franklin D. Roosevelt captured the other forty-six states in his landslide victory.

The 1936 debacle was not Hamilton's fault. He was a hard-hitting, energetic, and excellent speaker. But Roosevelt was at the peak of his popularity and Landon was not a good campaigner.

John D. M. Hamilton was born in Fort Madison in 1892 and thus was a small boy when the family moved to Topeka late in the 1890s. He was the first of his politically prominent family to become a Republican. His father was a Democrat, as was his grandfather who came to a tragic end. The grandfather's name was John S. Hamilton and he came to Fort Madison in 1854 from Pennsylvania where he served in the legislature.

The Fort Madison Democrats staged a big victory rally in November 1856 after James Buchanan had been elected president. Buchanan was a Pennsylvanian and the elder Hamilton was given the honor of firing the Fort Madison victory cannon since he was a Democrat from Buchanan's state.

The cannon exploded and killed Hamilton. Had he lived, says family lore, he would have been appointed governor of Kansas Territory by President Buchanan.

"I Never Miss Chicago"

AN ENTHUSIASTIC ADVOCATE of living in the city of Fort Madison was William E. L. Bunn, an artist and onetime industrial designer.

He painted the murals in the Fort Madison post office. He also wrote an article in 1955 for the *Saturday Evening Post* titled "I Never Miss Chicago."

Pointing out how life in Fort Madison did not require long-distance commuting, Bunn wrote that his home was "a two-minute walk to the center of the business district and eight minutes on foot to my office."

"The Mississippi borders the town on the south," he said, "and the rolling Iowa countryside is three minutes away by car in every direction. The rush hour doesn't exist here. If you work an 8-hour day, you actually spend the remaining 16 hours doing what you please."

He also said: "Despite everything you may have heard about cliquishness, money and social position play little part in determining who your friends are. . . . Because there is so much that parents and children can enjoy together, families are exceptionally close."

He described how he and his wife and two children had been happy to return to the easy and more leisurely living of a smaller Mississippi River city from the large metropolitan area.

The article was credited at the time by the chamber of commerce with bringing two new industries to Fort Madison.

BLACK HAWK

B *Black Hawk's Last Speech*

LACK HAWK, the legendary chief of the Sac and Fox Indians, spoke in public for the last time at a July 4 celebration in Fort Madison in 1838. He was seventy-one years old and had less than three months to live.

His last speech was both powerful and sad. Speaking in Indian dialect which was translated into English for the crowd, he talked of the loss of the fields and forests of his people to the white settlers, and of his defeat in the Black Hawk War.

It has pleased the Great Spirit that I am here today [he said]. I have eaten with my white friends. The earth is our mother; we are now on it, with the Great Spirit above us; it is good.

A few winters ago I was fighting against you. I did wrong, perhaps, but that is past; it is buried; let it be forgotten.

Rock River [in Illinois] was a beautiful country. I liked my towns and my cornfields, and the homes of my people; I fought for it . . . it is now yours; keep it as we did; it will produce you good crops.

I thank the Great Spirit that I now am friendly with all my white brothers; we are here together; we are friends; it is His wish and mine; I thank you for your friendship.

I was once a great warrior; I now am poor. Keokuk [a rival chief] is the cause of my present condition; but do not attach blame to him.

I am now old; I have looked upon the Mississippi River; I have been a child; I love the great river; I have dwelt on its banks from the time I was an infant; I look upon it now.

I shake hands with you and, as it is my wish, I hope you are my friends.

Black Hawk died October 3, 1838, in his lodge on the Des Moines River in Lee County.

TOM RUNYON

Writer in Prison

SHOULD Tom Runyon have been freed from the penitentiary? Would he have become a dangerous criminal again? Or was he a changed man? Those questions were argued nationwide in the 1950s.

The issue never was resolved because Runyon died of a heart attack at fifty-one years of age in 1957 after serving twenty years of a life sentence.

Those who wanted to give Runyon another chance included Erle Stanley Gardner, noted mystery story writer, and Fort Madison Warden Percy Lainson.

Those opposed included the state parole board, especially board member Virginia Bedell. The widow of a slain victim also did not want Runyon freed.

Runyon, perhaps the most famous lifer ever to serve in Fort Madison, was convicted of murder in 1937. He had been a member of the Barker and Gibson gangs in the 1920s and 1930s. They specialized in bank robberies around the Midwest.

Runyon was one of three criminals whose car was wrecked in a north Iowa ditch near Britt in the early morning blackness of November 2, 1935.

Farmer James Zrostlik came along the road, bound for early mass in a nearby church. Also in the car were Mrs. Zrostlik and their infant son.

When Zrostlik saw the car in the ditch, he stopped to help. His good intentions cost him his life. The gangsters shot and killed the farmer in front of his terrorized wife. She and the child were cut seriously by flying glass. The gunmen took the car and fled.

Runyon, then thirty-one, was caught and escaped a possible death penalty by helping in the prosecution of other members of the gang. Runyon got life in Iowa and later was given another life sentence in Minnesota for bank robbery, to begin when his Iowa sentence ended.

Runyon developed into a powerful writer in the Fort Madison penitentiary. His book *In for Life* was published nationally and netted him $4,000. He also had two articles published in the *Saturday Evening Post* and one in *Collier's* magazine. He served two extended periods as editor of *The Presidio,* prison magazine at Fort Madison.

He might have been *Presidio* editor continuously if he had not made a temporarily successful dash for freedom in 1943. He dug his way out of the penitentiary under an electrically charged fence.

In frantic efforts to avoid recapture, Runyon kidnapped five persons in Iowa, stole two autos and staged a number of robberies. But he was "free," if that is what it can be called, for only four days. He blundered into Fort Dodge and was caught by police.

He was whisked back to Fort Madison and placed in solid lockup. Not until 1948, five years later, was he restored to the *Presidio* editorship.

In urging Runyon's release in the 1950s, mystery writer Gardner wrote: "When a man takes advantage of the prison opportunities that are offered for rehabilitation, when by dint of hard work he begins to make over his character, society should give him some recognition.

"If we don't encourage rehabilitation in individual cases, it is foolish to claim that we are encouraging rehabilitation in prison."

Warden Lainson added: "Gardner maintains, and so do I, that Runyon has rehabilitated himself. We don't believe he would cause any more trouble."

But Mrs. Bedell said: "Personally I doubt if he has reformed. . . . How do you show rehabilitation from planned and cruelly executed acts? You can search Runyon's book from cover to cover and find no real expression of remorse or contrition. . . . If Warden Lainson will take care of his work and let us do ours, the State of Iowa will be better off." Mrs. Bedell and the warden did not get along.

Zrostlik's widow, who had remarried, also expressed opposition to freeing Runyon. She said she was afraid he would come after her.

Not generally known is the fact that Runyon also served as a correspondent for the Associated Press for some years inside the penitentiary walls. He sent news stories to the AP in Des Moines. Probably no other lifer in American history was ever permitted to do such a thing. The arrangement probably stemmed from the fact that Warden Glenn Haynes was World War I commanding officer in France of a unit to which T. M. Metzger belonged. Metzger was a good friend of Haynes and also was Associated Press chief in Des Moines. Haynes died in 1942 and was succeeded by Lainson.

Runyon wrote some good newspaper pieces reflecting the anguish of serving a life sentence. He told how a penitentiary "speaks with a thousand voices" to the wide-awake prisoner on a summer night.

"Coughs, grunts, and groans [of other prisoners] are loud in his sleepless ears," Runyon wrote. "There are snores in an unbelievable number of keys. A neighbor falls out of bed and grumbles drowsily as he crawls back. A man comes screaming out of a nightmare."

Runyon also heard the far-off music of a carnival in downtown Fort Madison, the bark of a distant dog, the mournful whistle of a train.

"I bat my pillow into shape and settle down to sleep," he said. "I know I am not alone in my longing for a part of the world that goes on moving."

One gets the feeling that Runyon would never have gotten into trouble again if, somehow, he could have been released after his first wide-awake night in a prison.

GLENN HAYNES

W *Greeted by Boos*

HEN Warden Glenn Haynes died in 1942, the penitentiary magazine said of him: "He found a prison where bedbugs and cockroaches were taken for granted . . . he left a prison that is cleaner than many civilian homes. . . . To the very end he fought for absolute impartiality in the treatment of all prisoners. . . .

"Warden Haynes gained and kept the respect of his charges . . . he will not soon be forgotten."

Haynes was cordially hated, however, when he first took over in 1933. He was a decorated veteran of World War I and had served in the Spanish-American War. He instituted iron army discipline in the prison.

He found the prisoners wearing better clothes than the guards. He ordered all inmates to wear the same prison-issued garb. He said prisoners no longer could have canaries. The next morning the lifeless bodies of the birds were strewn on the floor in the cell blocks. The prisoners had wrung their necks.

Discipline had been unbelievably lax. Outsiders were invited into the penitentiary to eat steak dinners and to play poker with the prisoners.

Haynes put an end to that sort of thing. When he walked into the dining room on Sunday morning he was greeted by a chorus of boos that "almost touched off a riot." He coolly stared at the booers and walked away without saying anything.

Haynes ordered a thorough housecleaning, including insect extermination and a general painting. He gained popularity and respect quickly by allowing prisoners to spend five evenings a week in the prison yard and by allowing them for the first time to get food from relatives and friends at Christmas. He started a sports program, organized a drum and bugle corps, opened a canteen, improved the school system, started the prison magazine, sponsored a minstrel show.

There never was a serious disturbance while he was warden. A state official said of Haynes, "He was utterly fair and he had an unusual ability to judge a man regardless of his own personal likes and dislikes."

A liquor cabinet in the warden's residence was left unlocked while some prisoners were painting the walls. They consumed the liquor, got roaring drunk. They were thrown into solitary. Haynes could not sleep that night. He said to himself, "It wasn't their fault, it was mine." He ordered the men released from solitary the next morning.

Haynes was twice elected state auditor and led the hard fight for paving Iowa's highways during an eight-year career as secretary of the Iowa Good Roads Association before becoming warden. He was a Republican but was appointed warden during the Democratic regime of Governor Clyde L. Herring (1933–1937).

He Lost School Money

J AMES D. EADS played fast and loose with a lot of money that belonged to the schools of the state.

He was a Fort Madison resident who was elected Iowa state superintendent of public instruction in 1854.

The state school fund was entitled to 5 percent of the money that the federal government collected from the sale of public lands in Iowa. Eads received the money from Washington.

He immediately started making loans to private borrowers, on mortgages and without security. There is no question but that he got out of line. He lent himself $20,000 and posted as security Fort Madison lots against which there were earlier mortgages and even mechanics' liens.

When loans went bad and the roof fell in, Eads turned fifty-four notes totaling $155,000 over to the state. Thirty-eight notes were secured by mortgages but fourteen of the mortgages were not even recorded.

Lending such public money to private borrowers would be unthinkable today.

One of the most interesting Eads loans was to a private Des Moines syndicate for construction of a public building. Eads lent the syndicate $47,350 to build a new Statehouse without expense to the state in Des Moines. (The building reputedly cost only $35,000 to construct.) A gift of a Statehouse was part of the bargain under which the state capital was moved in 1857 from Iowa City to the east side in Des Moines.

The Statehouse loan went sour in large part because the business district of Des Moines did not move from the west side over to the

Statehouse area as the syndicate had expected. Thus, the value of East Des Moines properties did not rise as anticipated. The syndicate lost heavily.

How much Eads's financial adventures cost the state apparently never could be determined. He purportedly kept no books of accounts. Estimates of the defalcations varied from $46,000 to $72,000, both huge sums in those pre–Civil War days.

Eads might have survived at that had good times continued. He lent money in the mid-1850s when business was prospering. The depression of 1857 knocked the props from under real estate values. Many of the loans went bad as a consequence.

Governor James Grimes removed Eads from office in 1857. The state found itself with a lot of unwanted real estate on its hands. The property had been posted as collateral for loans made by Eads.

The real estate included 90 city lots and 35 acres within Des Moines and Keokuk and 1,236 acres of land elsewhere. The state evidently did not realize very much from the sale of those properties.

W. A. SHEAFFER

J *Fountain of Ink*

EWELER W. A. SHEAFFER read with interest in 1908 an ad describing the advantages of a certain fountain pen.

Sheaffer decided there must be a better way to fill such a pen than the ad set forth (with an eye dropper).

He experimented in his jewelry shop and came up with a self-filling lever pen. He got a patent and spent the next five years developing, testing, and improving the pen. He opened a small factory in Fort Madison in 1913. Within a year after selling his jewelry store, the pen sales reached $100,000.

In the ensuing decades, the Sheaffer Pen Company became a world leader and several times exceeded $25 million in annual sales. The company was sold to Textron in 1965.

In 1951, when a new Sheaffer plant was opened, 1,800 employes were polled on what they expected the world to be like in fifty years, or in 2001. Their prophecies were sealed in a wall of the new building. Among other things, they predicted the common cold will have been cured, bald men will still be bald, passenger planes will fly faster than sound, the hydrogen bomb will have been used in war, a cure for cancer will have been found, Christianity will be as strong as ever.

One somber prediction already has been fulfilled: a majority foresaw another war in this century.

FORT DODGE

LORENZO COFFIN

W "Human Life Is Too Sacred..."

HEN railroad brakeman Albert Gaskell of Sanborn fell to his death between moving freight cars near Hull, Iowa, in 1888, the tragedy attracted little attention.

Such deaths were commonplace in those days. Brakemen died by the hundreds on American railroads each year. Another brakeman named Rossan was killed when he made a misstep and fell between cars near Hartley the year before. Two others from Sanborn, Jim Fee and Young Oleson, similarly lost their lives about the same time.

The life of a brakeman on a freight was particularly dangerous because he had to walk on tops of moving trains day and night in all kinds of weather, even in blizzards, to set the handbrake on each car. Automatic airbrakes operated by the freight engineer from his cab had not yet been perfected.

Coupling railroad cars (hitching them together) was similarly hazardous. Brakeman R. R. Shipley was crushed to death between cars at Villisca in 1887. Brakeman Dennis Murphy died the same way that year at Mystic. Automatic couplers were not yet in use.

Hardly anyone except the railroad men and their families and friends appeared too much concerned about the number of accidental deaths—until Lorenzo Coffin of Fort Dodge got stirred up.

Coffin, a successful farmer and preacher, was appointed a member of the state railroad commission in 1883. He was appalled to learn that 241 men had been killed and 474 injured in Iowa in falls from trains in a nine-year period. Accidents of all kinds, including those in which the victims were crushed between cars they were trying to couple together, killed or injured 1,880 Iowa railroad workers in the nine years.

Coffin demanded better and safer brakes on freight trains and automatic couplers for rail cars. He wrote in 1885:

How fearful to contemplate is this long list of fatal accidents and how terrible the reality!

That men, that human beings should be compelled to go at all times of the night, in all kinds of weather, from one end of fast-moving trains to the other on tops of cars, no matter how bitter the cold, how blinding the storm, how violent the wind, how icy and slippery the decks of cars . . . is a species of inhumanity that should not be tolerated among civilized people!

Human life is too sacred a thing to be trifled with, and put in the balance against a few dollars and cents.

Airbrakes were being used effectively on shorter passenger trains at the time but were not workable on freight trains of fifty or more cars.

After repeated failures, George Westinghouse of Pittsburgh, Pennsylvania, finally devised an effective airbrake for freights in 1888. Coffin was there when Westinghouse tested his brake at Burlington, Iowa. Said Coffin: "The long hoped-for thing was accomplished. An immense train [of fifty cars] could be hurled down the steep grade into Burlington at 40 miles an hour and, at a given signal, the brakes applied and the train brought to a standstill inside of 500 feet with scarcely a jar and not a man on top of the cars."

Coffin immediately went to work on the Iowa legislature. He was instrumental in getting laws passed over railroad opposition compelling installation of the newly invented automatic brakes. He also played a vital role in getting an act adopted requiring installation of automatic couplers on railroad cars.

He then went to Washington and lobbied vigorously (and ultimately successfully) for similar national laws. He recruited the help of President Benjamin Harrison who said in his 1889 inaugural address, "It is a disgrace to our civilization that men in lawful employment should be exposed to greater danger than soldiers in time of war."

It was estimated years later that the "loss of life of railroad employees" was "reduced by more than 60 per cent" through installation of automatic couplers on railroad cars.

Coffin's main interest in life was to help his fellowman. He donated twenty acres and $10,000 in 1891 for construction of a temporary home for convicts recently discharged from penitentiaries. He wanted to help them get started in life again. Name of the home, which was on his farm, was "Hope Hall."

He helped pay for a home at Highland Park, Illinois, for aged and disabled railroad men. He started a "white button" temperance movement among railroad men. He distributed 250,000 such buttons to railroad workers pledged not to use intoxicating liquor. And for sixteen years he rode horseback out in the country every Sunday and preached without pay or expenses in rural churches unable to support their own pastors. A county historian said of Coffin, "Who can measure the influence of such a life?"

Coffin died at ninety-three years of age in 1915 on his farm near Fort Dodge and is buried on a family plot there. The plot has been fenced by the railroad brotherhoods and is maintained by them.

Many tremendous and interesting personalities such as "Father" Coffin have enlivened Fort Dodge over the generations, and quite a few have been of major national and state importance. Most of them have been topflight

*citizens but some have been not too desirable. Those
with unusual traits have included a determined prose-
cutor who put major Chicago gangsters behind bars; a
courageous governor; a brilliant senator who came close
to the presidency.*

T Sent Capone to Prison

HE DISTRICT ATTORNEY chiefly responsible for sending gangster Al
Capone to federal prison for ten years was an Iowan from the Fort
Dodge area.

The DA was George E. Q. Johnson who was born in 1874 on a
Webster County farm and who grew up in Fort Dodge. He was a graduate of the old Tobin College in Fort Dodge.

Ganglords quickly learned to fear Johnson who was appointed
United States district attorney in Chicago in 1927. He relentlessly pursued law violators, particularly those who evaded income taxes.

Johnson sent Ralph Capone, Al's brother, to prison for 3 years;
Frank (the Enforcer) Nitti for 18 months; Jack Guzik for 18 months;
Beer Baron Frankie Lake for 18 months; and Terry Druggan, Lake's
partner, for 2½ years.

Johnson procured indictments against Scarface Al Capone himself
and sixty-eight of his lieutenants in mid-1932. Johnson then was appointed federal district judge, reportedly as a reward for his success in
nailing gangsters, particularly Al Capone who was imprisoned and his
power broken forever.

The flowing-haired, stern-faced Johnson was a Republican and
could not win confirmation as a judge from the Democratically controlled Senate, however, and he returned to the practice of law in Chicago in 1933.

A United States senator once said of Johnson, "He is slower than a
wet week but he never quits."

Johnson employed all sorts of tricks in catching gangsters in his
prosecutions, such as trapdoors, hidden panels, and the like. But he
made it a point not to glorify his tactics. He was only after results—
and how he got them!

Johnson died in Chicago in 1949 at the age of seventy-five.

T Stone Giant Found

HIS IS NOT a thing contrived of man but is the face of one who
lived on the earth, the very image and child of God."

Those somber words from a preacher drew nods of approval from
awed spectators standing in the dim light around the figure of a stone
giant prone in an open grave.

The body gave the appearance of a huge ancient man who had died in pain. One big hand was pressed against the stomach, the other against the back. One foot was drawn up. But the face was tranquil. A New York judge commented, "No one can look upon that grand smile of mingled sweetness and strength without being convinced that the giant once lived, and had a being."

The grave was enclosed in a large tent. The spectators paid fifty cents each to get in. They were not allowed to approach or touch the silent figure which had a brownish color, presumably from being buried for eons in the ground.

The big creature, 10 feet 4½ inches tall and weighing 2,990 pounds, had just been discovered by workmen digging on a farm in a New York community not far from Syracuse. The year was 1869.

Discovery of the giant touched off a nationwide wave of excitement.

Fifty thousand people came in the first forty days—and paid their half-dollar each to see the figure. The New York Central revised its schedule of trains to enable passengers to stop over and see the giant.

Scientists and artists were excited. One fossil expert called the giant "a most remarkable object" and expressed belief the figure had lain in that grave for ages.

A respected scientist called the giant "the most remarkable archeological discovery ever made in this country." A sculptor maintained the giant was a petrified man. Said the sculptor, "No chisel ever carved such a perfect man." One learned student advanced the theory that the figure was an ancient Phoenician god.

All this time, only a very few persons knew that the giant in a way was a refugee from Fort Dodge, Iowa, and was in fact a big phony.

Turn the clock back from 1869 to 1866. . . .

George Hull, a tobacco merchant of Binghampton, New York, came in 1866 to Ackley, Iowa, where his sister lived. Hull had sent 10,000 cigars to the sister's husband to sell. The guy never came through with any money and Hull came out to see why not.

Whether Hull ever collected his money is not known. But he did get into an argument with a Methodist evangelist in Ackley over whether there actually were giants in biblical days. The preacher said yes because the Bible says so and everything in the Bible is true. Hull, an atheist, said no.

The dispute ended in a draw. When Hull went to bed that night, he lay awake wondering why people believe those stories. Then he got an idea.

In June 1868, Hull and H. B. Martin, a Marshalltown blacksmith, came to Fort Dodge. Martin was familiar with the rock formations in that area.

They wanted a piece of gypsum rock twelve feet long, four feet wide, and two feet thick. Such a chunk was located at Shady Oaks, five miles southeast of Fort Dodge.

Fort Dodge residents were curious. They asked questions. The two men gave conflicting explanations as to why they wanted the rock. The mystery died down after they left with the rock in a big wagon and headed for the nearest railroad station, which was at Boone, thirty-nine miles away.

Moving the chunk that distance proved to be a monumental job. Wagons broke down. Horses had to be rested and changed frequently because of exhaustion. The trip took thirteen full days. A steep hill near Lehigh proved to be too much of an obstacle. Hull and Martin had to cut the 10,000-pound rock down to 7,000 pounds to get over the incline.

The gypsum section finally was loaded on a train and shipped to the shop of stonecutter Edward Burkhardt in Chicago. He and his assistants took a pledge not to say anything about the job they were hired to do.

When the work was done, a long and heavy box was shipped from Chicago to the farm of William C. Newell at Cardiff, New York, a village not far from Syracuse. Newell was a relative of Hull.

A hole was dug in a marshy area behind Newell's barn. One dark November night, the contents of the heavy box were lowered into the hole which was then filled and clover sown over the bare spot.

Hull, Martin, and Newell patiently went about their other business. They bided their time for nearly a year.

In October 1869, Newell hired two men to dig a well. Their shovels struck something hard three feet down. They uncovered a huge stone foot, then an entire stone body.

"Jerusalem!" exclaimed one digger. "It's a big Injun!"

Newell was watching close by. He immediately put up a tent to conceal the find. The story quickly got into the newspapers. Syracuse headlines screamed: "A Wonderful Discovery! . . . A New Wonder. . . . The Petrified Giant!"

Gate receipts at the Newell farm totaled as much as $3,000 a day. A Syracuse syndicate offer of $10,000 for the figure was turned down.

Other businesses sprang up close by. Newell's cowshed was turned into a restaurant. Two saloons opened.

The Hull-Newell interests sold a 75 percent share in the giant to three local men for $37,500 and retained the other 25 percent.

After a number of weeks, the figure was carefully lifted from the grave and taken to Syracuse and displayed to large crowds. Circus man P. T. Barnum tried to lease the giant for three months for $60,000. He was turned down. Barnum thereupon presented his own "giant," made out of paper mache, as a circus attraction.

One estimate placed the value of the "Cardiff Giant," as it came to be called, at $240,000.

Fort Dodge residents read the news stories with interest. Galusha Parsons, an attorney, said in a letter to a Fort Dodge paper, "I believe it [the giant] is made of that great block of gypsum those fellows got at Fort Dodge a year ago."

Also, W. H. Slauson of Fort Dodge said in a December 4, 1869, letter to his brother in Syracuse: "It is certainly amusing to those living in Fort Dodge to read the many accounts and theories regarding the

Cardiff Giant. There is scarcely a schoolboy here but could give you a solution of it."

The *North West,* a Fort Dodge newspaper, conducted a thorough investigation and published a pamphlet "exposing the fraud" and describing how the Chicago stonecutters had chiseled out the figure. The face, incidentally, was said to be a likeness of Hull.

The pamphlet created "great excitement among visitors" and "great consternation among the owners" in Syracuse. The owners "promptly published a statement denying every allegation."

Hull sold out his interest for $23,000, then admitted that he had perpetrated a hoax.

He much enjoyed the embarrassment of those he had sucked in, particularly the red-faced scientists and sculptors.

In all fairness, it must be said that not everybody was duped. Two Yale professors and a sculptor, plus some hard-headed newspapermen, cried "hoax" immediately upon the discovery of the giant. Lucky for Hull and his associates, such killjoys attracted little attention at first.

The Cardiff Giant is still "alive" today after over 100 checkered years. The Giant was in storage for many years in Massachusetts, then was exhibited at the Pan-American Exposition in Buffalo, New York, in 1901.

In 1913 Joseph R. Mulroney of Fort Dodge bought the giant for a reported $10,000.

In 1920 ten Fort Dodge residents purchased the giant for display in Exposition Park in that city. Admission was ten cents at first, later was free.

Another period in storage followed before the giant was acquired by Gardner Cowles, chairman of the board of The Register and Tribune Company in Des Moines. The giant was placed on display at the Iowa State Fair.

The Farmers Museum at Cooperstown, New York, bought the giant from Cowles in 1948. The museum has been the Giant's home ever since.

Nobody seems to have written about how the stonecutters fared. They should have had a great future after all that publicity and interest. But one report said the Giant is "defective in proportion and features and [is] simply a poor job of stone cutting."

The Giant since has been called "Iowa's largest native son" and "the American belly laugh in stone."

The Hull-Newell group never was prosecuted. Apparently hoaxes that give a lot of people a chuckle are to be forgiven. Said the *Louisville Courier-Journal,* "A hoax may become a valuable commodity . . . if in the end we can all laugh and particularly if the laugh is on us, and nobody has been hurt."

CYRUS C. CARPENTER

Grasshopper Scourge

W HEN the southwest wind blew, farmers shaded their eyes and anxiously scanned the sky. They were looking for—and hoping not to see—a blotch of shimmering white high in the heavens. All too often such a blotch was millions of grasshoppers, their wings glistening in the sunlight.

When such a 'hopper host landed, it was too bad for the farms in the area. The insects sometimes ate fields and gardens bare, even clothes off the line.

The grasshopper devastation was particularly bad in the spring and summer of 1873 when Cyrus C. Carpenter of Fort Dodge was governor of the state.

He might be called the grasshopper governor because he took such a keen interest in aiding early settlers blighted by the scourge. He said the effect on the pioneers was "most appalling." He estimated that in some parts of the northwest "one-fourth the farmers sold out at merely nominal prices and left the country."

The devastation was spotty but extended as far east and south as Webster County. Kossuth, Clay, Dickinson, and Emmet counties may have been hit hardest. At least their population either declined or stayed relatively static from 1873 to 1875 while neighboring counties were showing gains.

Kossuth slipped from a population of 4,251 in 1873 to 3,765 in 1875. Dickinson only held its own, going from 1,743 to 1,748, while Emmet dropped from 1,618 to 1,436. But Plymouth rose from 3,884 to 5,288 in two years, Crawford from 3,777 to 6,038, Sioux from 2,872 to 3,220, O'Brien from 1,865 to 2,349.

The population gains are not to be taken as meaning certain counties escaped major damage. On the contrary. O'Brien County was visited by hordes which arrived "with a roaring sound." The 'hoppers evidently came from "barren table lands along the eastern base of the Rocky Mountains." The insects and the settlers engaged in a race "as to which would gather the largest harvest."

At Carpenter's urging, the 1874 legislature voted $50,000 to buy seed for the hard-hit farmers and named a committee to investigate the situation. In addition, contributions of money, clothing, and food for the stricken settlers poured in from other parts of Iowa and from as far away as New England.

The response to the needs for help, the governor said, undoubtedly encouraged "a good many to stick to their farms, who [otherwise] would have given up this unequal contest."

What Iowa wanted most of all in those days was more population. Carpenter did not propose to allow grasshoppers to retard the state's growth. Iowa maintained a state board to attract new settlers. That board in 1873 distributed 20,000 pamphlets in eastern states describing Iowa's manufacturing and agricultural resources. Another 10,000 such pamphlets printed in German were distributed in Europe.

Some of the German ancestors of present northwestern Iowa residents may have been lured to Iowa by the pamphlets.

Carpenter was angry over losing a colony of Mennonites from Russia who thought of settling in an unnamed northwestern Iowa county. The Russians changed their minds, he said, when they learned of "the enormous debt the county authorities have contracted, and which will hang like a millstone upon every legitimate enterprise of the people for years to come."

Carpenter said the Russians in many instances possessed wealth and, what was better, they were people of "industrious habits and high moral principles." The governor said Iowa laws had failed to protect counties "from an extravagance which in some instances falls but little below criminality."

Carpenter may have been talking about Lyon County where early officials issued $170,000 in bonds that have been described as fraudulent, and school districts similarly floated bond issues ranging from $20,000 to $250,000 each. Some of those bonds, however, never had to be paid off. The courts ruled the issues illegal years later.

Regarding grasshoppers, Carpenter pointed out in a later report that 1873 was not the only year of such visitations. Farmers battled the insects sporadically beginning in 1867 and up to 1876 and later. Discussing the 1873 invasion, the report said, "This time they were early enough in the season to destroy nearly all the crops in [certain] counties; evidently having been hatched farther south and having attained maturity much earlier than in 1867."

The 'hoppers liked to gather by the millions at night on railroad tracks. Their crushed bodies actually brought a train to a standstill on the slippery rails on a slope near Arcadia, Iowa. The engineer had to back up the train and then "make a rush for the summit, sanding the track liberally as he did so."

Another time, North Western Railroad trains were halted for the same reason on the grades west of Jefferson, Iowa.

Farmers, scientists, and legislators conducted wide-ranging discussions as to how to get rid of the pests. Prairie fires were started and smudge fires lighted in vain efforts to eradicate the 'hoppers. Minnesota offered a bounty of a certain amount per bushel of grasshoppers.

Liquid pressed from half a bushel of grasshoppers at Spirit Lake was said to have had medicinal value. A St. Louis caterer reportedly said grasshopper soup "was pronounced perfectly delicious by many people." An entomologist also reportedly served a curry of grasshoppers and grasshopper croquettes to friends without "informing them as to the nature of the banquet." But an "unlucky hind leg, discovered in one of the croquettes, revealed the secret."

Carpenter first came to Fort Dodge in 1854, footsore and weary after walking eighty miles from Des Moines. He had but $1 in his pocket.

He was a twenty-five-year-old school teacher and a native of Pennsylvania.

Major William Williams, founder of Fort Dodge, took Carpenter by the hand and said that "the west was full of opportunities for young men who had the force and will to stick."

Carpenter got started by teaching Fort Dodge's first school.

Within three years he won election to the state legislature. In 1871, only seventeen years after his arrival in Iowa, he was elected governor of the state.

Carpenter served with distinction as an officer in the Civil War and was one of the first Iowa governors to begin forcing honesty into operation of the early railroads. He maintained that the rails overcharged the farmer for carrying his products to market. He attracted wide attention when he said, "The exorbitant rail rate is the skeleton in the Iowa corn crib."

Not only were the rail rates too high, he said, but the railroads also were guilty of discrimination. They gave shippers in one town lower freight rates than shippers in another and also granted special low rates to favored individuals or companies. Such policies were very unfair. A favored company would benefit by paying less for shipping its products, say, to Chicago. Another company having to pay higher rates could be forced out of business by the consequent higher operating costs.

In response in part at least to Carpenter's urging, the 1874 legislature established maximum limits on railroad charges both for freight and for passenger service.

Carpenter's messages to the legislature demonstrate that Iowa was by no means crime-free a century ago.

He offered eleven state rewards in two years for the arrest and conviction of persons responsible for murders in Iowa. The rewards were nearly all for $500 each. The list shows that these killings had taken place in all parts of the state: L. A. Billings, Floyd County Farmer; Francis Lassaux, Creston merchant; George N. Kirkman, Story County resident; Charles Howard, Henry Miland, Ella Barrett, John Hunter, and John Johnson, all of Polk County; Esther Alger of Olive Township in Clinton County; Elizabeth Brownlie of Winfield Township in Scott County, and John Raffety, a railroad engineer who died near Adair.

Raffety was killed when his train was deliberately wrecked in a holdup. Jesse James was believed to have been responsible but nobody ever was caught and convicted of that crime.

In 1876 Carpenter told the legislature at the end of his second and last term: "I can not refrain from calling your attention to the increasing number of . . . tramps who infest many parts of the country. . . . If legislative action can be devised to overcome this evil, I hope [you] will not be slow to apply it."

He also asked action against criminals "who haunt railroad trains and fleece passengers out of their money." Such sharpies perhaps got unsuspecting people into crooked card games on trains. Carpenter commented, "Through our state passes the great tide of California travel and it behooves our lawmakers to see that the fair name of our state suffers no detriment because of this modern variety of highway robbery."

After leaving the governor's office, Carpenter served two terms in Congress, then returned to the Iowa legislature in 1884 and helped pass a stringent antiliquor law.

He never feathered his own nest and he was hard up by 1889. Friends helped him get the postmastership in Fort Dodge that year.

Cyrus Carpenter "died poor" in Fort Dodge in 1898 at the age of sixty-eight. One of his warm friends said in a tribute that Carpenter had served as a public official "in a corrupt and profligate age [when] almost all channels of public life were more or less corrupt." Yet Carpenter's integrity was such that "no man could put a finger on a single act of his that was not honestly and faithfully done." The friend concluded, "His fellow citizens spent no time explaining his record for it shone with the same fixedness of truth and honor . . . as the North Star shines upon its fellow constellations of the universe."

Wrote Circus Music

T HE MANY MOODS of a circus are created by music of different tempos.

Karl King of Fort Dodge wrote dozens of pieces to fit each of those moods. He was one of the great circus composers and musicians of his time, and a topflight bandmaster as well.

He composed "Alhambra Grotto," a circus march used when a trainer enters with lions; "Broadway One Step," a clown parade number; "The Big Cage," a fast-moving piece used in the climax of an animal act; and such waltzes as "Enchanted Nights Waltz" and "In Old Portugal" for high trapeze acts.

"In Old Portugal" was written for Lillian Leitzel, famed aerial acrobat. The piece was being played when a brass swivel broke and she fell to her death in 1931 while performing in Copenhagen, Denmark.

King worked at various times with the Barnum and Bailey, Sells Floto, and Yankee Robinson circuses and directed the circus bands part of the time.

King began playing in circus bands in 1910. He came to Fort Dodge in 1919 when the big Ringling Brothers circus merged with Barnum and Bailey.

King is best known to Iowans for his thirty-eight-year career as conductor of the band in the grandstand each year at the Iowa State Fair. He performed that duty from 1921 to 1959.

He wrote numbers for such Big Ten universities as Minnesota, Wisconsin, Illinois, Indiana, Michigan, and Iowa. He once drolly observed, "I wrote a football number for the University of Chicago and the next year they quit playing football."

King was still director of the Fort Dodge municipal band when he died at eighty years of age March 31, 1971.

F *Terror in Winter*

AMILIES FLED for their lives over long distances through the snow and cold.

Terror gripped wide areas of Iowa and Minnesota—and with good reason. Indians had killed at least forty human beings—men, women, and children.

Some thirty had died in the Spirit Lake Massacre and seven more at Springfield, Minnesota, in March 1857.

William Williams set out from Fort Dodge with a force of volunteers to catch the Indians and to restore peace of mind to everyday pioneer life. He never found the Indians. The expedition did put an end to the Iowa killings, however. The Indians retreated and caused no more trouble in Iowa.

Major William Williams was the founder of the city of Fort Dodge. He had come as a sutler (canteen operator) with United States Army troops in 1850 when the Fort Dodge post was established to keep the Indians in check. The fort was named for Wisconsin Senator Henry Dodge who was the father of Iowa Senator A. C. Dodge of Burlington.

Fort Dodge was abandoned as an army post in 1853 and Williams bought the land (including eighteen log cabins) for a company of which he and other Iowans were joint owners. Williams was a native Pennsylvanian and not young. He was nearly sixty-two when he led a force of 110 volunteers who started from Fort Dodge three days after getting the news of the Spirit Lake Massacre.

The Indians probably felt they were justified in slaying the whites. Many settlers did not live up to land treaties very faithfully. They were forever invading areas supposedly reserved for the red men. And in Indian eyes, whites were all of the same ilk. It may have made no difference to the Indians that they had murdered innocent people who knowingly violated no treaties.

Although Williams's little Spirit Lake expedition engaged in no direct hostilities with the Indians, the volunteers fought a grim battle for survival against the weather which was unbelievably cold and snowy for late March and early April.

The expedition spent seventeen days looking for Indians north and west of Fort Dodge. Williams reported that 14 of the 110 men became "very badly frozen."

Two volunteers, Private William Burkholder of Fort Dodge and Captain J. C. Johnston of Hamilton County, lost their way and froze to death. Their skeletons were found eleven years later.

The terrorized settlers, especially the women and children, also suffered greatly from the cold. And the Indian killings left two small boys of Springfield, Minnesota, without parents. The youngsters were John Sheigley, four years old, and John Stewart, eight.

Williams saw the Sheigley child in a camp "wandering about the fires, wanting or asking for something to eat." He was "a particularly fine child but very lightly clothed, and his little feet were frozen." Touched by the plight of the little fellow, Williams adopted him and said he would rear and educate him.

Williams also put young John Stewart in the charge of J. W. Dawson of Fort Dodge who wanted the boy. Dawson may have adopted John Stewart.

Williams ardently promoted Fort Dodge. He lived an active life and did get into one scrape. He and John Duncombe were accused of putting tar and feathers on some newcomers who moved onto land claimed by Williams's son.

Williams and Duncombe were indicted and found guilty of "inciting to riot" but were freed after paying small fines.

Williams died in 1874 at seventy-seven years of age, an honored elder inhabitant.

JONATHAN DOLLIVER

Fought for Common Man

H OW THEY WORSHIPPED Senator Jonathan Dolliver in Fort Dodge!

When he came home in 1909 after losing a courageous battle over an important bill in the Senate in Washington, an estimated 15,000 people turned out to greet him in a warm demonstration of affection and respect.

Since the Fort Dodge population only totaled about 15,000 at the time, the estimate seems high. Yet many might have come from long distances to pay homage to the champion of the rights of the common man.

Rarely if ever has there been such a homecoming demonstration for any other United States senator from Iowa.

A newspaper account says Central Avenue in Fort Dodge was "ablaze with incandescent and arc lights [a lot of light in 1909!] and the national colors displayed from every business house and home along the route." Dolliver was escorted in state from his home on Second Avenue South to the "public square park where a public reception and ovation awaited him."

The demonstration was called the finest of all his homecomings, though such celebrations over the years had "grown to be an annual affair."

Dolliver was highly regarded nationwide. Mark Sullivan, the Washington columnist, called him "the greatest Senator of his time." Even though Dolliver was a Republican, Democratic Senator Ben Tillman of South Carolina said, "Great men are plentiful in this country but not as great as Dolliver." Senator Albert Beveridge of Indiana called the Iowan "our best, our most gifted man, our only genius."

Dolliver was a powerful orator. When word got around Washington that he was to deliver a major speech, the Senate galleries likely would be packed and the other senators would make it a point to be there to listen.

At the same time, Dolliver was despised by the monopolistic interests who sought to use government for their own financial gain, through unnecessarily high tariffs on foreign imports for example.

The battle that Dolliver and the other Liberal Republicans lost in the Senate in 1909 was over the Payne-Aldrich tariff which put high duties on iron, coal, hides, and other commodities coming into this country. Dolliver opposed such duties because the common man would have to pay the bill in unnecessarily higher prices for many of the things he had to buy.

Dolliver told the Senate in a speech that still rings with greatness:

I intend to fight without fear. I do not care what may be my political fate. For the day is coming—it is a good deal nearer than many think—when a new sense of justice, new inspirations, new volunteer enthusiasms for good government shall take possession of the hearts of our people.
The time is at hand when the laws will be respected by the young and old alike. A thousand forces are making for it. It is the fruitage of these Christian centuries, the fulfillment of the prayers and dreams of the men and women who have laid the foundations of the commonwealth, and with infinite sacrifice maintained these institutions.

Despite the strenuous efforts of Dolliver and the other opponents, the Payne-Aldrich tariff measure passed and contributed to Republican defeats at the polls in both the 1910 and 1912 elections.

Dolliver, a native of West Virginia, came to Fort Dodge as a young attorney in 1878 at the age of twenty. "Tall and muscular, his flashing eyes and glowing cheeks, his forceful gestures and clear-cut, fast-flowing eloquence" roused the 1884 Republican state convention to a fighting pitch. He made one statement in his convention speech, however, that he rued later. He said, "When Iowa goes Democratic, Hell will go Methodist." Iowa was a strongly Republican state in those days, but in 1889, only five years later, Iowa elected a Democratic governor.

Of all Dolliver's statements over a long political career, his "Hell will go Methodist" observation is the most often recalled.

Dolliver ran for Congress in 1886 but lost. He was elected in 1888 and reelected to the House the next six times.

Had things happened a little differently, Dolliver might have become president of the United States. Here is how things might have worked out:

Dolliver had strong support over the nation for the Republican nomination for vice-president in 1900. The belief was widespread that he would be nominated.

Theodore Roosevelt was Republican governor of New York at the time. He was an energetic and bothersome liberal who was intensely disliked by a New York party boss. The boss, who was a power in the party nationally, arranged to get Roosevelt out of New York by having him nominated for the vice-presidency. The Dolliver candidacy was dropped in deference to the New York plan.

Roosevelt was elected along with President William McKinley. The next year, in 1901, the president was assassinated. Roosevelt became president and is ranked among the great chief executives in American history. Dolliver might have advanced to the White House in the same manner had he not been sidetracked.

Dolliver was appointed United States senator in 1900 to fill a vacancy left by the death of Senator John Gear of Burlington. Dolliver spent ten notable years in the Senate. He was a strong liberal leader in the final years of his career.

The strain of the 1909 tariff fight was such that Dolliver's health was impaired. Yet he had sufficient strength left to deliver some telling blows in that 1910 Republican state convention. Among other things, he said:

While some think we are going to harm the Republican party by publicly admitting our differences, the fact is that popular government depends on discussion. Without that, it could never come into existence. Without that, it could not last very long.

The truth is found in controversy. It usually lies between the extremes of opinion, and the most important truth which the world cherishes has come down to us through the greatest trial and tribulation.

He said he had one ambition left "and that is to keep on the firing line in defense of public rights against the sordid private interests which are seeking to usurp the government of the United States."

But the end of his life was near. A little more than two months

later, on October 15, 1910, Dr. E. M. Van Patten came to see the ailing
Dolliver at his home in Fort Dodge.

Dolliver, who had had a fairly good day, was resting on a couch.
He rose and greeted the doctor.

Dolliver sat in a large chair for a medical examination. The doctor
placed a stethoscope against the senator's chest and counted fourteen
heartbeats. The doctor turned away for a minute and then applied the
stethoscope again. This time he could detect no heartbeat. He thought
the instrument had become faulty.

He was wrong. Death had come to Jonathan P. Dolliver at fifty-two
years of age.

DAVENPORT

WALTER L. BIERRING

T *Medicine from a Horse*

TWENTY-TWO PERSONS in Davenport, mostly children, became critically ill of diphtheria, a vicious disease.

Usually eight or ten would have been expected to die.

Thanks to a pioneering physician and a medication he brought from Europe, only one died. The other twenty-one recovered.

The physician was Dr. Walter L. Bierring, a native of Davenport and one of Iowa's great medical figures. The diphtheria outbreak which he fought so successfully occurred in the winter of 1894–1895. He "made" the medicine himself, inside a horse.

> *Dr. Bierring was one of many persons who have animated Davenport's bygone days. Others include William Conway, said to have once declared Davenport the capital of Iowa; Bix Beiderbecke, a legendary musician; murdered George Davenport, for whom the city is named; fat and capable Antoine Le Claire; Nila Cram Cook, who turned Hindu and lived in India; and Dred Scott, famed Negro whose lawsuit shook pre–Civil War United States.*

Parents of today cannot realize the deadliness of diphtheria a few generations ago. The disease has been all but wiped out by routine vaccinations of small children. But there was neither protection nor cure in the old days for diphtheria, which develops in the throat and interferes with breathing.

Frequently a family would lose four or five or even seven or eight children in a couple of weeks. As many as 9,000 cases of diphtheria a year were reported in Iowa. The death rate was often 40 or 50 percent.

A child, or adult, often recovered from diphtheria only when he was sturdy and in good condition, or when the disease was less virulent than usual.

Then, in 1894, came diphtheria antitoxin, a truly "miracle drug" of its era and science's first great step in the conquest of the disease. Dr. Bierring was in Paris that year. He saw antitoxin being used in an early series of tests. The death rate was cut in half in those tests.

Anxious to save children's lives, Dr. Bierring hastened back to Iowa City where he procured a horse for production of antitoxin. He first injected a small number of diphtheria germs into the horse's blood. Later and larger injections gave the horse immunity. Two quarts of blood were drawn from the horse and adapted as antitoxin serum. The process required 3½ months.

Dr. Bierring took the serum to Davenport where it was used with spectacular success in the twenty-one cases.

His serum was reputed to be the first produced in the United States west of New York where another physician had simultaneously embarked on the same type of undertaking.

Dr. Bierring told the Iowa State Medical Society meeting at Creston in April 1895 about the successful use of antitoxin at Davenport. After describing the almost unbelievable recovery of the twenty-one patients, and an additional six that had been similarly treated at Iowa City, Dr. Bierring suggested that a state appropriation be sought for making antitoxin. That would increase the supply and cut the cost, he said. He offered to produce the antitoxin himself "with no idea at all of deriving any personal benefit."

Some doctors at the society meeting were critical. One said a horse might not be free of other diseases. Dr. Bierring said every precaution had been taken, and added, "I assure the physicians of Iowa that it [antitoxin] will be used in very large doses on myself before being given out." Even so, the medical society declined to support his proposal for a state appropriation.

Before long, however, the serum came into wide use over the state.

Antitoxin is used only occasionally now as a treatment after a person becomes ill of diphtheria. The newer diphtheria vaccination provides complete advance protection against the disease. But antitoxin was the mainstay treatment for decades. A considerable number of patients continued to die of the disease. But tens of thousands of elderly Iowans are alive today because antitoxin overcame diphtheria infections in the earlier years of the century.

Dr. Bierring was active professionally in Iowa for more than sixty years. He served as state health commissioner for twenty years. He taught medicine at the University for twenty years and he was in private practice for upwards of twenty years. He was president of the American Medical Association in 1934. He remained active in public health work until close to ninety.

Dr. Bierring's personal health record should be of some encouragement to individuals with cancer. His right foot was crushed by a freight train in Davenport when he was fourteen years old. The foot had to be amputated years later when a cancerous growth appeared. He underwent surgery for cancer in the lymphatic glands in 1904 when he was thirty-six. In 1906 the right leg had to be amputated above the knee. Nevertheless, he lived until he was ninety-two. He died in 1961 of old age, not cancer.

Dr. Bierring was never a person to express regret. An admiring doctor once asked, "What would you have done with two legs?" He replied, "I would not have done as well."

In 1955, when he was eighty-seven, he said: "The older person needs constant contact with the spirit of the young. . . . I pity the fellow who does not have the privilege of talking with the young." Dr. Bierring never forgot this advice from Louis Pasteur, "Chance comes only to the mind that is prepared."

BIX BEIDERBECKE

"If That Boy Had Lived ..."

Sounds of jazz floated over the grave of Bix Beiderbecke in Davenport's Oakland Cemetery.

The musicians came from cities in eastern United States to honor Bix, "the greatest hot jazz player of them all."

They played such Bix favorites as "Louisiana" and "At the Jazz Band Ball."

The unusual graveside jam session was held August 6, 1971, the fortieth anniversary of Beiderbecke's death. He died at twenty-eight years of age in 1931. He was such a tremendous cornetist that his records still are selling in the 1970s.

The easterners, all of whom were members of the Bix Beiderbecke Memorial Jazz Band, wore lapel tags saying, "Bix lives."

A story long has been told that some of Beiderbecke's early musical pals once held an unannounced blow around his grave a few years after his death. Commenting on that legend, an admirer said, "All Bix would have asked was that the boys play with unfettered imagination, letting it ride joyously through the air, free and easy as the air itself."

That was the kind of music the jazz group played at his gravestone in the 1971 memorial which drew a crowd of 1,500. The spectators, many of them elderly and middle-aged, clapped in unison to the final tune, "When the Saints Come Marching In." In a eulogy to Beiderbecke, a Lutheran minister said, "His memory and his music belong to the ages."

His grave long was a shrine for jazz lovers from all over the world. Paul Whiteman, onetime great band leader, visited the spot in 1940, dressed in his bright yellow stage suit. Whiteman was performing in Davenport at the time. Bix, who was born in Davenport in 1903, played in Whiteman's band for eight years.

"Nobody could play 'Riverboat Shufflle' the way Bix could," said his brother Charles, a Davenport resident. "Some of the people who have written and visited here compared Bix to the Angel Gabriel."

Bix, whose real name was Leon Bismark Beiderbecke, composed such pieces as "In a Mist," "Candlelight," "In the Dark," and "Davenport Blues." He loved jam sessions. Said one report: "Beiderbecke was a brilliant exponent of improvisation, a feature of jazz music which has its roots in folk music, particularly that of the Negro. He, Bix, began playing on showboats while still in his teens."

He was careless of his appearance, of time, of money.

He could not read music at first even though he played superlatively. What he did with his battered cornet came not from written notes on a page but from his fiery and rhythmic soul.

As a sixteen-year-old, Bix sat on a Mississippi levee with the immortal Louie (Satchmo) Armstrong and listened to Armstrong blow. Bix then went home and practiced incessantly.

"I told Bix to just play and he'd please the cats," Armstrong said, "but you take a genius and he's never satisfied. . . . If that boy had lived, he'd be the greatest."

Somewhere along the line, Bix lost his way. His difficulties included too much liquor. Death came while he was in New York, reportedly from pneumonia.

Exceeded His Authority?

AN "ACTING GOVERNOR" proclaimed Davenport the capital of Iowa Territory in 1838, according to one early Iowa authority.

The acting governor was William Conway, a young Pennsylvanian. He was appointed secretary of the territory by President Van Buren. The president named Robert Lucas territorial governor. The Iowa Territory was created in 1838 from a western portion of Wisconsin Territory. Iowa did not become a state until 1846.

Conway reached Iowa a month before Lucas. Conway came to Davenport where he met Colonel George Davenport and Antoine Le Claire. Both were ardent boosters of Davenport.

No Iowa town had been designated a temporary capital as yet. Davenport and Le Claire told Conway that Davenport was "the only proper place for the capital." They said Davenport was "the greatest town in the Territory and had a magnificent future."

Since Lucas was not yet on the scene, Davenport and Le Claire persuaded Conway that he was "acting governor." At their urging and the urging of others, Conway named Davenport as the capital. The law did give the governor the right to designate a temporary capital.

Lucas arrived and put Conway in his place. Lucas designated Burlington as the territorial capital. Burlington continued to be the capital until 1841 when the seat of government was moved to Iowa City.

Conway died at Burlington in 1839 of typhus and was buried in Davenport.

Colonel Davenport Slain

COLONEL GEORGE DAVENPORT sat alone in his home on Rock Island. The rest of the household had gone to Stephenson (now Rock Island) for Independence Day celebration. The date was July 4, 1845.

Davenport heard a noise outside. He opened a locked door to investigate. Three men pushed their way in. "Seize him, Chunky," said one. At the same time somebody fired a pistol. The bullet wounded the sixty-two-year-old Davenport in the thigh. He was bound with strips of bark and blindfolded.

The bandits carried or pulled Davenport upstairs. He could not walk because of the loss of blood. Blood smears marked the trail on the stairs.

He was forced to open a safe. He fainted and was placed on a bed. The thieves took $600 in cash, a gold watch, and other loot and departed.

Davenport lived long enough to tell the story of the visitation, then died.

Justice was swift. Six outlaws were arrested. On October 24, less than four months later, three men were hanged for the crime on Rock Island. They were John and Aaron Long and Granville Young.

Davenport, a trader, was a friend of the Indians. He was buried behind his home and the Fox braves were there to pay him final homage. In an Indian ceremony, they told the Great Spirit that Davenport was their friend and they hoped the Spirit would open the door and take charge of him.

Davenport was an Englishman who had served in the United States Army. He was a member of the first expedition which came up the Mississippi to quiet hostile Indians. He was a member of the unit which located Fort Armstrong on Rock Island. He settled on Rock Island in 1816. When a new town was launched in 1836 on the Iowa side of the Mississippi, Le Claire insisted that the town be named for his friend Colonel George Davenport.

ANTOINE LE CLAIRE

Indians Got Fourteen Cents an Acre

Antoine Le Claire was one of the fattest and most important men of early Iowa. Half French-Canadian and half Indian, he was only five feet eight inches tall and he weighed at various times from 355 to 385 pounds. Yet he was "graceful and light of foot in a dance."

Le Claire was so highly regarded that the official Iowa State Bank put his likeness on its $5 bills in the late 1850s. Also, the first railroad locomotive to reach Davenport in 1855 carried the name "Antoine Le Claire."

When the Black Hawk War ended disastrously for the Sac and Fox Indians in 1832, a big tent was pitched at what is now Fifth and Farnam streets in Davenport. There the whites imposed upon the Indians the so-called Black Hawk Treaty.

Representing the Indians in the negotiations were Chiefs Keokuk and Wapello. Black Hawk could not be present. He was a prisoner at Prairie du Chien, Wisconsin. General Winfield Scott (for whom Scott County is named) represented the United States government. Illinois Governor John Reynolds was on hand. So was Le Claire who acted as interpreter.

Le Claire was a highly valuable person to have around such a conference. He could speak French, Spanish, and English as well as a number of Indian dialects. In addition, because he was half Indian (his mother was a Pottawattamie), the Indians liked and trusted him.

The Indians got the news in that big tent that they would have to surrender some of their "superfluous territory" on the Iowa side of the Mississippi. Having no other choice, they agreed. They gave up a strip of land 40 to 50 miles wide and extending 195 miles northward from the Missouri state boundary. Reserved for the Indians was a tract of 400 square miles through which the Iowa River flows.

The agreement provided for the Indians to get $20,000 a year for thirty years from the United States government. Counting other provisions of the agreement, what the Indians had to do was cede some five million acres to the whites for fourteen cents an acre.

The Indians insisted that Le Claire be given one section of land in Iowa opposite Rock Island (in what is now Davenport) and another section where the city of Le Claire stands. Also at the insistence of the red men, Le Claire got a section on the Illinois side. That land now in part is included in the city of Moline.

Le Claire later built his home in Davenport where the great tent stood.

Three and a half years after the Black Hawk Treaty, on February 23, 1836, Le Claire, Davenport, and six other men met in Davenport's home and signed an agreement for starting the town of Davenport. The townsite area totaled one-half section and was valued at $2,000. The boundaries of the tract were the present Harrison and Warren streets, the river, and West Seventh Street.

Le Claire, who died in 1861 at sixty-four, obtained from the Indians this explanation of how Iowa got its name: "A tribe of Indians was in search of a home or [were] hunting. . . . When they reached a point they admired and was all they wished, they said: 'Iowa—this is the place.'" The location is near the mouth of the Iowa River.

One of Le Claire's major contributions was his part in the writing of the autobiography of Black Hawk, a great Indian and a great human being.

Black Hawk wanted his story told and he asked Le Claire's help. Black Hawk talked in his Indian tongue, Le Claire translated, and J. B. Patterson, an Illinois newspaperman, recorded what Le Claire said.

The autobiography went through at least fourteen editions. Some of the language is a little fancy for an Indian, said one reviewer who nevertheless added, "Though Black Hawk was a thorough savage, he had yet a strong sense of honor, personal dignity and generosity."

The old chief never accepted the idea that the white man had the right to buy Indian lands. Black Hawk said: "My reason tells me that land can not be sold. The Great Spirit gave it to his children to live upon and to cultivate, as far as it is necessary for their subsistence; and so long as they occupy and cultivate it. . . . Nothing can be sold but such things as can be carried away."

Election Skullduggery

ELEVEN SLEIGHS loaded with Dubuque miners roared into Davenport to vote in the election called to select the county seat of Scott County.

The miners had no business voting in that election. They did not live in Scott County. But there they were.

Davenport was locked in a battle with Rockingham over which should be the county seat. Rockingham was a nearby town downstream from Davenport on the Mississippi.

Davenport paid the miners $1 a day plus food and whisky. Rockingham engaged in the same kind of skullduggery by importing "wood-choppers" from Cedar County to vote.

Davenport was filled with miners "patriotically drunk" on election day, February 19, 1838. They were described as a "wretched-looking bunch of rowdies" and the "fiercest, raggedest, most Godforsaken crowd under the sun."

The miners voted without hindrance. To have tried to interfere would have been "madness." It was said 300 gallons of whisky and other liquor were consumed during their stay. Their total expenses exceeded $3,000.

Davenport won that election but to no avail. The crookedness on both sides was too much for Henry Dodge, governor of Wisconsin Territory of which Iowa was still a part. He ordered a new election which was held the following August. Both sides again cheated on a large scale. Davenport was winner by two votes but a third election was called.

Rockingham withdrew from competition. Opposing Davenport this time was a settlement at the mouth of Duck Creek. The vote: Davenport 318, Duck Creek 221. Davenport won the county seat. The Rockingham area now is part of the city of Davenport.

Antoine Le Claire had agreed to contribute $3,000 and George Davenport $1,200 to help build a courthouse and jail if Davenport won. Both presumably honored their commitments.

A Effie Afton *Hit the Bridge*

BRAHAM LINCOLN had not yet become president when the *Effie Afton* hit the bridge.

Effie Afton was a new boat which rammed into a pier of a Mississippi River railroad bridge between Davenport and Rock Island in 1856. The ramming may not have been accidental.

The boat, valued at $40,000 to $50,000, caught fire. So did the bridge which was partly destroyed. As the bridge fell, other boats docked at Davenport and Rock Island sounded their whistles and bells in celebration. River men hated the new bridge. They tried to prevent its construction and they petitioned federal court to order its removal.

The St. Louis Chamber of Commerce called the bridge "unconstitutional, an obstruction to navigation, dangerous." St. Louis wanted Iowa grains and other farm products sent to that city for river shipment instead of to Chicago by rail.

The bridge was 1,582 feet long and an engineering pride of the times. The bridge came into Davenport between Third and Fourth streets.

Abraham Lincoln, a noted lawyer of the times, handled the case for the railroad in federal court. He reminded the jury that the river was closed to traffic by ice four months of the year whereas the bridge always was open to rail traffic.

He said east-west transportation was as important as Mississippi traffic and was growing rapidly with the enormous expansion of the

West. "This current of [rail] travel," he added, "has its rights as well as that of north and south."

Lincoln reported that the Rock Island Railroad had hauled 74,179 passengers and 12,586 freight cars across that bridge in eleven months. (Rare indeed is the railroad bridge with that much passenger traffic today!)

The trial ended with a jury disagreement and the case was dismissed. The outcome was described as "a victory for railroads, bridges and Chicago, as against steamboats, rivers and St. Louis."

B. J. PALMER

He Never Shaved

T EEN-AGE BEARDS are nothing new.

B. J. Palmer wore a beard from the time he was eighteen years old in 1899. He used to say that "no razor ever crossed my chin."

The bearded Palmer built the Palmer School of Chiropractic into a major Davenport institution. During the same period he engaged in a battle stretching over half a century with doctors of medicine and osteopathy.

Chiropractic began with Palmer's father who claimed in 1895 to have eventually restored a janitor's hearing by pushing a bump on his neck.

B. J. (his given names were Bartlett Joshua) was born in What Cheer, Iowa, in 1881. The Palmer family moved to Davenport in 1885. The father had been a rural schoolteacher, grocer, bookkeeper, and a student of phrenology, which is a method of analyzing character by a study of the shape of the head.

The father engaged in "healing" in Davenport and started the chiropractic school. B. J. went to Lake City, Iowa, at eighteen as a "doctor of chiropractic." B. J. got his diploma from the Palmer school in 1902 and took over management of the school at twenty-one years of age the same year.

B. J. defined chiropractic as "a method of eliminating the cause of disease by adjusting the spinal column without the use of drugs, medicines or instruments." The adjustments, he said, "relieve any impingement of the delicate nerve fibers which, by interfering with the free flow of Nature's life-giving force, results in impaired or abnormal functions."

Palmer's father went to jail in 1905 rather than pay a $500 fine for practicing medicine without a license. He left Davenport and died in California in 1913.

To publicize chiropractic, B. J. established Station WOC in Davenport in 1919 as the second station in the nation licensed for radio broadcasting. KDKA in Pittsburgh had gone on the air a few months before. Palmer organized Central Broadcasting Company and in 1930 acquired Station WHO in Des Moines. In 1949 WOC-TV became Iowa's first commercial television station.

Palmer gathered art objects all over the world, particularly in the Orient. He possessed the world's greatest collection of spinal columns, owned a $300,000 Egyptian princess mummy, and was known as a top circus fan. Still somewhat a man of mystery, he died at seventy-nine years of age in 1961.

NILA COOK

G *"I Hear the Mountain Stream . . ."*

EORGE CRAM COOK went to Greece for the final two years of his life.

His attractive daughter Nila became a disciple of Gandhi in India for a time and later was converted to Islamism in Iran.

The story of the Cooks of Davenport is strange, adventuresome, creative, and mystical.

The father, born in Davenport in 1873, wanted at one time to make his native city another "Athens" in culture. He was a notable writer who taught at the University of Iowa. In 1915 he and his wife Susan Glaspell, also of Davenport, founded the original Provincetown, Massachusetts, playhouse. There they helped Eugene O'Neill get his start by producing his first plays.

Susan Glaspell was a major playwright herself. She won a Pulitzer Prize in 1930 with her play *Alison's House,* which is based on the life of Emily Dickinson. Susan graduated from Drake University and was a newspaper reporter afterward in Des Moines. She became a successful novelist and short story writer as well as dramatist.

Cook did his best writing while collaborating with his wife. They turned out a number of plays. He was a novelist as well. He had a "rare gift of inspiring others." He loved Greece. In 1922 he took Susan and Nila, who was a daughter by a previous wife, to live in Greece. He wanted to "absorb without stint" the customs and habits of the common Greek people.

He died in 1923 "among the shepherds of Mount Parnassus." He is buried at Delphi near the Temple of Apollo of ancient Greece. At the grave are two stone plaques containing beautiful bits of poetry in English. Over the grave itself is this verse:

> I hear the mountain stream
> > Pouring in beauty. That
> > rhythmic water
> Does not need to be more
> > than itself
> But I,
> Spirit,
> Have no reason for living
> Unless somehow for Spirit
> somewhere
> Life is immortal.

The second plaque nearby on the cemetery wall contains these lines:

> Not in the Parthenon
> > The temple of the shaper
> > of the mind.
> Thrust upward on the Attic
> > promontory
> > In proud self-affirmation
> To be forever
> > The image of intellectual
> > beauty
> Knowing its worth
> > More deeply here
> In the heart that is us all
> > The instinct of the hollow
> > of the hills
> Not knowing its own aim
> > Built blindly for the Greece
> Which could not be.

Cook's name is engraved under both poems. Perhaps he wrote them.

Susan Glaspell returned to Provincetown after his death and continued her writing. She died in 1948 at sixty-six years of age.

Nila Cram Cook, a dark and classic beauty, was born in Davenport in 1910. She started studying theology when only fifteen years old.

She learned Sanscrit and other oriental languages from sages in the king's court in Greece.

She presented a striking appearance in the flowing robes of old Greece and with only sandals on her feet.

In the late 1920s, she married a young and aristocratic Greek by whom she had a son. In 1929 she left Greece and her husband and went to India where she caused a worldwide sensation by becoming a follower of Gandhi and a devotee of Brahma in the Hindu religion. She lived for two years in a convent to prepare herself for "a life of ascetism, sacrifice and service." She gave up her money and ceded her property to her son to be "better fit to serve the greatest spiritual figure in the world," Gandhi.

Nila saw little of Gandhi, however. He apparently never quite approved of her. In 1933, less than two years later, she left her bed of hard bricks in Gandhi's "asham" and went to New Delhi where she announced: "My heart is leaping for thrills. I want speed. I want to fly. I want to attend orchestra dances."

She immediately experienced one unwanted thrill when she drove a car into a ditch while traveling seventy miles an hour. She was injured but recovered. The British, then rulers of India, deported Nila back to this country. When she landed in New York in 1934 she sang "America the Beautiful." She puzzled customs officials when she said she had no baggage "except the flower seeds in my heart."

She married a ship's steward but soon got a divorce.

Nila served as a war correspondent for a time in Greece during World War II. Early in the war she outwitted the German Nazi police and escaped, presumably into the wild fastnesses of Parnassus above Delphi. They never did find her.

In 1945 she turned up in Teheran, Iran, as director of Persian state theaters and censor of all movies shown in that country. She formed the first modern Iranian opera company. She was called the "Luther of Islam" for her new compilation and translation of the Koran, bible of the Islamic religion.

In 1954 she was back in India where some recalled that she once had been known as the "blue goddess." She was last heard of doing archeological research in Sykia, Greece. She reportedly left no forwarding address when she left Sykia.

Sold Washers for $10

WILLIAM Voss did not like the sight of his mother laboring over a steaming tub washing clothes in their Davenport home.

Voss was twenty years old. The year was 1877. The family had come from Germany five years before.

The youth went to work and produced an almost entirely wooden washing machine operated by a hand lever. It worked.

Word of the marvelous new machine spread around the neighborhood. Other housewives wanted machines. Voss started production. He sold his wooden models for $10 each. He was manufacturer, designer, and salesman.

Voss became president of Voss Brothers washer manufacturers in Davenport. He died in 1939 at eighty-two years of age.

C Exposed Corruption

CHARLES RUSSELL, a leading "muckraker" and notable author, was born in Davenport. His father was editor of the old *Davenport Gazette*. As a boy in the 1870s, young Russell spent all the time he could learning newspapering in the *Gazette* office.

He later became a top newspaperman in Minneapolis and New York and was publisher of the Hearst *American and Examiner* in Chicago at the turn of the century.

Becoming a magazine writer in 1903, the intense Russell brought corrupt practices to light in a number of fields but principally in meatpacking and corporations. He became widely known as a "muckraker," a small group of dedicated writers who exposed corruption in government and business.

Russell became a Socialist in 1908 and later was Socialist candidate for mayor of New York City and governor of New York. He turned down the Socialist nomination for president in 1916. He then left the Socialist party and accepted several foreign-duty appointments from his friend President Woodrow Wilson.

In 1926 the British government did not want him in England because he had espoused the cause of rebels in Ireland. Italy denied Russell admittance to that country because of his attacks on Mussolini.

Russell wrote thirty-four books, including a 1927 Pulitzer Prize winner dealing with the American orchestra. Music was his lifelong hobby.

Russell also helped found the National Association for the Advancement of Colored People (NAACP).

OCTAVE THANET

G Iowa Fed Hungry Russians

GOD BLESS MISS French and you."

That was the telegram which Clara Barton, founder of the Red Cross, sent to Benjamin Tillinghast at Davenport in 1892.

Tillinghast was associate editor of the *Davenport Democrat*. Miss Alice French was a noted Davenport author who wrote under the pen name of "Octave Thanet."

Together Tillinghast and Miss French had headed an Iowa drive which resulted in the donation of upwards of 200 railroad cars of corn for shipment to Russia where millions were starving. Other states also contributed but the drive had most verve in this state. Said Miss Barton of the campaign, "In Iowa it took the form of a veritable crusade for a most holy cause."

Tillinghast gave five full months of his time and about $1,000 of his own money. Miss French traveled the state stirring up interest among women, "enlisting sympathy for the hungry in Russia."

Tillinghast was named an American delegate to the International Red Cross Conference in 1902 at St. Petersburg. He and Miss Barton were received by the Czar and Czarina of Russia at that time.

Miss French was one of the nation's ablest novelists and short story writers for thirty some years beginning in the late 1880s. Titles of her stories are inviting: "Knitters in the Sun," "Expiation," "The Missionary Sheriff," "A Slave to Duty," and others. She was interested in the welfare of the working man and she tackled the Negro problem of her times in her book *By Inheritance*.

Miss French, who never married, opposed giving women the right to vote. She thought the voting privilege might interfere with the man remaining as head of the American home. But once the women suffrage amendment was adopted, she strongly supported its enforcement. She died in 1934.

Tragedy in Hotel Room

L ONG BEFORE there was any NAACP, a famous Negro slave was brought into the Davenport-Rock Island area.

His name was Dred Scott.

His owner, Dr. John Emerson, died late in 1843 in the Le Claire hotel in Davenport where he had started to practice medicine. Before dying of tuberculosis, the doctor drew a will which left Dred Scott to Mrs. Emerson and their infant daughter in trust.

A court battle developed over whether Scott should be freed. He had been taken in the previous ten years into such free territories as Illinois and what are now Iowa and Minnesota. Slavery was forbidden in all those places. Was he therefore automatically entitled to his freedom?

The Missouri Supreme Court said no, that he was still a slave. (He lived in St. Louis at the time of the lawsuit.) The United States Supreme Court in 1857 upheld the Missouri ruling and said he was still a slave. The whole country was shaken.

Antislavery advocates raised a storm of protest. The Dred Scott decision "did much to precipitate the bloody [Civil War] struggle four years later," says one report. Speaking of Dr. Emerson's bequeathing Dred Scott to his wife, one history writer said: "Grave consequences . . . grew out of the will made in a sickroom in Le Claire House in Davenport on a cold December day. . . . Because a certain black man . . . was included among the assets which Mrs. Emerson was directed to conserve, there are many monuments at Gettysburg and Antietam [Civil War battlefields]. . . . Tragedy abided unseen in that hotel room in Davenport on that December day."

Dr. Emerson was a surgeon in the United States Army in 1833 when he first brought Dred Scott with him to Fort Armstrong on Rock Island. When Emerson was sent to Fort Snelling in the present Minnesota in 1836, Scott went along.

Before leaving, Emerson staked out a claim of land in what is now Bettendorf and built a log cabin there. Tradition says Dred Scott was left behind to farm but there is little reason to believe that that is true.

Emerson quit the army in 1842 and returned to Scott County, Iowa. He bought some property on what is now Pershing Avenue in Davenport and started construction of a brick home. He died before the house was finished. He was buried in Davenport.

Mrs. Emerson married a Massachusetts physician in 1850. He was strongly opposed to slavery and he did not want his wife named as a defendant in the pending Dred Scott case. The ownership of Dred thereupon was transferred to Mrs. Emerson's brother. The brother freed Scott after the 1857 United States Supreme Court decision.

One interesting angle is the report that Dred Scott did not like to work. He was described as "one of the most shiftless and lazy members of his race." Mrs. Emerson is said to have never really wanted him.

JAMES GRANT

Restless Pioneer

J AMES GRANT was on the go all his life. He was born in North Carolina, practiced law in Chicago for a time, and then settled in the village of Davenport in 1838.

Few attorneys in Iowa history have been so successful. He and his partner won a verdict of nearly $1 million for their clients in an early case involving the Rock Island Railroad. Their fee was $100,000.

He was elected to the legislature and served as Speaker of the Iowa House of Representatives in 1852. He wore a stovepipe hat regularly and had "a voice like a Stentor that made everything resound."

When the legislature decided the Iowa Supreme Court should hold two sessions a year in Davenport, Grant provided the courtroom and made his extensive law library available to the justices.

He could not stand delaying tactics. While serving as a district judge, he became impatient over the slowness of two attorneys arguing a motion for a new trial. He was listening to the arguments in an up-river county when the sound of a steamboat whistle was heard.

Grant quickly sustained the motion for a new trial, adjourned court, "grabbed his carpet bag and ran for the river bank." He was going home on that steamboat no matter what legal questions were left behind, and he did.

After retiring with a comfortable fortune, Grant found it impossible to sit still. He went east at sixty-eight years of age to study mining engineering at the "Massachusetts School of Technology." At sixty-nine, he reported, he was at Fresno Flats, California, "50 miles from a railroad and managing a gold mine."

He was one of those restless, hard-hitting, capable pioneers who made America what it was in the nineteenth century.

Grant loved Iowa. When he was seventy-three years old in 1885, he wrote: "No matter where I go, whether . . . in the mountains of Colorado or the vineclad hills of California, my mind is ever going back to Iowa, its bar and its Judges and its people. . . . Iowa is my home and if I die away from that I suppose somebody will bring me there."

They did. He died in 1891 at the age of seventy-nine in Oakland, California. He is buried in Oakdale Cemetery in Davenport.

BIBLIOGRAPHY

T HIS BOOK is based principally on research collected from the following sources:

NEWSPAPERS

Albia Republican	*Iowa City Republican*
Bloomfield Democrat	*Keokuk Gate City*
Burlington Hawk-Eye	*Marshalltown Statesman*
Cedar Rapids Gazette	*Marshalltown Times-Republican*
Christian Science Monitor	*Mason City Globe-Gazette*
Clinton Herald	*Miami Daily News*
Council Bluffs Nonpareil	*Muscatine Journal*
Davenport Times	*New York Herald*
Davenport Times-Democrat	*New York Herald-Tribune*
Des Moines Capital	*Ottumwa Courier*
Des Moines Register and *Tribune*	*St. Louis Globe-Democrat*
Dubuque Herald	*Waterloo Courier*
Fort Dodge Chronicle	Waterloo, *Iowa State Reporter*
Fort Madison Democrat	

STATEWIDE PUBLICATIONS

Annals of Iowa, State Department of History and Archives.

Annual Reports of Board of Railroad Commissioners, State of Iowa.

Biennial Reports of Board of Health, State of Iowa.

Biennial Reports of Superintendents of Public Instruction, State of Iowa.

Census of Iowa, 1836–1880, State of Iowa.

The Constitutions of Iowa, B. F. Shambaugh, State Historical Society, 1934.

Historical Atlas of the State of Iowa, A. T. Andreas, Andreas Atlas Co., Chicago, 1875.

History of Iowa, B. F. Gue, Century History Co., New York, 1903.

Iowa Clubwoman, 1938.

Iowa Colonels and Regiments, Addison Stuart.

Iowa Democracy, John D. Denison, Democratic Historical Association, 1939.

Iowa, a Guide to the Hawkeye State, sponsored by State Historical Society, 1938.

Iowa, Its History and Its Foremost Citizens, Johnson Brigham, S. J. Clarke Publishing Co., Chicago, 1915.

Iowa Journal of History, State Historical Society.

Iowa Official Registers (redbooks).

Iowa Supreme Court Reports.

Iowa in Times of War, Jacob A. Swisher, State Historical Society, 1943.

Ioway to Iowa, Irving B. Richman, State Historical Society, 1931.

I Remember I Remember, Cyrenus Cole, State Historical Society, 1936.

Messages and Proclamations of the Governors of Iowa, edited by B. F. Shambaugh, State Historical Society, 1905.

A Narrative History of the People of Iowa, Edgar R. Harlan, American Historical Society, Chicago and New York, 1931.

The Palimpsest, State Historical Society of Iowa.

Proceedings of Pioneer Law-makers Association of Iowa.

Recollections and Sketches of Notable Lawyers and Public Men of Early Iowa, Edward H. Stiles, Homestead Publishing Co., Des Moines, 1916.

Roster and Record of Iowa Soldiers in the War of the Rebellion, State of Iowa, 1908.

The Story of Iowa, William J. Petersen, Lewis Historical Publishing Co., New York, 1952.

Transactions of Iowa State Medical Society.

IOWA COUNTY HISTORIES

Black Hawk	Lee	Pottawattamie
Cerro Gordo	Linn	Scott
Clinton	Marshall	Wapello
Des Moines	Muscatine	Webster
Dubuque	O'Brien	Woodbury
Johnson	Polk	

BIOGRAPHIES

William Boyd Allison, Leland Sage, State Historical Society, 1956.

Artist in Iowa, Darrell Garwood, W. W. Norton & Co., New York, 1944.

Carrie Chapman Catt, Mary Gray Peck, H. W. Wilson Co., New York, 1944.

The Dillinger Days, John Toland, Random House, 1963.

Grenville M. Dodge, Stanley P. Hirshson, Indiana University Press, 1967.

Jonathan Prentiss Dolliver, Thomas R. Ross, State Historical Society, 1958.

U. S. Grant, Louis A. Coolidge, Houghton-Mifflin, 1917.

Life of James W. Grimes, William Salter, Appleton, 1876.

Invincible Louisa, Cornelia Meigs, Little, Brown and Co., 1933.

Samuel Jordon Kirkwood, Dan E. Clark, State Historical Society, 1917.

Fred L. Maytag, A. B. Funk, privately printed, 1936.

One Foot in Heaven, Hartzell Spence, McGraw-Hill, 1940.

A Peculiar Treasure, Edna Ferber, Garden City Publishing Co., New York, 1938.

Christian Petersen, Sculptor, Iowa State University Press, 1962.

Rickenbacker, Edward V. Rickenbacker, Prentice-Hall, Englewood Cliffs, N.J., 1967.

Billy Sunday, the Man and His Message, William T. Ellis, 1914.

Carl Van Vechten and the Irreverent Decades, Bruce Kellner, University of Oklahoma Press, 1968.

OTHER HISTORIES AND BOOKS

An Alphabetical List of the Battles of the War of the Rebellion, published by G. M. Van Buren, Washington, D.C., 1883.

Antique Dubuque, M. M. Hoffmann, Dubuque Telegraph-Herald Press, 1930.

John Brown and His Men, Richard Hinton, Funk & Wagnalls, London and Ontario, 1894.

Crimes of the Civil War, Henry Clay Dean, W. T. Smithson publisher, 1868.

Davenport Past and Present, Franc Wilkie, Luse, Lane & Co., Davenport, 1858.

Morris Fishbein, M.D., an Autobiography, Doubleday, New York, 1969.

The History of Early Fort Dodge & Webster County, edited by Edward Breen, 1950.

A History of Iowa State College, Earle D. Ross, Iowa State College Press, 1942.

How We Built the Union Pacific Railway, Grenville Dodge, privately printed at Council Bluffs about 1911–1914.

In Cabins and Sod-Houses, Thomas H. Macbride, State Historical Society, 1928.

The Indian Wars of Minnesota, Louis H. Roddis, Torch Press, Cedar Rapids, 1956.

Life on the Mississippi, Mark Twain, Harper & Brothers, 1935.

Personal Recollections of Abraham Lincoln, Grenville Dodge, privately printed at Council Bluffs, about 1914.

The Pioneer Era on Iowa Prairies, Julian E. McFarland, 1969.

Pioneers of Polk County, L. F. Andrews, Baker-Trisler Co., Des Moines, 1908.

A Raft Pilot's Log, Walter A. Blair, Arthur H. Clark Co., Cleveland, 1930.

Rebirth of Freedom, Thomas Bray, Record and Tribune Press, Indianola, 1957.

MAGAZINES, PERIODICALS, MISCELLANEOUS

Paper on button industry by Mrs. Marshall Hurd of Sioux City.

Cardiff Giant Hoax, by James Taylor Dunn.

Central Constructor.

Diaries of Frederick M. Hubbell

Fresh Water Pearl Button Rush of 1890, from Laura Musser Art Gallery and Museum.

The Iowan (1917–1919 volume).

Reprints of Maytag-Mason Motor Company catalogues.

The Presidio of Fort Madison Penitentiary.

Saturday Evening Post (August 1955).

PERSONAL CONVERSATIONS . . .

. . . over the years with: Virgil Allen, Virginia Bedell, Walter L. Bierring, Jessie Binford, Russell Bobzin, Addie and Effie Cherry, A. C. Conaway, E. A. Conley, T. Nelson Downs, Will Durant, Charles Friley, J. F. Glassco, W. Earl Hall, Muriel Hanford, Arthur J. Hartman, Glenn Haynes, Clyde L. Herring, Harry Hopkins, George Keller, Nile Kinnick, Lawrence Krause, P. A. Lainson, Herschel Loveless, Arch McFarlane, Hanford MacNider, Frank O'Connor, Jake Perkins, Charles D. Reed, Theodore Schultz, Sim Smith, John Sokolovske, Frank Spedding, Mat Tinley, Henry A. Wallace, Frank West, J. W. Willett, Meredith Willson, and David Wine.

INDEX

Addams, Jane, 134, 135
Airplane, first flight in Iowa, 25
Allison, William, 6
American Friends Service Committee, 196
American Legion, 45
American Medical Association, 105, 106, 227
American Telephone and Telegraph Company, 20, 21
Ames, 93–103
Anderson, Daniel, 195
Andre, Hazel Beck, 97
Annie Wittenmyer Home, 88
Anson, Adrian, 120
Anson, Henry, 124
Appanoose, Chief, 191
Armstrong, Louie (Satchmo), 229
Army of the Tennessee reunion, 168
Associated Press, 165, 205
Atom bomb, 99, 100
Audubon Republican, 161
Automobiles, early speed of, 58

Bagley, Willis G. C., 37
Baird, Bil and Cora, 42–43
Baird, George, 43
Baker "hospital," 105–6
Baker, Norman, 105–8
Baldwin, John, 166, 167
Ball, Bill, 15
Banghard, Basil (The Owl), 72
Barbed-Wire Trust, 175
Barnum, P. T., 214
Bedell, Virginia, 204, 205
Beiderbecke, Bix, 228–29
Belknap, William, 90
Berry, W. H., 169
Bierring, Walter L., 226–28
Big Ten, 153, 161, 220
Binford, Jessie, 134–35
Black Hawk, Chief, 25, 26, 29, 81, 203, 204, 231, 232
Black Hawk steamer, 16
Black Hawk Treaty, 231, 232
Black Hawk War, 4, 8, 12, 81, 203, 231
Blacks, 23, 24, 26, 57, 58, 59, 60, 94, 95, 111–12, 130–31, 239–40
Blew, Father, 158
Bloomer, Amelia, 147–48
Blythe, James E., 71
Blythe, Joseph, 32, 175
Boepple, John, 112, 113
Boies, Horace, 197
Bootlegging, 128–29, 186
Bowen Guards, 124
Boxer Rebellion, 171–72
Brewer, Luther, 74
Bridge collapse, 113–14

Browne, Jesse, 200–201
Brownlee, O. H., 98, 99
Bruguier, Theophile, 186
Bryan, William Jennings, 192
Buchanan, James, 38
Buchanan, William I., 187
Bull Run, Battle of, 126
Bunn, William E. I., 202–3
Burlington, 22–34
Burlington Gazette, 29
Burlington Hawk-Eye, 29
Burlington Railroad, 32, 138
Burlington reservation, 32

Camanche, 55–56
Campbell, C. S., 59, 60
Cancer, 97, 105–7, 227
Candidates barred from speaking on campus, 154
Capitol commission, Iowa, 165–68
Capone, "Scarface" Al, 212
Cardiff Giant, 212–15
Carpathia, 66, 67
Carpenter, Cyrus C., 216–19
Carroll, Tommy, 37–39
Carver, George Washington, 94–95
Casino Theater, 165
Catfish Creek, 3
Catt, Carrie Chapman, 40–42
    International Woman Suffrage Alliance, 40
    League of Women Voters, 40
    National American Woman Suffrage Association, 40
Cedar County, voting of residents, 232
Cedar Falls, 17, 18
Cedar Rapids, 62–75
Cedar Rapids Republican, 74
Cedar River, 16, 18
Cemetery, national, at Keokuk, 88, 89
Central Intelligence Agency (CIA), 45, 46
Chalmers, John, 173
Chapman, Leo, 41
Chase, Salmon P., 27, 154
Cheek, Mrs. Allie Smith, 89
Cherry Sisters, 63–65
Chicago slums, 134–35
Chippewa Indians, 11, 12
Chiropractic, 234–35
Chouteau, Auguste, 4
Cigarettes, illegal in Iowa, 169–70
Cilley, Jonathan, 9
Circus music, 219
Civil War, 5, 6, 24, 27, 31, 58, 60, 77, 78, 86, 87, 89, 91, 109, 110, 118, 125, 126, 127, 131, 132, 140–42, 156, 168, 184, 186, 190, 195, 239–40

Civil Works Administration (CWA), 159, 160
Claims clubs, 30
Clamshells, 112–13
Clarke, George W., 125, 153
Clarke, William Penn, 154
Clark, Samuel Kirkwood, 156
Clarkson, James, 80, 142
Clark, Susan, 111–12
Cleveland, Grover, 182
Clinton, 50–61
Clinton Herald, 55, 57
Coffin, Lorenzo, 210–11
Cole, Cyrenus, 74, 75
Collier's magazine, 205
Collins, Keith, 138, 139
Conaway, Aaron C., 128
Confederate Army, 31
Conger, Mr. and Mrs. Edwin H., 171–72
Conley, E. A., 123
Constitutional Convention, state (1844), 110
Conway, William, 229–30
Cook, George Cram, 235–36
Cook, Nila Cram, 235–37
Cooper, Hugh, 84, 85
Cooper Lake, 85
Corn Palace, 182
Corse, John M., 7, 31, 32
Council Bluffs, 137–48
Courthouse elections
    Black Hawk County, 17–18
    Marshall County, 124–25
    Scott County, 232–33
Cousins, Robert, 6
Cowles, Gardner, 215
Cow War, 123
Crimes, 10, 36–39, 71–72, 107, 114–15, 128, 138–39, 150–51, 165–67, 178–80, 188, 192, 200, 204, 205, 207, 212, 218, 219, 230
Crocker, Marcellus, 7, 168
Cubbage, George, 12
Cubs, Chicago, 120
Cummings, Henry J. B., 195
Cummins, A. B., 32, 175–76
    Esch-Cummins law, 176
Curtis, Charles, 45, 106
Curtis, Samuel, 7

Dairy controversy, 97–99
Daughters of Revolution, 69
Davenport, 225–41
Davenport Democrat, 238
Davenport Gazette, 238
Davenport, George, 229–30, 233
Davis, James C., 174
Davis, Jefferson, 7, 8
Dawson, J. W., 221
Dean, Henry Clay, 77–80
Dean, John S., 166
Death penalty, 146, 200
Democratic National Convention, 10, 29, 79
Depew, Chauncey, 6

Des Moines, 163–76
Des Moines Art Center, 148
Des Moines Leader, 63–64
Des Moines Rapids, 84
Des Moines Register, 80, 142
Des Moines Register and Tribune, 102
Des Moines River, 90, 118, 192, 193, 195, 196
Des Moines Valley Line, 89
d'Georg, Amber, 165
Dick, escaped Negro slave, 23, 24
Dickinson, L. J., 107
Diet kitchens, Civil War, 87
Dillinger, John, 36–39
Diphtheria antitoxin, 226, 227
Dodge, Augustus C., 8, 9, 33–34, 156
Dodge, Grenville M., 7, 140, 141–42, 166
Dodge, Henry, 33, 34, 220, 233
Dolliver, Jonathan, 221–24
Douglas, Mahala, 66, 67, 73
Douglas, Stephen A., 24, 25
Douglas, Walter D., 66
Downs, T. Nelson, 133
Draft officials murdered, 78
Drake estate swindle, 178–80
Drake, Francis M. (Governor), 170–71, 190
Drake University, 82, 83, 91, 170, 171
Dred Scott, 239–40
Drought conference, 168, 169
Dubuque, 2–12
Dubuque, Julien, 3, 4
Duck Creek, 233
Duesenberg, Fred and August, 18, 19
Duncombe, John, 221
Durant, Will, 136
Dyer, Charles, 18

Eads, James D., 207–8
Edmundson, James D., 148
Edwards, James, 29
Effie Afton, 233–34
Ellis, L. A., 169
Emerson, Dr. John, 239–40
Envoy, 60–61
Explosions damage Muscatine homes, 114–15

Factor, Jake (The Barber), 71–73
Faith, Don, 164, 165
Farmers Protective Association, 175
Farm prices, 172, 188
Farm troubles, 123, 172–73, 175, 182, 187, 188, 216
Ferber, Edna, 191–92
Finkbine, Robert S., 157
Fires, 55, 127
Fisch, Mike, 172, 173
Fisher, Harry, 36, 37, 38
Fisher, William, 127
Floods, 192, 193, 195, 196
Floyd, Sergt. Charles, 186
Folsom, Amelia, 84
Foreign languages banned in Iowa, 74, 75, 182, 183
Fort Des Moines, 164–65

Fort Dodge, 209–24
Fort Dodge, army post, 220
Fort Madison, 198–208
Fort Madison Penitentiary, 146, 199–200, 204–7
Foster, Suel, 115–17
Foster, Thomas D., 196, 197
Francis, May E., 19–20
Frederick, John T., 27
Free tuition, 96
French, Alice (Octave Thanet), 238–39
Friley, Charles, 98, 100
Frisbie, J. H. H., 129
Fugitive slave law, 23, 156

Gallagher, J. P., 20
Gardner, Erle Stanley, 204, 205
Gaskell, Albert, 210
Gear, John H., 32, 33
Germans, 112, 133, 182, 183
Glaspell, Susan (Mrs. George Cram Cook), 235–36
Glassco, J. F., 129
"Glory Song," 123
God, 11, 42, 80, 94, 95, 110, 121, 122, 145, 153
Goodno, David, 109
Goodrell, Stewart, 167
Grand Army of the Republic (GAR), 126
Grange, 70
Granger law, 32, 70
Grant, James, 240–41
Grant, Ulysses S., 87, 142, 168
Grasshoppers, 216–18
Graves, J. K., 9
Graves, William, 9
Graybeard Regiment, 109–10
Great Western Railroad, 129–30
Greece, 235, 236, 237
    Temple of Apollo at Delphi, 236
Green, Eddie, 37–39
Gregory, Catherine (Amber d'Georg), 165
Griffith, John, 153
Grimes Hall, 24
Grimes, James, 26, 27, 208

Half-breed tract, 89
Hall, W. Earl, 49
Hamilton, Augustus, 190
Hamilton, Billy, 63–64
Hamilton, Hale, 201–2
Hamilton, John, 37–39
Hamilton, John D. M., 202
Hamilton, John S., 202
Hammerstein, Oscar, 63
Hanford, Muriel, 185–86
Hangings, 10, 192, 199–200, 230
Hanley, Charles, 107, 108
Harding, William, 74, 75, 182–83
Hardy, O. E., 17
Harrison, Benjamin, 6, 211
Hartman, Arthur J., 25
Hartzell, Oscar, 178–79
Harvey, John L., 10
Hastings, Serannus, 116

Hawkeye Rangers, 58
Hawkeye State, 29
Hayes, Walter I., 59
Haynes, Glenn, 200, 205, 206–7
Haynes, Jim, 113
Heinz, Marlo, 199–200
Henderson, David, 5
Hennepin Canal, 59
Hepburn, William P., 6, 125
Hepburn Act, 125
Herrick, Mrs. Mary, 150–52
Herring, Clyde L., 145, 168, 169, 173, 207
Herron, Francis, 6, 7
Hershey, Ben, 108, 109
Highway Commission, state, 101, 102
Highway Patrol, state, 39
Highways, 49, 58, 101, 102
Hilton, Milo, 128
Hinton, Richard, 26
Hobby, Oveta Culp, 165
Hoffmann, the Rev. Albert, 10
Hog cholera, 100
Hohn, Franz, 196
"Hold the Fort," 31
Homestead Law, 33
Honey War, 28, 29
Hoover, Herbert, 106, 182
Hope Hall, 211
Hopkins, Harry, 181–82
Howell, James B., 78
Hubbard, Nathaniel, 32, 69–71, 175
Hubbell, Frederick M., 184–85
Hughes, Rupert, 85
Hull, George, 213, 214
Hull, J. A. T., 6
Hummer, Michael, 152–53
Huncke, Mary, 170
Hutchison, Joseph G., 196–97
Hybrid Seed Corn, 95, 174

Illinois Central Railroad, 14, 21
Indians, 3, 4, 11, 12, 25, 29, 81, 89, 186, 190–91, 203, 220, 221, 230, 231, 232
Industrial Workers of the World (IWW; "Wobblies"), 187
International Woman Suffrage Alliance, 40
Invincible Louisa, 91, 92
Iowa City, 149–62
"Iowa Corn Song," 102
Iowa Equal Suffrage Association, 147–48
Iowa Farm Holiday Association, 172–73, 188
Iowa Good Roads Association, 207
"Iowa, It's a Beautiful Name . . .", 48–49
Iowa, origin of name, 232
Iowa State Medical Society, 227
Iowa State University, 42, 48, 94, 95, 96, 97, 98, 99, 100, 101, 102, 103, 115–16
Iowa Suffrage Association, 41
Iowa Territory, 9, 229, 230
Iowa, University of, 43, 48, 69, 82, 91, 131, 150–53, 158, 159, 160, 161, 162, 235
Iowa Wesleyan College, 80
Irish, John, 150–52

Jacobs, Cyrus, 29
Jacobsen, Franz, 199–200
James, Edwin, 23, 24
James, R. L., 38
Japanese, 14, 15, 44, 100
Jefferson Hotel, 151, 155
Jennie Edmundson Hospital, 148
Jessup, Walter, 161
John Morrell Packing Plant, 196, 197
Johnson, Francis, 98
Johnson, George E. Q., 212
Johnson, Wendell, 160–61
Jones, George W., 6, 7–9
Jones, Laurence, 130–31
Juneau, U.S. Cruiser, 14, 15
Juvenile Protective Association, 134

Kansas antislavery conflict, 26
Keller, George, 159–60
Kelly's Army, 192
Kelly, Thomas, 10
Kendall, Nate, 170
Keokuk, 76–92
Keokuk Aid Society, 86
Keokuk, Chief, 81, 231
Keokuk College of Physicians and Surgeons, 90
Keokuk Gate City, 78
Keokuk Medical College, 91
Keokuk power dam, 84, 85
Keokuk & Western Railroad, 85
Kessenger, E. M., 114
Key, Francis Scott, 89
Khrushchev, Nikita, 102
Kincaid, George, 109
King, Karl, 219–20
Kinnick, Nile, 153
Kirkwood, Samuel, 33, 34, 78, 155–57
Klipto Loose Leaf Company, 45, 46
Knights of the Golden Circle, 78

Lacey, John F., 6
Lainson, Percy A., 146, 204, 205
Lake LaVerne, 96
Lamb, Chancy, 55
Lambert, John, 190
Landon, Alfred M., 168, 169, 202
Land sales, 30, 89, 172, 207, 231
Lead mining, 3
League of Nations, 42, 168
League of Women Voters, 40, 42, 148
Le Claire, Antoine, 229, 230, 231, 232, 233
Leen, the Rev. William, 136
Leffingwell, William E., 58, 59
Legislature, Iowa, 69, 70, 71, 82, 162, 170, 172, 173, 211, 216
Lewis and Clark Expedition, 186
Lewis, Sinclair, 17
Lichty, Ben, 17
Lincoln, Abraham, 8, 24, 77, 79, 140–42, 154, 156, 197, 233, 234
Liquor, 17, 28, 29, 59, 88, 100, 114, 115, 120–22, 128–29, 145, 170, 183, 186, 207, 211
Liquor laws, 59, 114, 115, 145, 186, 197

Lobbyists, 175, 176
Logging, 18, 54, 55, 108
Long, John and Aaron, 230
Loras, Bishop Mathias, 11
Louisiana Territory, 4
Louisville Courier-Journal, 215
Loveless, Herschel, 193–94
Lucas, Robert, 25, 26, 28, 29, 110, 229, 230
Lumber production, 54, 55, 108, 116
Lyon, Harrison, 166
Lyon, Nathaniel, 186

Macbride, Thomas, 159
MacNider, Hanford, 44–45
Mahaska, Chief, 148
Mahin, John, 114–15
Mahony, Dennis, 9
Main Street, 17
Marietta, 124, 125
Mark's Mill, battle of, 190
Marshall County conflict, 124–25
Marshalltown, 119–36
Marston, Anson, 102
Martin, H. B., 213, 214
Mason, Charles, 30
Mason City, 35–49
Mason City Globe-Gazette, 49
Mason City Republican, 41
Mason, Edward B., 18
Maxwell, Elsa, 83, 84
May, Samuel L., 16
Maytag cars, 18, 19
Maytag, F. L., 18–19
Maytag-Mason Motor Company, 18, 19
McFarlane, Arch W., 21
McGee, W. J., 10
McGowan, Clarence, 39
McKinley, William, 100, 101, 223
Meigs, Cornelia, 91–92
Meigs, Montgomery, 91
Mennonites, Russian, 217
Meredith, Edwin T., 183
Metzger, T. M., 205
Midwest Free Press, 106
Miller, Allen, 190
Miller, Jack, 193
Miller, Samuel Freeman, 90
Mills, C. A., 10
Mines of Spain, 4
Mississippi River, 4, 5, 8, 23, 24, 28, 54, 55, 59, 60–61, 84, 85, 86, 90, 91, 108, 112, 113, 118, 192, 233–34
Mississippi River Power Company, 85
Missouri River, 140, 183, 186
Missouri, state of, 23, 28, 29
Mormons, 145–46, 152–53
Morrow, Honore Willsie, 197
Mother Bloor (Mrs. Andrew Omholt), 187, 188
Mott, David, 161
Mott, Frank Luther, 161
Mount Pleasant, 80
Mullan, Charles, 16
Mulroney, Joseph R., 215
Murphy, Louis, 6

Murray, William G., 194
Muscatine, 104–18
Muscatine Journal, 114
Music Man, The, 47, 48
Muskets, theft of, 26

National American Woman Suffrage Association, 40
National Guard, Iowa, 123, 144, 188
Nelson, Baby Face, 37–39
Newell, William C., 214
Nixon, Mr. and Mrs. Richard, 194–95
Northwest, The, 215
North Western Railroad, 32, 69, 71, 127, 217
Nuclear research at Iowa State, 99

O'Connor, Frank, 10
O'Connor, Patrick, 10
Odeboldt Chronicle, 63
Oleomargarine, pamphlet on, 97–99
One Foot in Heaven, 28
Ottumwa, 189–97
Ottumwa Courier, 190

Packard, Stephen, 131–32
Palmer, B. J., 234–35
Pammel, Louis H., 95
Papoose Creek, 117
Parsons, Galusha, 214
Parvin, Theodore, 115, 117–18
Payne-Aldrich tariff, 222
Pearl buttons, 112–13
Pearl Street, 183
Pegram, Benjamin, 166, 167
Perkins, the Rev. Jacob R., 142–43
Petersen, Christian, 103
Phillips, Merl, 138, 139
Phillips, Orville, 138, 139
Piney Woods Industrial School, 130–31
Plumbe, John, 10
Plum Grove, 29
Poffenberger, Fred, 138, 139
Polygamy, 145
Population, in Iowa, 54, 216, 217
Potosa, 4
Potts, George, 20
Prairie Rapids, 16
Prairie Rapids Crossing, 16
Prayers, 95, 110
Presidio, The, 205
Prohibition amendment, 59
Provincetown, Mass., playhouse, 235
Public Instruction, state superintendent of, 19–20, 51–54, 81–83, 207
Public Works Administration (PWA), 159
Pugsley, Sergeant, 144
Pulitzer prize winners, 102, 161, 191, 235, 238
Pusey, W. H. M., 140

Quick, Herbert, 186, 187

Railroads, 129–30, 174, 175, 176, 183, 218, 219, 240

accidental deaths, 210–11
free passes on, 32, 69–71, 176
rates, passenger and freight, 218
Rainfall, 117–18
Rand Park, 81
Red Cross, 238–39
Red Rock Dam, 196
Reed, Charles D., 94, 95
Reid, Hugh T., 89
Republican National Conventions, 6, 45, 154
Republican party, in Iowa, 110, 155
Rewards for apprehension of murderers, 218
Reynolds, John, 231
Rickenbacker, Eddie, 180–81
Riding, Henry, 183
"Riverton," 28
Road building, 101, 102, 183, 207
Rockingham, 232, 233
Rock Island Railroad, 234, 240
Roe, N. C., 60
Roosevelt, Franklin D., 144, 168–69, 182, 202
Roosevelt, Mrs. Franklin D., 15
Roosevelt, Theodore, 5, 86, 223
Rorer, David, 29
Rosenberger, N., 114
Runyon, Tom, 204–6
Russell, Charles, 238
Russell, Lillian, 56–57
Russian farm delegation, 102–3

Sabin, Henry, 51–54
Sac and Fox Indians, 203, 231, 232
St. Katherine's School, 91
St. Lawrence River Treaty, 45
St. Louis, 3, 4, 18, 26, 233, 234
Sales tax, state, 193
Salt, price of, 16
Samuelson, Agnes, 20
Saturday Evening Post, 202–3, 205
Schools, 19, 20, 40, 41, 51–54, 81–83, 87, 130–31, 158, 207–8
attendance problems, 52, 53
fund scandal, 207–8
health hazards, 51–52
Negro controversy, 111–12
one room rural, 20
teacher problems, 53
Schultz, Theodore, 98
Scott, Alexander, 166, 167
Scott, Winfield, 231
Sells, Elijah, 110, 111
Seward, William, 7, 154
Shambaugh, Benjamin, 162
Shaw, Leslie, 5–6
Sheaffer Pen Company, 208
Sheaffer, W. A., 208
Sheigley, John, 221
Sherman, Buren, 157
Sherman, William T., 31
Shiloh, Battle of, 89
Shipley, John C., 38
Short, Wallace M., 187

Simpson College, 94, 95
Sioux City, 177–88
Sioux Indians, 11
Slater, Fred (Duke), 57–58
Slauson, W. H., 214
Slavery, 8, 23, 24, 25, 26, 33, 59, 60, 80, 95, 156, 239, 240
Smallpox, 90
Smith, Ida B. Wise, 169–70
Soldiers Home, Iowa, 126
Soldiers and Sailors Monument, at Des Moines, 6, 7
Soth, Lauren, 102
Spanish land title, 4
Spedding, Frank, 99–100
Spence, Hartzell, 27–28
Spiked beer, 129
Spirit Lake Massacre, 220
State capitol, 157, 165–68, 172–73, 207
Stewart, John, 221
Street, Joseph, 190, 191
Stuart, Addison, 195
"Sucker," nickname, 29, 141
Sullivan brothers, 14–16
Sullivan, Genevieve, 15
Sullivan, Mr. and Mrs. Thomas, 14–16
Summers, Samuel, 195
Sunday, Billy, 120–23
Supreme Court, Iowa state, 30, 59, 64, 71, 111, 112
Supreme Court, Missouri state, 239
Supreme Court, U.S., 4, 28, 89, 239
Swale, Douglas, 38

Taft, William Howard, 74, 75
Tattooed Countess, 73
Teeters, Wilbur, 158
Thanet, Octave (Alice French), 238–39
39th Iowa Regiment, 31
Tillinghast, Benjamin, 238–39
Tinley, Mat, 143–45
Titanic, 66–67
TNT magazine, 105
Tofte, Hans V., 45–47
Tornado, at Camanche, 55–56
Touhy, Roger, 72, 73
Train robbery, 138–39
Tuberculosis, 123
Turner, Dan, 123
Turner, David, 69
Turner, John, 68
Twain, Mark, 79, 83, 111

Underground railroad, 59–60
Union Army, 5, 7, 78, 86, 87, 109, 110, 126, 156
Union Pacific Railroad, 10, 140, 141, 142
University hospital, at Iowa City, 161
Unknown Soldiers, 88
Uranium, 99

Vail, Theodore, 20–21
Van Meter, Homer, 37–39
Van Vechten, Carl, 73–74

Vietnam War, 45, 89
Voss, William, 237

Wade, Martin, 139
Wallace, Henry A., 10, 95, 100, 154, 173–74
Wallace, Henry C., 95, 174
Wallace, "Uncle Henry," 100
Walters, Tom, 37
Wapello, Chief, 190, 191, 231
War Eagle, Chief, 186
Waterloo, 13–21
Waterloo Courier, 17
Weare, John, 71
Weather observations, 117–18
Weaver, James B., 195
Western Union, 21
West, Frank, 128
Westinghouse, George, 211
Weston, George, 59, 60
Wheatcraft, William, 113
White, Fred, 101, 102
Whiteman, Paul, 229
Wicklund, Charles E., 129
Wilkins, Mary, 184–85
Willett, James W., 126, 127
Williamson, James A., 167
Williams, the Rev. Willis K., 136
Williams, William, 218, 220, 221
Willkie, Wendell, 153
Willson, Meredith, 47–49
Wilson, James "Jefferson Jim," 100
Wilson, James "Tama Jim," 6, 100–101
Wilson, Thomas S., 4, 12
Wilson, Woodrow, 168
Windmill destroyed, 96
Wine, David, 132–33
Winslow, Edward, 195
Wittenmyer, Annie, 86–88
Wobblies (IWW), 187
Woman suffrage, 40–42, 239
Women's Army Corps (WAC), 164–65
Women's Christian Temperance Union (WCTU), 88, 170
Wood, Grant, 67–69
Woods, Matt, 115
Work, Henry Clay, 184
Work relief, 159, 160, 181
Works Progress Administration (WPA), 159, 160, 181
World War I, 44, 45, 85, 144, 168, 170, 174, 205, 206
World War II, 10, 14, 15, 44, 46, 47, 98, 99, 100, 123, 133, 153, 164, 165, 173, 194, 237
Wright, Herbert R., 131
Wright, J. C., 81–83

Yewell, George, 157
Young, Brigham, 84, 145, 146, 152
Young, Courtland, 55
Young, Granville, 230
Young, William J., 54
Younker, Samuel, 90

Zrostlik, Mr. and Mrs. James, 204